A Historical Political Economy of Capitalism

In order to understand the resilience of capitalism as a mode of production, social organization, and an intellectual system, it is necessary to explore its intellectual development and underlying structure.

A Historical Political Economy of Capitalism argues that capitalism is based on a dominant intellectuality: a metaphysics. It proposes the construction of a history-based 'critique of political economy', capable of revealing the poverty of capitalism's intellectual logic and of its application in practice. This involves a reconsideration of several classical thinkers, including Smith, Marx, Berkeley, Locke, Hobbes, Hume and Rousseau. It also sketches an emancipative methodology of analysis, aiming to expose any metaphysics, capitalist or none. In doing so, this book proposes a completely new approach in materialist philosophy.

The new methodology in political economy that is proposed in this volume is an alternative way to organize a materialist approach. Some basic aspects of what is argued by the author can be found in Marx. This book is well suited for those who study political economy and economic theory and philosophy, as well as those who are interested in Marxism.

Andrea Micocci is Professore Straordinario of Political Economy, Link Campus University, Rome, Italy.

Routledge Studies in the History of Economics

A full list of titles in this series is available at www.routledge.com/series/SE0341

Recently published titles:

A Historical Political Economy of Capitalism

After metaphysics

Andrea Micocci

Routledge
Taylor & Francis Group

LONDON AND NEW YORK

First published 2016
by Routledge

2 Park Square, Milton Park, Abingdon, Oxfordshire OX14 4RN
52 Vanderbilt Avenue, New York, NY 10017

Routledge is an imprint of the Taylor & Francis Group, an informa business

First issued in paperback 2019

British Library Cataloguing in Publication Data
A catalogue record for this book is available from the British Library

Library of Congress Cataloging in Publication Data
Names: Miccoci, Andrea, author.
Title: A historical political economy of capitalism : after metaphysics /
Andrea Miccoci.
Description: London ; New York : Routledge, 2016. |
Includes bibliographical references.
Identifiers: LCCN 2016001164| ISBN 9781138193734 (hardback) |
ISBN 9781315639192 (ebook)
Subjects: LCSH: Capitalism – History.
Classification: LCC HB501 .M6266 2016 | DDC 330.12/209 – dc23
LC record available at http://lccn.loc.gov/2016001164

ISBN: 978-1-138-19373-4 (hbk)
ISBN: 978-0-367-87693-7 (pbk)

Typeset in Times New Roman
by Florence Production Ltd, Stoodleigh, Devon, UK

Contents

Acknowledgements

Brunella Antomarini carefully read the whole manuscript, helped me find books and was very encouraging. Sergio Cabras also read and commented on the whole manuscript. There have been conversations on some parts of it with Carlo Scarfoglio and Oscar Cetrangolo. Alex Allen helped me with the English, and, wherever there are errors or clumsy constructions, it is because I did not follow his advice. Massimiliano Biscuso, besides everything else, corrected some philosophical mistakes. Chuck McCann was very supportive in many ways. Nadine Valat, Claudio Micocci, Marshall Langer, Mark Mascal, Mino Vianello, Elena Caramazza, Flavia Di Mario, Sergio Vellante, Mariella Eboli, Corrado Ievoli and Patrizia Pugliese spent time and energy supporting me and discussing some of the theoretical issues. I am also obliged to Alex Callinicos for debating some fundamental questions, and to Ia Pardjanadze and Luarsab Jandieri for moral support. I thank Laura Johnson and Emily Kindleysides at Routledge. All the students of my courses in all the universities where I have been teaching are due a heartfelt thank you. Also, Dr Forleo, Dr Torrelli, Dr Filippetti and everybody at IFO must be thanked. All the above-named people have no responsibility for any statement or, obviously, any mistake contained in the book. Apologies go to those I have forgotten to mention. Finally, the usual special thanks go to Nino Pardjanadze, Alessandro Micocci and David Micocci.

1 Introduction

1.1 On capitalism

It is customarily expected of a work on the political economy of capitalism that it should open with a discussion of what capitalism is, leading to the production of a working definition to be used in the text. This book, however, is based upon a completely different logic. Unlike the present literature in the field, it seeks to identify its subject matter by a continuous sceptical doubt of its material reality. At the core of its argument is the hypothesis that capitalism is an intellectual construction that aims to provide an ultimate system of meaning to reality: a metaphysical construction. Such metaphysics, as we will see, is logically wrong, limited and limiting to such an extent as to completely inhibit individual understanding. As a consequence, to work as a social glue, it can only exist in the belief that it is universal to mankind, thus powerfully effacing, with human understanding, material reality itself.

As a preliminary illustration of what we will endeavour to demonstrate in the rest of the book, a few suggestive images are offered here. The first is as familiar and unthreatening to most people as it is appalling under a less frivolous analysis. Its implications are momentous in politics, and it is crucial in anticipating what this book is about. Scores of people are continually dying, suffering and starving all over the world as a consequence of the absurdity of capitalist politics, and, before that, many similarly fell victim to the absurdity of non-capitalist politics, so there is nothing new there. However, in capitalism, one finds that there is always a minority willing to volunteer to 'raise awareness' about this or that form of death or suffering (usually, never more than one issue at a time). If that social function were truly necessary, it would simply mean that the capitalist individual lacks the capacity to partake of the joy and pain of the others, or that such a capacity can be worn at will, like a prosthesis.

Is that truly so? Is humankind in capitalism capable of alienating itself from its own feelings, which can nonetheless be regained by the sharing of a conversation, or a blood-curdling photo, documentary film or book? If that were so, the creation of a perfect society would be an easy task: one would simply ban negative sentiments and use only the socially useful ones. This paradox is one of the core questions this book faces: the relationship between the vague, yet apparently existent, things we call sentiments, intellect, instinct and society. In capitalism, we will argue, we find awareness-raisers because humans are homogenized, by a passively enforced intellectual socialization, to be less than they could be as individuals. This grants social cohesion within injustice: the presence of this last is the awareness-needing safety valve the system needs to keep in touch with its 'speakable' sentiments. The search for justice and equality is a tool, in other words, to preserve capitalism. We should all be seeking something else: emancipation from the intellectual insanity of capitalism itself.

The implications of this matter are momentous. The study of capitalism becomes the study of its metaphysics as a socialized intellectual system, which we will also examine in the form of 'human understanding'. Such study must probe into the illusory security of the intellectual methods of capitalism itself. Studying capitalism can only be a process of analysis, and radical criticism, of capitalism's structures of thought and scientific methods. Here, no compromise is possible: if you are frightened, you can only go back to the known intellectual environment. Our search will take us, in fact, to what we shall call perfectly unconceived shores instead. The reader is warned.

For a second image, the artificiality and substitutability of human sentiments are also visible if we take a bird's eye view of one of the cornerstones of capitalist literature: the novel. Novels are narratives that constantly re-spin the same elements. Some describable human feelings, lost, gained and regained, are meant to disinter in the reader the realization that social life comprises sentiments that are socially developed and conditioned. Some novelists denounce this as a problem, some just take it as it is, some point out issues of social injustice. Even new offshoots of the genre, say, science fiction or fantasy, that claim room for the construction of new worlds seem unable to offer an intellectually alternative perspective. Sentiments and society cannot be split, and they are not. The lesson one learns from reading novels is that capitalism is sad and limiting, and you can only pine or fight for your own, or your class's, or kin's, share of humanity and justice, as long as it can be described in words and speech. No emancipation is offered, other than by proposing perfectly capitalist alternatives – for example, a well-known historical instance that still finds many supporters: socialism.

Economics and political economy present us with the same dismal landscape. Like the awareness-raisers, the literati and their readers, economists and political economists can only offer the results of their brooding over the unjust consequences of capitalism. As we shall submit in the course of the book, all they produce is a reshuffle of the various categories that their disciplines deal with: the logically flawed concepts of capitalism's metaphysics. Socialism thus becomes something to do with distribution and production organization, and anarchism becomes a set of autonomous communities that trade – capitalistically – with each other and the rest. To such silly goals, further lives, sufferings and starvation are sacrificed. The reason, as we shall see, is that, in the metaphysics of capitalism, diversity is confused with utopia and otherness.

This last consideration leads us to the role of language. In capitalism, we will seek to demonstrate, language confuses rather than clarifies issues, because its words and speech, in the general, moderate dialectics capitalist metaphysics is about, are simultaneously precise and approximate. Without this self-contradictory nature, language would do things (e.g. identify objects unequivocally, thus freezing their characteristics into what they are and not what the flawed capitalist dialectics requires) that would destabilize capitalism's mechanisms of functioning. These last points, as outlined above, mix together a cold, bounded rationality and a limited set of sentiments that need not be expressed together, or fully: to this inexact combination, language and speech must correspond.

Take an innocent metaphor: the idea of blue skies. Such an expression is simultaneously overdetermined, for blue is the colour of the sky, and approximate: celestial features connected with blue shades of colour become features of ethereal connections with feelings and idealizations (of the beauty of the universe, of religious issues, of love, of some peculiar objects, of foods and drinks, or of emotional aspects whose only common feature is that they are hard to pick up, let alone express, and whose material nature is highly uncertain), but skies are also, in children's understanding and in some languages, white, black or even red. Such intense colours identify their dense profundity and the mystery to the human eye of whether they are finite or not. These are perfectly meaningful as metaphors, in that there is no other way of rendering the density of sensual mystery.

The complex image above conveys the third outcome of the reasoning that is being proposed: the necessity to go beyond the sad capitalist metaphysics, to posit the potential presence of what we shall term the unconceived. This last is simply whatever the human mind and senses (of which much will be said throughout the book with the means supplied by philosophy and the social sciences) conceptualize as deprived of perceived and understandable determinations. We aim to break open the metaphysics of capitalism by returning 'human understanding' to an attitude that does not a priori avoid – like capitalism does – the unconceived. The idea is to move from the melancholy capitalist intellectual boredom to the excitement of mystery, from the iteration of known categories to the possibility that new categories might be all of a sudden forthcoming. This is, we submit to the reader, the basis for what is meant here by materialism.

Nature, i.e. the concrete (the material), must be recovered to the human mind and body by breaking free of the boundaries of the metaphysics of capitalism. Needless to say, there is a chance that the concrete itself is an illusion produced precisely by the intellectual barriers that the metaphysics of capitalism has erected to protect itself from such. To do so, we shall show, the metaphysics of capitalism, with its dialectical features, conflates the concrete (material reality, in common parlance) and the abstract (solid logical thinking, e.g. arithmetic) into an inter-`mediate object that is neither the former nor the latter, and prevents the contemplation of both: the metaphysics itself. This whole alienated bubble must be rendered by a language and speech that are, and can only be, simultaneously precise and approximate, to signify the equivocal ontological nature of the capitalist intellectuality and of its actual social and economic organization.

In such a framework, our task is no longer that of producing a working definition of capitalism. We have done that by saying that we are going to study its flawed metaphysics. The problem we have now is that, having doubted the material reality of it all, we are in trouble as to how to identify, and be sure we grasp, the actual items capitalism is made of. We refer, obviously, to the time-honoured economic and political categories that social scientists of all types have been studying. Can we use them in our highly sceptical framework? As our task is that of proving that we need a materialistic, historical political economy to criticize capitalism's metaphysics, on the grounds that such metaphysics itself can be transcended, and that such a transcension could leave us completely without capitalism, we need to build a bridge between theoretical argument and empirical (doubtable, but at least at this initial stage of our argument, kind of present) reality.

A bridge solution is available to deliver us to the final theoretical argument about the emancipation from capitalist metaphysics we are seeking here. It is provided by the sceptical, Epicurean and materialistic thinkers we shall study in the course of the book, within one of their most remarkable productions: the so-called Classical political economy. As we shall analyse in detail throughout the book, Adam Smith provided the method we can provisionally adopt until we reach Chapters 5 and 6, where an alternative proposal will be put forward. For Smith's solution, to put it with the approximation that is required at this introductory stage, capitalism is what calls itself so, whether true, imagined or potential. We will stay with this rule until Chapter 5, for it will let us put together theoretical ideas such as the market with the actual material items related to what markets materially appear like. Thus, terms such as individual and fact should be understood in this sense, unless otherwise indicated, until Chapter 5.

We will see that we need to use a language that is not the language of capitalist metaphysics, but cannot be – for emancipation is beyond what we can do here – very different to the present words and speech of capitalism. A mode of expression such as we need was started by the empiricist philosophers (we take Francis Bacon as our ideal ancestor, as discussed in Micocci, 2008/2010) and brought to its highest degree of utility for us here in the eighteenth century by such writers as La Mettrie, d'Holbach, Rousseau, Berkeley, Hume and Smith. We shall study these authors in the course of the book, but our goal is not to borrow, refine or improve upon their attempts. We need and shall use their tools like the tools of political economy: as 'historically dated' instruments that can only go as far as their limited historical nature. Our task is precisely that of creatively going beyond them and beyond anything we can conceive of in capitalism as we know it, to make room for what we cannot say.

In developing this argument, it will be evident that one cannot do without the work of Karl Marx. Here, a warning to the reader who is used to present-day literature in the human sciences is necessary. We shall read Marx directly, that is (as far as this is possible), without the mediation of the prejudices of his main interpreters. We shall thus discover that Marx was always an anti- or non-Hegelian thinker, i.e. a revolutionary and not a socialist. Such a Marx we have called 'Marx the anarchist', and he will accompany us throughout the whole book. A pleasant outcome of this way of reading Marx is that, as with the other thinkers we are going to consider, the reader cannot, and must not, even try to stick the '-ist' suffix to what is being submitted here. Erudite critics might detect in all this a typically

Epicurean dislike of the intellectuals. To this observation, à la Epicurus, the warning against all 'isms' applies with all the associated irony.

The highly inspiring view Epicurus introduced into Western philosophy, that material reality might have no better explanation than a type of chance whose logic escapes human understanding, certainly is one ideal influence behind what is being proposed here (see Micocci, 2002, 2008/2010). We shall also see that it lies behind Marx's work. Finally, it explains why nobody can call the present theoretical proposal Epicurean. Nor can it be called a contingency-based approach, for contingency itself can be doubted, and indeed there is a chance that we could well do without it. We can summarize by saying that the present book is an invitation to stand back and watch things with a mind unburdened of the capitalist connection between intellectual activity and socialized, moral worrying. Here is another Epicurean/non-Epicurean puzzle for the pedantic reader.

It is time for us to announce, with the utmost clarity, that the message of the book is the following: capitalism as we know it works well in practice as a mode of production, and might even last a long time, but the price of its functioning is the repression of human prerogatives and the annihilation of individuality. Its speech-based, flawed logic pervades every nook and cranny of human under-standing, killing it. This lets the capitalist observer notice its internal injustices and atrocities, do something about it and get nowhere, justice-wise. Precisely this continuous process of mending mistakes that appear system- and life-threatening while they are not (for they are always vulgar, Hegelian, dialectical relationships) is the reason for the survival of capitalism. Such anxiety to always work and do good is also the cause of capitalism's evil-doing.

Those who love capitalism as we know it do not, as a consequence, love capitalism as a concept. Pro- and anti-capitalist activists are sadly deceived when they think they are operating to put their utopias into practice. They are instead participating in those sad iterations of the same flawed, speakable actions that we can have intuition of from what has been anticipated so far, and that will be explained in detail throughout the course of this book. The only liberation we can seek, provided, that is, that we do not like capitalism as we know it for reasons more general than its cruel injustices, is an intellectual emancipation from it. We have called it silence, and it is outlined in Chapter 5. As an intuitive, provisional image, for the time being, we can offer Hume's idea of 'liberty as chance'.

Let us move on, starting from this new, provocatively Epicurean expression. The first thing to do is to make a few preliminary remarks about method.

1.2 This book's method

The first explanation that is due to the careful reader is whether the materialism that is developed here is also a type of naturalism. In a general sense, and for the present, initial purposes of clarity, the answer is a qualified yes. The idea of capitalism as we know it, erecting barriers to keep nature (the material and its unpredictable and inconceivable catastrophes) out, implies that it is nature that we want to recover. Such an interpretation might appear strengthened by our having referred to the importance of the sentiments, instinct, senses and intellect connection, but it is not so easy.

If, as we shall endeavour to show, the metaphysics of capitalism (this term, and the basics of the reasoning, come from Micocci, 2002, 2008/2010, 2012, which are thoroughly re-elaborated here) is flawed in the direction of providing a limited and limiting, iterative understanding of reality, then one cannot help having doubts about reality itself. Worse, we could never know how to prove when we have finally grasped material reality itself, for below the one metaphysics we have criticized there might be yet another, even subtler and more flawed. Let us put it plainly: the true problem we are considering here is the insidious connection between individual and social understanding and the senses. All the dangers to human understanding that we shall face, and that can be envisaged from any perspective, even other than the one offered here, come from human society and its metaphysics.

In other words, in capitalism, the main hindrance to a solid understanding of the empirical (which includes the possibility that the empirical itself, the material, may not exist) is the individual–society connection. No philosophical or scientific problem can be solved without looking at this character of all intellectual problems. This is the historical basis on which the materialism used here is built. The more pervasive and organized and efficient society is, the more it impinges upon human rationality and human feelings, the more we are incapable of knowing reality, for this is substituted by metaphysics. That means the challenging notion that we may not know anything about reality itself, not even its material existence. Knowledge, if the logic of this book is correct, is an antisocial operation.

The alternative conception of a reality potentially ruled (in our minds, that is) by 'liberty as chance' necessarily implies that knowledge must be a process of individual emancipation from the social and the political. These last are not human values, but intellectual and sentimental fetters. The role of political economy, and the reason why it should be materialistic and historical, should now be unequivocal. Political economy is a tool to analyse, in a negative way, the metaphysics of capitalism (i.e. capitalism itself), without replacing it with similar systems of thought, let alone projects of actual social systems. That is what is meant by historical: it must always be a backward-looking enterprise. Its role is that of sitting upon the debris of the past political economy it has itself caused.

To continue with our qualified naturalism, we can compare such political economy to the apical meristem of developed plants: a remarkably creative cellular formation that reproduces itself by always leaving its own production behind, down at the bottom. This process materializes the whole plant, while the meristem keeps moving upwards, oblivious to what happens to what it leaves behind and what holds it. The limitations of language compel us to use, to signify the solution to this complex and unresolved set of tangled problems, a word that has always had bad publicity: anarchism. There is no other term for what is meant here, however, and so the reader should always understand it as such and not according to its various equivocal meanings under capitalism as we know it.

Thus, if it is a naturalistic argument, this is of a reverse type. It is a materialistic attempt towards a naturalistic argument and, from there, to the verification of whether nature does exist. It is a naturalism that challenges naturalism, just as the historical, materialistic political economy proposed here debunks political economy. It needs no words and speech in the capitalist sense, and yet it needs to be communicated. Thus, the next problem is that, along with and after emancipation from capitalism, we need to reconsider language and speech. This comes down, again, to the individual–sociality question. Let us accept the hypothesis that we want to be social and live together.

We need to use a language that does not come from the metaphysics of capitalism, and yet that is compatible with it. As we are concerned with a political economy, it must be able to signify economic, social and political concepts and structures of thought without belonging to them, while being in touch with the normal communication of capitalism as we know it. The solution that has already been announced is to resort to a critical use of the language of the materialistic, naturalistic and sensist philosophers. Such a type of philosophical expression, we will argue, constitutes the intellectual structure of the Classical political economy of Adam Smith and Karl Marx. We are undertaking a perfectly legitimate operation; however, it might look peculiar to the reader used to the Byzantine logic of mainstream economics and of Marxist political economy. Yet, it is hoped that this will help the reader keep his/her balance in the course of an argument that is unsettling for the reasons put forward in Section 1.1.

The aim is to grant communication, while also allowing that degree of intellectual detachment that is needed to follow the present theoretical proposal through. To summarize: the argument, as well as the way it is expressed, is neither fully philosophical (although it uses philosophical tools) nor fully economic, although it is political economy that we are dealing with here. It is, rather, a critical analysis of both of them, delivered in a language and with a logic that belong to neither. Its goal is to summarize the complexity of technical debates, delivering them in the most straightforward way available. Some terms that are laden with the typically capitalist mixture of precision and approximation (market, anarchism, revolution, silence and the like) are, then, to be taken carefully. Explanations are attached as needed.

By reviewing some extreme forms of scepticism of the materialist kind, the book construes a fairly traditional European philosophical and economic argument, symbolically represented by the discussion of Marx the anarchist that connects all its chapters. At the end, the reader will not find a solution to the problems raised, but – it is hoped – a framework for a solution. The most powerful implication of the analysis of capitalism as we know it that is proposed here is, in fact, the recovery of individuality, i.e. of individual rationality, sensuality and instinct (or anything else these terms signify in a framework of liberty as chance and emancipation). The most important and intriguing consequence of such a move is that there could be a plurality of alternative, incompatible solutions.

If such an outcome is possible, then it is evident that social life must be completely rethought, as well as the social sciences. No known political philosophy makes room for such wild diversity to seek to compose a sociality. Such a feature makes the question of naturalism inescapable. Is social life natural? The only way to find out is to go looking for nature abandoning the metaphysics of capitalism. That, however, as signalled more than once, does not grant the desired result. This dynamic and endless difficulty makes, at least to the present author, the need to go beyond the metaphysics of capitalism compelling. The purpose of this book is to excite in the reader the same wild curiosity that has motivated its author in its writing.

With such a goal, the result that is reached here, that a materialistic, historical political economy is a tool not for managing society but for dissolving its intellectual illusions, is fundamental. There are, as we shall see, remarkable regularities in some material phenomena related to human action (agriculture above all) that are as helpful in this sense as they are peculiar. The capitalist anxiety to regulate nature, we will argue, may be completely misguided. There is the possibility that the need for social and natural regulation is overstated. This calls for a discussion about the similarity in the structure of thought between the social and the natural sciences that is long overdue, but cannot be confronted here.

If everything presented so far holds, we have a few final points. Capitalism as we know it and its metaphysics had been well intuited by Marx the anarchist and by those who criticized Hegel's logic and theory of history. The polemics against the dialectics initiated by Feuerbach and Marx and furthered, for our purposes here, by Colletti and Della Volpe are at the origin of what is being proposed here. However, they have been reworked and simplified in what follows, liberating the present author from too strict a connection with the aforementioned. Yet basic they remain, even in the new formulation put forward in particular in Chapter 2.

Marx's triple alienation is also fundamental, for it remains the best way to render the effects of the metaphysics of capitalism: the individual's estrangement from his/her own self, other individuals and nature in general. Although the nature of this triple alienation as proposed here is different in many respects from that of Marx, still, the reference to his term has been kept as a grateful homage to his beautiful intuition.

Finally, a warning that summarizes the present discussion on method: What is offered here is delivered with the maximum thoroughness possible: the simultaneous vagueness and precision of capitalist concepts are avoided as much as possible. This might, at times, result in surprising statements that, to the experience of the present author, are only outwardly and formally so. This is the emotional result of the useless verbosity of the metaphysics of capitalism. The author begs the reader, therefore, for some patience.

1.3 Clearing the ground

The customs of academia and of monograph writing impose on this introduction a further task: that of explaining why some apparent similarities with other authors, past and present, do not apply. Hopefully, this is going to be a relatively straightforward task, after the explanations about the contents and method that have been supplied so far.

The first, general similarity that does not apply is to the current criticisms of mainstream economics. The present work is no such thing, because it is much more radical. Mainstream economics is described in what follows as a discipline that works well enough in capitalism as we know it, precisely because of its illogical structure and its doing without material reality in principle. Mainstream economists are the most coherent interpreters and users of the metaphysics of capitalism. The mainstream illogical structure and refusal of reality are, instead, the two most common criticisms levelled at it by the majority of dissenting economists, as an explanation of its supposed failure to work. In what follows, it is also argued that those who criticize and those who are criticized are closely bound. They talk about the same things from the two sides of a dialectical relationship. Criticism is not possible, we propose instead, without implying a real opposition, a revolution: the elimination of the very mentality behind the ideas under examination.

The above difficulty is the main problem plaguing heterodox economic thinking worldwide. Most criticisms of the economic mainstream do a valuable job in showing its obstreperous absurdities (we will see the most important in due course), only to then – inexplicably – seek to rebuild economic theories on similar (metaphysical) bases, i.e. bases compatible with the metaphysics of capitalism. Instead of considering, for a current instance, that the preponderance of finance that is superseding material production in entrepreneurial and political choices is capitalism itself (pure metaphysics), they hanker after or reinvent former ideas, based first of all on the notion that economic activity is about material production and exchange. We shall see this to be a hopeless mistake that fails to register the historically metaphysical nature of capitalism as we know it, which is the same nature as that of money and finance.

Thus, works such as, for a well-known recent instance, Fine and Milonakis (2008) present much that is valuable, and this author has no major quarrel with their observations on technical issues. The problem is that their book, like most works in that field, stops at technicalities and gives you no indication as to what to do next: should we reform economics or start a revolution against it, or against capitalism itself? The three options are wildly different, even if by revolution against capitalism we just mean revolutionizing theory. Backhouse, in the 2012 Symposium on *Historical Materialism*, notices, with much less force, this very political point.

As a consequence, the present book needs not engage with such works as Fine and Milonakis (2008). Nor will it engage in Marxist analyses, such as Callinicos's (2014). In this case, the differences in scope, aim and method are the fundamental reason. Callinicos seeks to reread Marx in a fresh way, without departing from the Marxist tradition and the Marxist debates. This is the very opposite of what is being done here. Engaging in such an effort would require a book-length work in itself, and a punctual exegesis of Marx would be insufficient, for there would be a requirement to discuss the enormous body of literature.

Thus, the pages that follow can do without discussing the type of Marxist literature of which Callinicos (2014) is a leading example. This is not supposed to mean that such discussion is not important and momentous: on the contrary. But it is not strictly necessary to the development of the argument that is our object here. The thorough, critical consideration of the interpretation of Marx comprising the one put forward here must wait for another occasion, which the present author eagerly awaits.

It is, instead, very instructive to take a brief look at a work by the maverick Marxist Sohn-Rethel: *Intellectual and Manual Labour: A critique of epistemology* (1978). Such a book is highly representative of his fairly independent approach, the position of which in the development of Marxist thought has always been that of a disquieting concern in the mind of all. Yet, its impact has been hardly felt, in general. Commentators on the work of the present author (gratefully acknowledged for their kindness) have pointed at similarities between a few of its features and some of the Sohn-Rethel (1978) proposals. It will be argued below that there is no relevant similarity, on the grounds of the precision–vagueness of the language question that will be developed throughout the book – hence the importance of this preliminary discussion. The few apparent analogies evaporate if looked at from such a perspective.

The most commonly observed similarities people notice concern the so-called 'real abstraction' and money. One should consider to start with that, very importantly, Sohn-Rethel's book has perfectly mainstream Marxist conclusions that make whatever intuition one finds in the first part rather useless to the second.

Let us start from what he calls (1978, p. 5) 'social synthesis', 'the socially necessary forms of thinking of an epoch [. . .] in conformity with the socially synthetic forms of that epoch'. This would seem like an alternative formulation of what is called here the metaphysics of capitalism. In fact, Sohn-Rethel goes on (ibid.), noting the 'conceptual foundations of the cognitive faculty vis-à-vis nature', again evoking what we do here. Further, similarly to what is submitted in the present book, he says that, in societies based on commodity production, such social synthesis is based on the functions of money as Marx's 'universal equivalent' (p. 6).

However, to Sohn-Rethel, crucially, money is 'abstract' (ibid.) and manifests itself as concrete objects. Such abstraction contributes to the making of 'abstract human labour' (ibid.). '[The] constituent elements of the exchange abstraction unmistakably resemble the conceptual elements of the cognitive faculty emerging with the growth of commodity production' (ibid.). A 'true identity exists between the formal elements of the social synthesis and the final constituents of cognition. [. . .] The conceptual basis of cognition is logically and historically conditioned by the basic formation of the social synthesis of its epoch' (p. 7). Hence, the manual and intellectual labour distinction.

Let us delve further into what he says without being misdirected by the approximation of the metaphysics of capitalist communication. Sohn-Rethel is suggesting that a 'social synthesis' does materially exist. No such thing is proposed with the metaphysics of capitalism: this last is merely a theoretical hypothesis whose aim is to summarize some recurrent capitalist phenomena recorded à la Adam Smith in order to show their flawed logic. The relation of such phenomena to material reality (nature), as we shall endeavour to show, may or may be not determined. If it were, the metaphysics hypothesis would transform itself into the usual capitalist illusion that words, political economy and science represent reality, and that reality exists and is what words, political economy and science talk about.

In fact, in Sohn-Rethel, nature is out there, and so is society, and so is 'real abstraction'. It follows that even 'abstract human labour' exists, and manual and intellectual labour can, as a consequence, be identified. Such a notion is predicated upon a simple mistake: to Sohn-Rethel, as to mainstream Marxists, the abstract coincides with what we call here metaphysics. This error is one that they share with mainstream economics (Micocci, 2002, 2008/2010, and the rest of the present book). Their logical problem is precisely the confusion between the abstract and material, which, to them, must correspond with one another, in the mistaken illusion that this is the only way to represent things in order to operate upon them; this is, as we shall point out throughout the book, very Hegelian. The abstract and the material are collapsed together, and their distinction is effaced.

The consequence is a surprising looseness in the use of words and speech. Suddenly, 'social synthesis' and 'abstract human labour' reappear as manual and intellectual labour, but they are similar because they are transcended into a metaphysics, the metaphysics of capitalism. Only by keeping the idea of 'abstract human labour' abstract, for a powerful instance, can we instead observe its horrifying human consequences: triple Marxian alienation and the bizarre idea that there can be a fair wage for human exertion (both of which will be discussed in this book). Also, we lose our theory's capacity to be, and remain, outside the dominant mentality of capitalism; on the contrary, we immerse ourselves in it, thus condemning ourselves to being forever entangled in its vulgar Hegelian dialectical relationships.

Manual and intellectual labour become, rather than two precise concepts, two large sets of variable objects–concepts, which ends up blurring the very difference between these two categories. True monsters are thereby begotten. Take the celebration of work as human achievement (which, we will show, Marx resisted all his life), rather than as a sheer necessity and a hindrance to happiness, and its Leninist aberrations, the most recent of which is 'collective intellect', another item this book is going to discuss. From such vagueness of meaning further vagueness can be produced by more and more subtle splitting of the concepts into sub-concepts or degrees of intensity. The paradoxical outcome of such a process is the generalized impression that it is precision that is being pursued. This is identical to what happens in mainstream economics, as we shall see in due course.

The above makes Sohn-Rethel's invocation of Kant versus Hegel (1978, p. 19) as an aid to Marx perfunctory. In fact, to him, 'abstractions' are no metaphors (p. 20):

> While the concepts of natural science are thought abstractions, the economic concept of value is a real one. It exists nowhere other than in the human mind

but it does not spring from it. Rather, it is purely social in character, arising in the spatio-temporal sphere of human interrelations. It is not people who originate these abstractions but their actions. '*They do it without being aware of it*'.

(p. 20; emphasis in the original)

How does he know? Of course, he does not, but he wants to operate in practice, and cannot do it without coming up with such precise approximations.

As a consequence, 'The abstractness of their action is hidden to the people performing it' (p. 30). People are thus exonerated from any responsibility for what is going on, and the general capitalist dynamics is also exonerated. This collective lack of responsibility can only make room for active, operational intervention. The one or many who get a glimpse of the situation can intervene, but the overall meaning is still missing. What is it that he is describing: concepts of the theories or natural material objects? In this general lack of awareness conveyed by vague words, meaning is malleable to circumstances. Abstract manual labour, like hidden abstractions, can mean a wide number of things, in theory and in practice; most importantly, it can take up just as many erroneous or correct meanings, let alone shades of meaning.

There is, in fact, a basic, and only apparent paradox here: if we follow Sohn-Rethel's logic, i.e. the normal logic of the social sciences (our metaphysics), everything appears somehow determined. Concatenations of causes can be produced and iterated at leisure, to which similar but different concatenations can be compared. Everything seems to be in a state of continuous flow and discussion, while nothing moves, because the ontological status of what is being dealt with is uncertain and substitutable by degree (never, however, completely). This book proposes to invert the process, basing itself upon a complete lack of determinations (liberty as chance at first) as a way to do (if at all possible) what the metaphysics of capitalism cannot do: make right or wrong assertions. This means to discover the actual existence of things, without ever expecting to do so.

The result is that, in such a process, we liberate ourselves from the limited and limiting mental framework of the metaphysics of capitalism. The alternative is to find oneself, like Sohn-Rethel, imagining for instance (1978, ch. 34) that automated labour processes transform the subjectivity of labour into a 'social power of machinery' (p. 175). That is not all: such social power can 'be transformed into means of production for socialism' if the power of capitalism has been 'broken' (p. 177)! His observations on science and the environment (pp. 179–80), again apparently similar to what we shall say in the course of the present book, can as a consequence be returned to the flawed division between manual and intellectual labour. There follows the further nonsense that 'in socialism [. . .] [technology] must be made the instrument of the relationship of society to nature' (p. 181). It could mean anything.

The discussion of Sohn-Rethel (1978) has afforded us a chance to glimpse at the difference between the method that is being proposed here and the method of mainstream economics and mainstream political economy. It also affords us a word of caution about the way we distribute our 'isms'. If technology can be lifted from capitalism to socialism by simply 'breaking capital', then it is easy to see why all socialist and communist movements have failed badly, and have given a bad name to their ideals. A word of caution is therefore due here: the present book is not a way to alert us to the possible presence of the formation of a 'false consciousness' that misdirects us towards mistaken goals. A false consciousness is as vague and meaningless a concept as Sohn-Rethel's social synthesis or real abstraction.

1.4 A historical political economy of capitalism: after metaphysics

A historical political economy of capitalism is our materialistic task here. It must have the ability to analyse capitalism, initially in the spirit of Adam Smith's Classical political economy, and then in the highly sceptical, materialistic environment of 'liberty as chance', to finally deliver us to emancipation from both, as well as, of course, from the metaphysics of capitalism. This theoretical process is a form, therefore, of individual liberation from the homogenization induced by the intellectual and sentimental massification capitalism is all about. This is not to say, however, that we must emancipate ourselves.

The book's goal is not a call for action, but an attempt to put the analysts of capitalism before their responsibilities, which can be summarized as a culpable lack of radicalness in their methodology. Then, one can choose to side with or against capitalism, or its economic intellectual structure. However, those who are looking for an encouragement to rise against it should look somewhere else. They will find inflammatory calls for subversion in the capitalist literature that is criticized here. If they want to fight, they must go back to capitalism and immerse themselves in it. Here, we simply seek to invite the reader to enter the world of the recovery of individual thinking, which is a truly revolutionary task.

As a consequence, the book is fashioned, rather than as a common multidisciplinary study, as a sort of literary composition (without, it goes without saying, any artistic pretence) that seeks to put in succinct and linear language what parts of philosophy, economic theory and the social sciences must be used to build the required argument. To fashion a proposal that is 'other' than what is usually done in one's field, this is the least that is required. Practitioners of the various single subjects that are being handled could, as a consequence, occasionally feel lost, for they will not find well-known items coated in the usual words and sentence types. This, however, should help communication across disciplines, thus helping all readers follow the development of the argument. Provided, that is, that the present author has been capable of doing what he has set out to do.

Conventionally enough, Chapter 2 ('Capitalism as we know it and its metaphysics') opens with a description of the technicalities of the metaphysics of capitalism. In so doing, it reworks arguments that have been presented in previous publications in different and, for the obvious reasons, more tentative ways. It is crucial to understand, from the very beginning, that what is proposed is very unlike, in its economic part, the 'normal' premises and structures of political economy, even of the materialistic types. The basis on which to build economic considerations is not the metaphysics itself: commodities, exchange, the market and all the rest originate there, and we do not wish to end up positing the existence of objects whose ontological status cannot be proved.

This chapter also introduces the two authors whose work we shall keep discussing throughout the whole book: Adam Smith and Karl Marx. The wealth of material available for the latter will obviously make for different uses and roles for these two classics. The intent in Chapter 2 is, in other words, that of clearing the ground by offering a general framework for the main concepts used, and starting the discussion of the main technicalities.

Chapter 3 ('Nature and liberty') widens the issues raised in Chapter 2. First, it introduces nature and some of its interesting puzzles (which are, and remain, puzzles even for the theory proposed here, thus proving one of its basic contentions: lack of determination is indeed possible, and does not hurt). The main question it deals with can be described as the trouble with the regularities of nature, and whether they match the artificial and logically flawed regularities of capitalism as we know it and its metaphysics.

The chapter also introduces the idea of 'human understanding', which is borrowed from eighteenth-century philosophy. It is found to be useful because, not only does it describe the social–individual connections of intellectual endeavours, but also because it is from here that Adam Smith starts his own analysis. If we want to keep within the boundaries of a materialistic political economy, we cannot do without it. It is a defining issue of the metaphysics of capitalism.

Chapter 4 ('Economic discipline') seeks to explain how, on the basis of what we have argued up to then, economic discourse organizes capitalism in all walks of life. It is in this chapter that the problems related to capitalist speech and words that lead, as hinted earlier on, to the paradox of vague expressions being mistaken for precise concepts (and the other way around) are introduced. This is just another way to keep showing the intrinsically vulgar Hegelian dialectical character of all intellectual endeavours in capitalism as we know it.

It is here that the need for political economy to free itself from the fetters of being a 'practical' discipline, meant to help the organization of production, makes itself felt. This last is in fact the task of mainstream economics, to which political economy should be a perfect 'other', but is not. To reach all these results, the theoretical background is progressively shifted by continuing the discussion of the sceptical, Epicurean and materialistic work of a number of French and British eighteenth-century authors, whose work is introduced in Chapter 3. The Humean concept of liberty as chance is here brought to its completion.

But liberty as chance, however radical, unsettling and frightening to behold for the capitalist mind, is not sufficient to our task. We need to answer questions on the very existence of reality and, above all, we need to get as close as possible to a definition of liberty in a general, not in a political, sense. Thus, building on the argument so far, Chapter 5 ('Silence') proposes an idea of liberty/emancipation as a form of silence. Liberty is, first of all, for nature to be the way it is. To have that, you need to make room for what you cannot know and is perfectly other from you. The chapter thus divides the imaginable from the unimaginable, which are the two basic capitalist categories, in order to make room for the 'unconceived'.

The 'unconceived' symbolizes the possibility of a complete lack of determinations. It should be clear by now that this does not necessarily means lack of determinations in material reality. That is possible and thinkable and, therefore, is not the unconceived. The unconceived is the sudden apparition of itself, what throws human understanding back to the beginning: what the metaphysics of capitalism has refused to see by erecting barriers that are impassable to it, by making no intellectual and emotional room for it. In other words, there may be things all around us that we simply do not see for lack of means or will to perceive them. We are thus back, with the unconceived, to that intellect–senses connection we cannot fully explain, or know about, until we emancipate ourselves from the metaphysics of capitalism. If such a thing exists, that is.

There are, in the development of this complex argument, some side issues of a political nature. In fact, if you have chosen to side against capitalism the reasoning of this book can only deliver you to anarchism based on the elimination of economic intercourses (we shall call this last feature 'communism'). However, for evident, logical reasons, the reader interested in this possibility will not find a theory of anarchism here. In fact, once again, Marx had the right intuition: in such cases, his Thesis XI on Feuerbach is all there is to say about it. Philosophy, however, and it is well worth pointing this out plainly, can perform its task of changing the world only when it is radically pursued. This last is, the present author dares hope, the most important political message this book is meant to convey. This is what it is meant by revolution here.

A second political consequence is that a theory of political evil can be worked out from the present argument. The flawed, partial and obstinately bounded reasoning of the metaphysics of capitalism can in fact be, at least for the purposes of illustration, identified with evil. Forced intellectual socialization, in other words, produces socialized evils. Here, we may recall, and partly explain, the capitalist need for awareness-raisers. If the present reasoning holds, evil is an enforced, partial and defective socialized understanding of one issue, helped by the presence of Marxian triple alienation. Natural sentiments can be, and in fact are, in capitalism as we know it, taken on and cast off at need, like a prosthesis.

The conclusions will come back to these issues, adding some others, but the point of the present book is not in the single conclusion. It is in the solidity of the argument itself, which is for the reader to judge.

References

Callinicos, A. (2014) *Deciphering Capital*, Bookmarks, London.

Fine, B., and Milonakis, D. (2008) *From Political Economy to Economics*, Routledge, London.

Historical Materialism (2012) Symposium on Fine and Milonakis, 20:3, 3–96.

Micocci, A. (2002) *Anti-Hegelian Reading of Economic Theory*, Mellen Press, Lampeter, UK.

Micocci, A. (2008/2010) *The Metaphysics of Capitalism*, Lexington, Lanham, MD.

Micocci, A. (2012) *Moderation and Revolution*, Lexington, Lanham, MD.

Sohn-Rethel, A. (1978) *Intellectual and Manual Labour: A critique of epistemology*, MacMillan, London.

2 Capitalism as we know it and its metaphysics

2.1 Introduction

Within capitalism, there is, at the intellectual and bodily level, a pressure to conform to given patterns of thought and syllogisms, even at the most trivial level. Nothing is exempt from this unpleasant influence. A few minutes of application to anyone of the mass media, and the sad banality and repetitiousness of capitalist reality talking about itself cannot fail to register. Yet, it is clear that it is precisely this repetitious banality that ensures capitalist survival, for in most cases it engenders habituation. From the housewife with her TV set that is never switched off, to the teacher of any high-level academic subject, failure to conform to the over-arching logic means not to communicate, or so it seems. As a consequence, the only space left for criticism appears to be to concentrate on the faults of this or that particular, instead of considering the whole.

Consideration of the whole would in fact bring everything back to another time, when philosophy replaced the single scientific disciplines and harsh battles were fought over the primacy of metaphysics and its connection with ontology. This chapter builds upon the present author's previous work on the intellectuality of capitalism, which is defined as a metaphysics. The main difficulty is that, if 'capitalism as we know it' (i.e. not the theoretical capitalism that most Classical and non-Classical authors discuss in political economy and economics) is a metaphysics, then an ontology of capitalism by capitalist means is perfectly impossible. Let us introduce this aspect, which will be developed in this chapter and in the rest of the present book.

The very concept of metaphysics implies the construction of a general framework that puts in place the various subjects and forces of the system that is being analysed. Indeed, the negative connotation of metaphysics in our time comes from its presumption of being able to organize what is behind what is visible, at the risk of abusing reality by bestowing on it a logic that is not necessarily its own. The metaphysics of capitalism does this by construing an intermediate rational system, suspended between the material (the concrete) and the abstract (pure thought constrained only by logical needs).

If capitalist metaphysics replaces reality with a (inevitably flawed) mental construction, then the practice of ontology (in itself highly difficult, given the impossibility to know the material essence of things without making up an ad hoc framework) becomes impossible. Capitalist metaphysics, lying between the abstract and the concrete, prevents direct access to both. In other words, capitalist metaphysics lacks a discussion of ontology and is, therefore, in a continual state of drift, with no clear aim, owing to a lack of material as well as philosophical reference.

Naturally, one can argue that, without a metaphysical frame, concepts cannot be discussed. The urgent problem, however, is that the metaphysics of capitalism as we know it is global and all-pervading: it forms the very basis of the system. Thus, fighting metaphysics equals fighting capitalism. Whatever theoretical framework[1] is available, pursuing the concrete, to a materialist, has to be the first step towards an attempt (mind you, just an attempt) to study (the ontological nature of) whatever item of reality is under consideration. Yet, as we shall show in the rest of the book, an ontology is likely to be precluded for materialists too, and this is fortunate.

In the metaphysics of capitalism, words replace reality and cannot in any way, given that they are amenable to connection with neither the abstract nor the concrete, help towards the knowledge of reality itself, nature. They cannot be used to gain knowledge of capitalism either, for they only signify a mistaken or missing relationship to a concrete, material object, as well as to abstract, logically correct reasoning within capitalism, both of these being, as said above, completely out of reach and impossible to retrieve. Capitalist words can only exist in capitalism, where they mean nothing in practice, but they are the only commodity that communication peddlers (i.e. everybody) can deal in.

Potential readers imbibed with analytical philosophy, communitarian ideas, cognitive sciences, philosophy of language, dialectical materialism and most other present-day theories produced by the cultural debate of 'capitalism as we know it' will feel lost at this point. After the initial bewilderment, however, they will triumphantly conclude that these are just the intemperances of a radical mind intent upon provoking outrage. Upon further consideration of the issue, those with a more benign character will conclude that this is, if at all justifiable, only an abstract possibility, and they will relax as if the problem has been solved. These are the emotional consequences of capitalist metaphysics, which we will discuss through political economy.

If an intuition of the abstract is at all possible in 'capitalism as we know it', it only serves to simultaneously terrify and reassure the person who dares venture as far as to dabble in such things. Anything abstract appears not to be wrong, but rather impossible, and so not worth considering. The most important consequence is not just that abstract thinking is abhorred, but rather that, in order to abhor it, instinct and intuition must, as a consequence, be repressed.

The number of ideas that we feel might be worth exploring is drastically cut down to non-abstract notions and hypotheses only. As a consequence, only what can be rendered with words and the few basic, known syllogisms is kept. We will see in the course of this chapter and in the subsequent chapters that this argument is an enlargement and development of an original intuition put forward, in its first modern sense, by Karl Marx, among others. It suffices here to quote from a very well-known (and so all the more surprising to the average reader) text: his 'Preface to the critique of political economy' (1975).

> In considering such transformations [social revolutions, AM], a distinction should also be made between the material transformation of the economic conditions of production [. . .] and the legal, political, religious, aesthetic or philosophic – in short, ideological forms in which men become conscious of this conflict and fight it out. Just as our opinion of an individual is not based on what he thinks of himself, so can we not judge of such a period of transformation by its own consciousness [. . .] this consciousness must be explained by the contradictions of material life [. . .] Therefore mankind always set itself only such tasks as it can solve; since, looking at the matter more closely [. . .] the task itself arises only when the material conditions for its solution already exist or are at least in the process of formation.
>
> (p. 182)

As is well known, Marx here is discussing the base–superstructure relationship. He argues that no period can understand itself and make revolution unless the material conditions have so deteriorated that the legal, political, religious, aesthetic and philosophical forms can let some repressed ideas break free, thus allowing retrospection with detachment (some Marxists might want to connect such ideas to those 'extraneous standards' in relation to history Marx has called for in *The German Ideology*; Marx and Engels, 1985, pp. 59–60), and move forward with the capacity to produce novelties, ideas about social-economic organization that are 'different' from anything hitherto devised. In what follows, we shall go beyond this mechanistic relationship. Before doing so, however, the concept of difference needs a word of caution, in relation to Marx as well as to the argument of this book. In a dialectical environment such as capitalism as we know it, difference and otherness are conflated, as in Hegel's *Phenomenology of the Spirit* (2008c). We shall argue throughout the present book, however, that otherness and real opposition are also at work, and reality becomes, as a consequence, unpredictable.

Capitalism as we know it can only be transcended and revolutionized (i.e. destroyed completely, and fully replaced, which is the equivalent of saying that no dialectical relationship is possible here) by going beyond its structure of production as well as its culture, intellectuality (its metaphysics) or ideology, as Marx prefers to summarize it (1975). However, unlike Marx, we will argue that there are no necessary connections between the operations of the contradictions internal to the mode of production and the evolution that will lead to a social revolution, or any other kind. A social revolution à la Marx might still be possible perhaps, but revolution-wise it is much more effective, and necessary if one considers humankind as a genus of potentially infinitely creative individuals, to leave at once the culture/ideology of capitalism.

In other words, on the one hand, capitalism consists of a system of intellectual metaphysics that is clearly illogical and unsatisfactory, both in theoretical terms and in the unjust conditions of material life it engenders. On the other hand, it is precisely this impoverished and impoverishing metaphysics that produces a perverse and binding habituation, thus jeopardizing Marx's own mechanistic 'social revolution'.[2] The intellectual structure of the metaphysics encapsulates even those mental operators (philosophers or economists, for instance) who should see the situation clearly. Collective intellectual slavery and repression ensue, which, being logically flawed, always produce working problems. These last are routinely and iteratively interpreted, by Marx himself in some places and by most 'Marxists', as the birth pangs of a never-to-come new order. We will argue here and further on that they are instead the very tools of preservation of the capitalist system itself.

Normal life in capitalism as we know it thus comes down to a repetitive routine of generalized intellectual (hence, instinctual, psychological and sexual) repression, and of appalling injustices meted out at random. However, for the latter, a cause and a logic are always found within the general (limited and flawed) intellectual framework, for this continuously repeats itself. The metaphysical nature of this whole business, detached both from logical abstraction and from the concrete objects and logic of nature itself, makes 'scientific' and even just rigorous discussion impossible. What is done instead is an exchange of verbal constructions accompanied by a pompous attitude, easily described as what we earlier called the abhorrence of abstract ideas. Power structures survive by the continuous discussing and even challenging of themselves that capitalism is about, *pace* Luhmann.

The words, grammar and syllogisms of all kinds allowed by the metaphysics of capitalism come to gain a peculiar primacy, and, as we shall see for the case of political economy and economics, the boundary between words and material objects becomes blurred. In the metaphysics of capitalism, a word can easily and seamlessly shift from its ontological status of word to that of item endowed with a spurious, metaphysical, yet perfectly working quasi-ontological status of object, and even of relationship of objects and persons. By outlining the nature and functioning of capitalism as we know it, this chapter constitutes the first step towards a complete demonstration, which we shall achieve, hopefully, at the end of the book.

In conclusion, what we will do here is point out the main features of capitalism as we know it, which will serve us by doing two things that are necessary to the argument of this book. The first is discussion of the actual and epistemological differences between the social and human realm of economy and society (in the next chapter) and that of nature in general. The second thing we must do is a critique of political economy and economics. This will be done in Chapter 4, using the arguments of the two preceding chapters. Chapter 5 will sketch a way forward.

In Section 2.2, we will first discuss what was meant by capitalism in Classical political economy, and how the anti-Hegelian analytical attitude proposed here changes all of that radically. The old communism/liberalism alternative will be reconsidered, and the necessary link that binds these last two together – anarchism – will be introduced. This will help us return to them their long-lost, radical method.

Section 2.3 outlines the metaphysics of capitalism itself, with its non-existent market and its almost impossible realization. It will also indicate the intrinsic intolerance of the capitalist set-up, determined by its dialectical, moderate working.

Section 2.4 introduces the momentous issue of liberty, which directly ensues from the repressive nature of capitalism as we know it. This section also introduces the issue of the Humean problems in the description of capitalism and of nature in general. Such a set of questions will be developed in Chapters 3 and 4. The idea here is to start working out the naturalistic side of the argument of the present book.

Section 2.5 will discuss, quite inevitably, the issue of emancipation. A materialistic political economy can, in fact, only be a way to emancipate individuals from the grip of the intellectual metaphysics of capitalism as we know it. The issue of language follows suit: this will accompany us throughout the whole book.

The conclusions will place us in front of the radical implications of the whole line of reasoning: if capitalism is based upon an intellectuality reduced to a logically flawed metaphysics, no compromise is possible. Avoiding or going beyond capitalism can only be achieved by destruction of the metaphysics of capitalism. This is fundamental to the purpose of understanding the true role of a political economy of a materialistic and historical kind, which is neither normative nor positive, but merely negative. Here, again, language plays a major part.

2.2 Classical approaches

Although it is fairly common and useful, as acknowledged by almost all writers in the field, to commence short accounts of the economic characteristics of capitalism and of political economy with Adam Smith, it is much less common to start from Smith's *The Theory of Moral Sentiments* (2009).[3] Given the broader than economic purposes of our enterprise, however, that is where we must start. On page 25 (Part I, 'Of the property of action'), Smith claims to 'have no other way' to judge like faculties in other men than by the same faculties: reason by reason, love by love, resentment by resentment, ear by ear, sight by sight.

However, although sympathy is natural:

> Every calamity that befalls [them; great kings, AM], every injury that is done to them, excites in the breast of the spectator ten times more compassion and resentment than he would have felt, had the same thing happened to other men.
>
> (p. 65)

This, he acutely notices, resembles 'the misfortunes of lovers' (ibid.), because lovers supposedly partake of a 'happiness superior to any other' (ibid.). In other words, the common man has the intuition of higher states of mind and higher emotional states than he can ever hope to experience, but whose actual existence and nature he nonetheless believes to know for sure: not because they are visible, but because they are thought and talked about as embodied, indeed inevitable, in the happier classes who are, or can be, thought of (and talked about) as being masters of themselves.

In other words, envy engenders, instead of violence, artificial participation and identification, i.e. a discursive attitude predicated on the illusion that class differences are not iron-tight.[4] Acutely blissful or dejected states can be attained, but they pertain to those who have power over themselves and over the mass of the less fortunate (who admire their lives, thus vicariously partaking of their supposedly full emotions). However, these few powerful people have (we have moved to Part IV, 'On the effect of utility upon the sentiment of approbation') 'eyes larger than the belly' (p. 214). 'The capacity of their stomachs bears no proportion to the immensity of [their] desires' (ibid.) and 'will receive no more than that of the meanest peasant'. In fact, by 'selecting from the heap what is most precious and agreeable' (p. 215):

> They are led by an invisible hand to make nearly the same distribution of the necessaries of life, which would have been made, had the earth been divided into equal portions among all its inhabitants, and thus without intending it, without knowing it, advance the interest of society, and afford means to the multiplication of the species.
>
> (p. 215)[5]

As a consequence, it often happens that, 'There have been men of the greatest public spirit, who have shown themselves in other respects not very sensible to the feelings of humanity' (p. 216).

In fact – and this mixture of rational thinking, practical deeds and (artificial) emotional arousal will follow us throughout the book:

> Upon this account political disquisitions, if just, and reasonable, and practicable, are of all the works of speculation the most useful. Even the weakest and meanest of them are not altogether without their utility. They serve at least to animate the public passions of men, and rouse them to seek out the means of promoting the happiness of society.
>
> (p. 217)

On to Part VII now ('Of systems of moral philosophy'):

> There is, however, another system which seems to take away altogether the distinction between vice and virtue [. . .] wholly pernicious: I mean the system of Dr. Mandeville. Though the notions of this author are in almost every respect erroneous, there are, however, some appearances in human nature, which, when viewed in a certain manner, seem at first to favour them. [. . .] Dr. Mandeville considers whatever is done from a sense of propriety, from a regard to what is commendable and praise-worthy, as being done [. . .] as he calls it from vanity.
>
> (p. 362)

However, for Smith, there are three different feelings (he calls them, appropriately, passions) involved: the desire of rendering ourselves the proper object of honour and esteem, the desire to '*really*' deserve honour and esteem, and the frivolous desire for praise at any cost:

> There is an affinity between vanity and the love of true glory, as both these passions aim at acquiring esteem and approbation. But they are different in this, that the one is a just, reasonable and equitable passion while the other is unjust, absurd and ridiculous.
>
> (p. 364)

In order to understand this difference, we have to stray into the realm of the unjust, absurd and ridiculous. This is problematic. How could anybody possibly get there, in a world in which an invisible hand holds the greed of the powerful in check, thus letting them, on average, consume the same (though better in quality) or just a little more than the poor, advancing the interests of society, despite politicians of great public spirit not necessarily being sensitive to the feelings of humanity? What is the connection between the natural equilibrium of the invisible hand and the presence of unjust passions? Why should we worry about them? For the solution is easy: they are absurd, and what is absurd cannot make sense, being by definition opposed to reason and incongruous with reality.[6]

Adam Smith is describing a world in which:

(a) Passions are thought by all to exist for everybody, even though most of them only can be sympathetically and vicariously observed in privileged others; these others are supposed to feel them, and whatever they do is read by everybody else as if that were true. But, of course, the truth of such belief cannot be proved: watchers can only theoretically bestow their unexperienced idea of passions on some people, who are limited to doing what they do, whether they do or do not have, or feel, such passions themselves. The result is that those passions exist because they are pronounced to exist, and their existence is materially proved by the concrete existence of the lucky people whom have been pronounced to be holders of them by virtue of belonging to the powerful classes.

(b) Passions in any case are no problem to the establishment and to society in general, for the presence of a powerful minority is not a major source of destabilizing injustice: an invisible hand sees to that. A funny consequence of all this, to which, perhaps, Marx would not object, is that class difference becomes class struggle and, hence, social revolution only in very special cases (we shall see them when discussing *The Wealth of Nations*). In all other historical configurations, the upper classes emotionally complement the lower classes, like the two halves of sex in Plato's *Symposium*.

(c) Nonetheless, there are 'erroneous' systems, created by the likes of Dr Mandeville, that see all of the above as a collective concession to the 'frivolity' of 'absurd' passions. Unfortunately, the 'frivolous' passions look very much like the worthy desire of primacy that is, instead, the leading cause of noble deeds and of strong and virtuous societies. It is very hard to disentangle the two, especially in the acts and in the persons of politicians, however eminent.

(d) The question, then, seems to be that there indeed are some truly worthy passions, which do not correspond to those in point (a) and which must be aroused by means of such edifying activities as 'political disquisitions', provided they are 'reasonable' and 'practical', i.e. not 'absurd' like Dr Mandeville's system.

A world of attribution of fake or unprovable passions, which are then observed rather than lived, must by necessity be rescued from admissions of frivolity by the rational creation of true, useful passions in political disquisitions. These, however, must be sound not in logical terms, but 'reasonable' (i.e. they must follow the same intellectual pattern as society) and useful (i.e. non-absurd, non 'other' from society). Now, we can turn to *The Wealth of Nations* (Smith, 1999).

Those precious few economists who have actually read Smith (1999) know very well that in there the invisible hand is hardly mentioned, despite what the vast majority of their colleagues purport to believe. The supposed definition is in Book IV, Chapter 2, page 32.

We have seen that, in Smith (2009), the invisible hand is an inertia inbuilt in social relations, the very opposite of what it is supposed to be in the dynamics of the perfect market in standard microeconomics. What matters to modern times is the coming to life of the 'commercial man', who can only fully express his natural 'propensity to truck, barter and exchange one thing for another' (Smith, 1999, Vol. I, p. 117) when the division of labour is at its peak of structuration.

In fact:

> By nature a philosopher is not in genius and disposition half so different from a street porter, as a mastiff is from a greyhound [. . .] These different tribes of animals, however, though all of the same species, are of scarce any use to one another. [. . .] The effects of those different geniuses and talents, for want of the power or disposition to barter and exchange, cannot be brought into a common stock. [. . .] Each animal is still obliged to support and defend itself, separately and independently. [. . .] Among men, on the contrary, the most dissimilar geniuses are of use to one another [. . .] by the general disposition to truck, barter, and exchange, being brought, as it were, into a common stock, where every man may purchase whatever part [. . .] he has occasion for.
>
> (Vol. I, pp. 120–1)

We are fully in Smith's kind of environment (2009), in which the invisible hand performs its miracles of preventing consumption-side injustice, though not justice in possession, as Marx was quick to notice. In fact, 'When the division of labour has been thoroughly established [. . .] Every man thus lives by exchanging, and becomes in some measure a merchant, and the society itself grows to be what is properly a commercial society' (Vol. I, p. 126).

In a commercial society you need money: a numeraire for exchange calculations and a store of wealth to accumulate. 'In all countries [. . .] men seem at last to have been determined by irresistible reasons to give the preference, for this employment, to metals above any other commodity' (Vol. I, p. 127).

From money and value, we move on to Chapter V on the price of commodities, with all the doubts Smith himself had about the labour theory of value (see Micocci, 2008/2010, 2011a, 2011b) and its use, which have no consequence here and will be dealt with later on in the book. Smith famously distinguishes between market value and natural value and goes on to describe (we need not challenge the literature here, for this matter is uncontroversial) what economists mistake as the invisible hand: 'The quantity of every commodity brought to a market naturally suits itself to the effectual demand' (Vol. I, p. 160). It is in everybody's interest, he continues, that the quantity should never exceed or fall short of that demand. This requires some elaboration.

In the first place, we must remember that Smith has a view of society as a harmony, as proved by his *The Theory of Moral Sentiments* (2009). This led Jean-Baptiste Say (another harmony adept)[7] to bring himself to show what Smith had achieved, and then to indicate 'some of the points in which he erred' (1863, p. XI). It is enlightening that Say agrees with Smith's view above, which in fact can be easily reformulated as the so-called Say's law: given that value is (differently from Smith) given by utility, people produce in order to exchange (by means of money) that production, and they do that when they feel they can successfully do it, and not as a compulsion. That is why 'produce opens a vent for produce';[8] gluts and overstocks are entirely possible, but can be corrected, and will inevitably be corrected, not by the mechanistic and mistaken invisible hand of the mainstream economist, but by human decisions.

Smith in fact says that, 'enhancements of the market price are evidently the effect of particular accidents, of which, however, the operation may sometimes last for many years together' (Vol. I, p. 163).

'The natural price itself varies with the natural rate of each of its component parts [wages, profit, rent, AM; according to society's circumstances], their advancing, stationary or declining conditions' (ibid., pp. 165–6).

It is very unfortunate that masters 'being fewer in number, can combine much more easily' (ibid., p. 169). Hence:

> Masters are always and everywhere in a sort of tacit, but constant and uniform combination, not to raise the wages of labour above their actual rate [. . .] sometimes enter into particular combination to sink the wages of labour even below this rate [. . .] Such combinations, however, are frequently resisted by a contrary defensive combination of the workmen.
>
> (ibid., pp. 169–70)

There is, in other words, a social inertia – the invisible hand – that, by allowing the market never to take the features of the perfect market of mainstream economics (which is, instead, mistaken by mainstream economists to be the embodiment of the invisible hand) allows for a (not necessarily immediate) solution to the gluts. By balancing the relative power, influence and capacity to collude, it also allows the working of what Marx later on called class struggle. We are outside mainstream economics, in a world that is stuck, and can only fall or progress by means of a major catastrophe. But Smith, and Say had no desire to explore this possibility, whereas Marx did, as we shall see soon.[9]

We need to complete the picture by pointing the reader to the celebrated pages in Chapter I of Book V of *The Wealth of Nations* (1999), where Smith notices that the 'progress of the division of labour' (Vol. II, p. 368) makes people 'as stupid and ignorant as it is possible for a human creature to become' (ibid.). This exposes opulent and civilized nations to the threat of 'barbarous societies' (p. 369), in which 'every man has a considerable degree of knowledge, ingenuity and invention' (p. 370).[10] Civilization is great, but full of insidious enemies, simultaneously weak and strong: their threat can never be assessed and is, therefore, terrifying.

From the study of Adam Smith, we can gather a first type of conclusion: we are not in a world that has anything to do with mainstream economics, though what Smith says is undoubtedly amenable to be of inspiration to it. Rather, we are in a typically eighteenth-century political-philosophy environment. Let us gather the threads, for we shall discover, in so doing, some surprising logical problems that will accompany us through the rest of the book.

In the first place, society is characterized by a basic inertia in production and consumption and their encroaching relations, which Smith labels the invisible hand. As a consequence, the market is not the theoretical place of present-day microeconomics in which an infinite multitude of price-impotent individuals meet in perfect knowledge of each other's actions.[11] It is, instead, a real place, in which Say's law can operate because nobody gropes in the dark, given the presence of the invisible hand. The condition for this to happen efficiently is the overwhelming presence of the commercial man within the framework of the division of labour and of class society.

This whole situation engenders some intellectual and emotional consequences: specialization makes men stupid, and potentially at the mercy of more 'natural' men (but we should not forget the presence of nations, and the advantage of technology given by the division of labour, which makes, with firearms, wars too expensive for barbarous nations (1999, Vol. II, p. 296)). Feelings are only rationally imagined by the majority, to then be attributed to the precious few who can afford the luxury of having the emotional inebriation of lovers, though we can only presume this and watch what they do, assuming that their deeds are the consequence of their passions.

In fact, Dr Mandeville places us in front of a most obnoxious entanglement: passions are similar, and it is hard to tell whether an individual, although nobly stirred by Smith's political disquisitions, is operating out of frivolous or serious motives. The only criterion for knowing what is right, Smith has to admit, is to stick to what is reasonable and avoid what is absurd. In other words, we must not venture out of the intellectual and emotional framework of our times. No intellectual revolution can be allowed, unless you are ready to risk your society and economy. These last two are potentially at risk in any case, for we do not know how long our technological superiority can keep more natural populations from overcoming us, using the unpredictable intellectual and practical superiority of their barbarous individuals.

It is customary to move from Smith to David Ricardo when dealing with Classical political economists. For our purposes here, however, Ricardo is of little or no use. In fact, his approach is much more similar to that of modern mainstream economists: he tends to stick to 'technical' items, implicitly referring the reader to Adam Smith for whatever lies beyond that limited realm. We can only check whether he agrees with Smith on the issues we have been concerning ourselves with here.

Not surprisingly, this is so. Only, Ricardo's point of view is much weaker than Smith's, being entrusted to a very weak anti-metaphor:

> Man from youth grows to manhood, then decays, and dies; but this is not the progress of nations. When arrived to a state of the greatest vigour, their further advance may indeed be arrested, but their natural tendency is to continue for ages, to sustain undiminished their wealth and their population.
>
> (1962, p. 177)

Another inertia is at work.

Needless to say, Ricardo reproduces Say's law in his own way: 'No man produces but with a view to consume or sell, and never sells but with an intention to purchase some other commodity' (ibid., p. 192). In fact, 'Commodities are always bought by commodities, or by services; money is only the medium by which the exchange is effected' (ibid., p. 194). A glut, he continues, might affect one commodity, not repaying the capital invested, but it can never happen with respect to 'all commodities' (ibid.).

In the years around 1803, Vincenzo Cuoco, the celebrated historian of the Neapolitan revolution, worked on his *Statistica della Repubblica Italiana* (1991). He was already complaining about the division between history, politics and economics, from which it followed that:

> *le osservazioni economiche si sono avute a spezzoni, separate dalle osservazioni politiche. [. . .] per mancanza di unione di queste osservazioni noi, delle nazioni [. . .] sappiamo meglio le epoche del loro accrescimento e della loro caduta che le cagioni.*
>
> *Le osservazioni statistiche così interrotte son divenute inutili per l'economia.*
>
> (1991, p. 67)

This translates as:

> Economic observations come piecemeal, separated from political observations.
> [. . .] because of these disjointed observations we know better, of nations
> [. . .] the ages of their rise and fall than their causes.
>   Such interrupted statistics have become useless for economic analysis.
>
> (trans. A. Micocci)

Cuoco then moves on to caution us about the poor, and about believing that
we should take from the rich to help them. He thus produces an argument that is
very similar to that of Smith's invisible hand:

> *Coloro i quali odiano i grandi non intendono che, senza di essi, una nazione
> sarebbe sempre piccola, perché mancherebbe quell'immenso superfluo, che
> nell'uguaglianza di divisione, sarebbe ripartito tra tutti, e che in tanto è
> necessario che sia accumulato in poche mani, onde possa accrescere, con
> nuove industrie, la ricchezza dell'intera nazione. I grandi proprietari appunto
> son quelli che sviluppano il* gusto *in una nazione e che lo rafforzano.*
>
> (ibid., p. 148; emphasis in the original)

Translation:

> Those who hate the wealthy do not understand that without them a nation
> would remain small, because it would lack that immense superfluity which,
> in an equal sharing, would be fairly distributed, while it is necessary that it
> is accumulated in few hands, so that it can increase, with new industries, the
> wealth of the whole nation. Large owners are precisely those who develop
> the prevailing taste of a nation, strengthening it.
>
> (trans. A. Micocci)

Such 'prevailing taste' is a way to define a dominant culture, which he identifies
(p. 150) with autonomous, in the sense of aboriginal, inventions. A prince (p. 151),
however, can get his people used to Haydn or Mozart, and this might lead to the
establishment of civilizations as powerful and influential as Ancient Greece. In
other words, as for all Classical political economists – and for present-day
economists, although this is not often made explicit – societies progress, and the
need for political economy (pp. 8–9) grows with the progress of society, i.e. of
history, à la Gianbattista Vico, whom Cuoco often invokes on matters concerning
science and prudence.

In this intellectual coincidence between a dominant (modern and developed)
culture, with its 'prevailing taste' (a topic that Smith and Ricardo did not evoke
so explicitly and so narrowly), and political economy, Cuoco notices the puzzling
problem of the 'stationary state', very much à la Ricardo. Countries grow and
evolve, become powerful and yet seem unable to detect the creeping arrival of
the stationary state (pp. 23–4). This last depends upon 'indolence' (p. 24), and
for nations '*spesso quello che noi chiamiamo stazionario si chiamerebbe vero stato*

di decadenza e di languore' (ibid.; 'what we call stationary state would often be called decadence and languor', A. Micocci). That is because '*per difetto di calcoli esatti, non sappiamo riconoscere né la decadenza né il progresso* [. . .] *Quando la decadenza di una nazione è divenuta tanto rapida che si avverte, allora per lo più il rimedio è già vano*' (ibid.; 'for lack of exact calculations, we can recognize neither decadence nor progress [. . .] When the decline of a nation has become so fast that it is perceived, then all solutions are in vain', A. Micocci). The 'vain security' (ibid.) of the stationary state deceives us, but, on a closer examination, does it not look like Smith's invisible hand? This last, in fact, works the same way, in times of plenty and in times of crisis.

Cuoco is adamant that, in order not to perish owing to an undetected stationary state, like the Egyptians, the Persians, China and 'many European examples' in his days (p. 56), '*Il principal soggetto dell'aritmetica politica dovrebbe essere quell'appunto di stabilire le formole necessarie a riconoscere ed esprimere questi cangiamenti politici*' (Translation: 'The main subject of political arithmetic should be that of establishing the formulas that are necessary to recognize and express such political changes', A. Micocci).

He continues (ibid.) that '*aritmetica politica*' is not a '*scienza a parte*' (a separate science), as some proposed. It is the application of calculation to both those objects (ibid.) that cannot be directly known and those amenable to a proportion or measure. '*Aritmetica politica*' is the art of comparing and putting together these two types of object ('commerce, population, arts, money'; ibid.). Only thus shall we have '*un'idea intera di tutte le parti che costituiscono la pubblica economia*' (ibid.; translation: 'only thus shall we have a complete idea of the parts that constitute the public economy, A. Micocci).

We have started drifting from that inevitable mixture of facts and trends of the historical kind announced in Chapter 1 that Smith deals with, towards a more 'theoretical' attitude that seeks, with Ricardo, Say and Cuoco (but please refer to any book on the history of economic ideas for a complete list of authors, with all the internal diversities), to encapsulate some selected facts within a 'scientific' and 'arithmetical' conceptual framework. In so doing, these authors are compelled to crystallize concepts, facts and even numbers, not only in limited meanings and uses, but also in limited webs of reciprocal interactions. Smith's historical inertia, the invisible hand, loses its general validity related to its open meaning and becomes 'the stationary state'. This typically could be measured if only (Cuoco, 1991, p. 57) '*l'aritmetica politica fusse perfettissima*' ('if political arithmetic were as perfect as possible'). You certainly cannot reach the 'perfect perfection', but you can '*avvicinarvisi quanto più possa*' (ibid.; 'come as close to it as you can'), our duty being of '*tendervi sempre*' (ibid.; 'always tending to that').

With this last move, the path has been opened to the only tool to tend to social scientific perfection: calculus. The mathematical properties of limits, derivatives and integrals seem to fit the need to approach a never-to-be-reached point perfectly, which nonetheless is, in the abstract, 'precise and does correspond to a mathematically significant property of the function' (Allen, 1960, p. 96). Surely there is the powerful limit that, for this mathematics, continuous functions are required, which are rarely found in nature and in human endeavours. But, 'The differential calculus is [thus] of almost immediate application in all scientific studies' (ibid., p. 150). In fact, 'it is found mathematically convenient to assume, wherever poss-ible, that the variables and functions are continuous [. . .] Sometimes it is necessary to retain discontinuous variables, but the theory thus becomes mathematically much more difficult and much less elegant' (ibid.).

Much has been written on this issue concerning the Neoclassical approach and its use of calculus. What we need to do here instead is to show how this was encoded in what the Classical political economists after Smith sought to do. Let us see.

We are progressively shifting from Adam Smith's dynamic and open eighteenth-century philosophical scenario – which nonetheless has all the problems we find in his followers and adversaries of positing a social inertia that devolves understanding to a shared rationality that can supposedly detect absurdity and frivolity – to a world that takes the same shared rationality for granted in order to reach as closely as possible some firm arithmetical laws. All these authors rely on an inbuilt inertia that historical systems have (similar to Smith's invisible hand) and that allows them to withstand both their own internal disruptive forces, the undetectable threat of the stationary state, and the external menaces from lesser civilizations. We need, to keep to this type of reasoning, a narrower, more political philosophy.

As acknowledged by the greater part of the literature, the position as of one of the most accomplished of fully capitalist philosophers belongs to John Stuart Mill. His liberal philosophy and his political economy will accompany Anglo-Saxon students well into the twentieth century. It is well worth starting from his justly celebrated essay 'On liberty' (1859, in Mill, 1986). On page 130, he discusses the need to have 'rules of conduct'; these must be imposed by laws only in part, for there are some that cannot be so enforced. We need then to use 'opinion' (ibid.), 'but no two ages, and scarcely any two countries' have agreed on them. Mankind constantly deceives itself by believing that the customs of one age and one country are anthropological constants. 'This all but universal illusion is one of the examples of the magical influence of custom, which is not only, as the proverb says, a second nature, but is continuously mistaken for the first' (p. 131).

In fact, there is not even any need to give reasons for rules of conduct. They are given by customs, they are unjustified rationally and, therefore, 'can only count as a person's preference' (ibid.), and reasons that are given come down to appeals to similar preferences 'felt by other people' (ibid.). This extends to morality, taste and propriety. Fundamentally, for our general argument, 'Wherever there is an ascendant class, a large portion of the morality of the country emanates from its class interests, and its feelings of class superiority' (p. 132). 'The likings and dislikings of society, or of some powerful portion of it, are thus the main thing which has determined the rules laid down for general observance, under the penalties of law or opinion' (ibid.)

The wide meaning of Smith's inertia and the multiple possibilities it entails are narrowed down to a simple, arid relationship. There is little use, then, in stating (p. 135) that, 'Over himself, over his own body and mind, the individual is sovereign', for such sovereignty is belied by the above reasoning. In fact, Mill continues, in such world he regards 'utility as the ultimate appeal on all ethical questions' (p. 136). The whole of Chapter II ('Of the liberty of thought and discussion') has a different, more limited dimension.[12]

It follows logically that customs are far from making a proper human being (ch. III, 'Of individuality as one of the elements of well-being', p. 187). A note of caution: Mill is adamant that individuals should take their destiny in their hands and act without letting anybody or anything 'choose his plan of life for him'. Nonetheless, action is so atrociously narrowed as to take us straight to a whole new world, 'capitalism as we know it': 'The human faculties of perception, judgement, discriminative feelings, mental activity, and even moral preference, are exercised only in making a choice. He who does anything because it is the custom makes no choice' (p. 187).

What a condition! Customs count but make no individuals; but individuals are such only in that they choose, whether from custom or from other sets of items. Creativity is dead and buried, for in this context no novelty can appear. In fact, there have been earlier states of society 'when the elements of spontaneity and individuality was in excess, and the social principle had a hard struggle with it' (ibid., p. 189).

There is a conflict between individuality and the need for power and institutionalized society. As a consequence, 'conformity is the first thing thought of; they like in crowds; they exercise choice only among things commonly done [. . .] human capacities are withered and starved' (p. 190), which Calvinists deem a good condition. Instead, we must not foster uniformity:

> It is not by wearing down into uniformity all that is individual in themselves, but by cultivating it [. . .] within the limits imposed by the rights and inter- ests of others, that human beings become a noble and beautiful object of contemplation [. . .] human life becomes rich, diversified and animating [. . .] there is greater fullness of life about his own existence, and where there is more life in the units there is more in the mass that is composed of them.
>
> (ibid., p. 192)

Or is there?

Individuality is development, nearing the best thing one can be (p. 193), and liberty is the goal. 'Genius can only breathe freely in an *atmosphere* of freedom' (ibid., p. 194; emphasis in the original). Mill goes on to notice that England is losing individuality, and conformity is rife in his day; what little 'energy' there is 'finds business as its only outlet' (p. 200), and he is sorry. 'Free trade' rests on grounds (ch. V, 'Application') different from, though equally solid with, 'the principle of individual liberty asserted in this Essay' (p. 227). He goes on producing examples of necessary restrictions to trade. Confusion piles up on confusion for those of us who are used to the limpid openness of Smith's theorization.

The only conceptual difference with the other Classical political economists, including Smith, is that the common rationality produced by the leading classes (whether it is practised or just vicariously enjoyed) must supply some criteria whereby one can recognize what is absurd (as Smith says) and the power of customs, in order to tend towards an individual autonomy. However, such autonomy comes down – if the above holds, and in the very words of Mill – to choice among given alternatives. All that can be done is to use one's brain in a rational (common and socialized) way to avoid falling prey to custom, conformity, or absurd and pernicious ideas such as Mandeville's, which are subtle and, after all, contain a grain of truth.

Mill has an inkling that this is a miserable state and appeals to the vague and undefined hope that mankind might still be a 'noble and beautiful object of contemplation', and that freedom can breed 'genius', but what genius? A genius who can only pick from the alternatives offered! No wonder the only outlet for individual energy is business: there is the kingdom of choice in it, as the Neoclassical economists were to propose later, driving the last nail into mankind's intellectual, creative and emotional coffin, and as a consequence into liberty's coffin too. It is also important to notice that this world still has some aspects that are not amenable to arithmetical treatment, but reason as choice makes for a perfect environment for the use of calculus, and for behaving as if functions were all continuous. Instead of going somewhere or doing something, we 'tend' towards that.

We should not forget that we are not yet in the realm of perfectly pure theory that distinguishes the Neoclassicals. These Classical authors still refer to given, historical facts. They observe reality. Let us now turn to Mill the economist.

In a world in which the last vestiges of individual creativity can only be spent in business, political economy acquires quite different meaning and importance to those in the preceding authors. Thus, although 'The laws and conditions of the production of wealth partake of the character of physical truths' (1998, p. 5), 'We cannot alter the ultimate properties of matter or mind, but can only employ these properties more or less successfully, to bring about the events in which we are interested' (ibid., p. 6). We cannot foresee any changes in the modes of production (p. 5) and must make do with what we have – quite a disconsolate beginning.

It follows that:

> Any disposal whatever of them can only take place by the consent of society, or rather of those who dispose of its active force [. . .] The distribution of wealth, therefore, depends on the laws and customs of society. The rules by which it is determined, are what the opinions and feelings of the ruling portion of the community make them.
>
> (p. 6)[13]

Mill goes on, reminding us of the combination of the laws of human nature and the existing state of knowledge, social institutions and 'intellectual and moral culture', but the point is that, 'Society can subject the distribution of wealth to whatever rules it thinks best' (ibid., pp. 6–7). One must ask, however, what this thing is he calls society, with its shared culture and its customs.

In the development of his argument, which starts from private property, Mill seems to stick to the view that society evolved by adjusting to what was expedient given the circumstances. This, of course, is open to historical criticism, but what interests us here is rather that society and its culture tend to lose historical clarity, becoming more and more just what they are. Thus, Mill can introduce theoretical 'communities' (p. 10), which end up doing this or that by taking community decisions about what is expedient. This naturally needs small communities. Hence, Mill has to introduce the concept that, 'History bears witness to the success which large bodies of human beings may be trained to feel the public interest their own' (p. 12), which is very similar to Smith's reasonable political disquisitions versus Mandeville.

Mill's example is extreme, in that he refers to 'communism'. But the idea is clear that the hawk-eyed power of the community can control, to whatever degree (communist or liberal), individual actions and even participation (i.e. emotions). He, in fact, goes on (pp. 17–18) repeating the liberal conditions of maximum liberty with the limit of doing no injury to others. This might lead to dangerous epistemological shores, and Mill realizes it.

In Book III (*Exchange*, ch. 10, 'Of value'), he says:

> It is a case of the error too common in political economy, of not distinguishing between necessities arising from the nature of things, and those created by social arrangements [. . .] causing political economists to class the merely temporary truths of their subject among its personal and universal laws [. . .] leading many persons to mistake the permanent laws of Production [. . .] for temporary accidents arising from the existent conditions of society – which those who would frame a new system of social arrangements, are at liberty to disregard.
>
> (p. 54)

Nonetheless, all 'civilized' nations increase gradually in production and population (p. 66) and in 'the security of person and property'. Capitalism is, to him, a universal law.

If society and community merge into one another and can exert a coercion on individuals that is not inimical to individuality, and if there are universal laws leading to capitalism, it is no wonder that, 'there is no more certain incident of the progressive change taking place in society, than the continual growth of the principle and practice of cooperation' (p. 69). The difference from Smith's invisible hand is, however, fundamental: Mill's own version of the invisible hand, which holds society together, is the result of 'voluntarily combining their small contributions' (ibid.). Rather than Smith's own invisible hand, this is very similar to the Smith of *The Wealth of Nations* and the quest for 'opulence' of a nation.

In fact, to Mill (Book IV, *Influence of Progress*, ch. IV, 'Of the tendency of profits to a minimum'), life in modern times has fewer vicissitudes and engenders a habit of perseverance and of sacrificing ourselves for the future. It engenders 'capacity of forethought and self-control' (p. 106). Rates of profit can and do go down. The increase of wealth is not boundless. At its end lies the 'stationary state' (ch. VI, p. 124). This is ultimately 'impossible to avoid', and it would be, Mill believes, 'A very considerable improvement on our present condition' (p. 126), ending the trampling, crushing and elbowing of the existing type of social life. 'But the best state for human nature is that in which, while no one is poor, no one desires to be richer, nor has any reason to fear being thrust back, by the efforts of others to push themselves forward' (p. 127).

Here, one can glimpse at an apparently open-minded, socialistic John Stuart Mill, but, with more careful consideration, this is not so. On the contrary, this statement only brings to bear upon political economy the customs and habits, rationally shared ideas, and decisions on what is expedient that characterize his political economy and that of all the other writers of the Classical period.

In fact (Book V, *Influence of Government*, especially ch. VIII, 'Of the ordinary functions of governments, considered as to their economical effects'), governments have the same functions as in Adam Smith's *The Wealth of Nations*. Mill only allows for concessions to the creative power of lawless ages, with their 'degree of insecurity' (p. 257). In fact, governments should not 'choose opinions for the people' and should not (p. 322) enforce repressive laws of any kind. Spain and Portugal were held back by the presence of the Holy Inquisition and they failed their historical, 'Smithian' pursuit of opulence.

This last observation by Mill is very appropriate to make us notice the typical internal incoherence of all the Classical approaches we have examined here. On the one hand, we are told that society and the economy are held together and kept (even well beyond their golden age of dynamic growth) by an economic, social and cultural inertia and by a tendency to conform to whatever general intellectuality is available in each given era. On the other, there is a need for 'genius' and originality that is perfectly artificial (for it only exists as choice and as something different from conformism) and that can only be defined by sketching the ominous contours of its reciprocal: obscurantism.

Yet obscurantism cannot exist as such in this general framework. Like Smith's potential barbarian enemies, it needs to be defined as a hazy, general theoretical presence (rather than possibility) and, hence, needs to be embodied into occasional, symbolic, actual instances. The Holy Inquisition above is one of them, an easy target to shoot at, for it indeed was a concentration of all that is bad: repression of ideas, torture, executions, Catholic integralism, injustice and a desire to extend control over practically everything. In other words, it is an object abject and evil enough to be a monster, and, like all monsters, is identified through our common understanding of it, rather than through a precise record of its misdeeds (at least at the level of common discussion; one may assume that somewhere there must be a scientist who holds all the facts).

To summarize, concepts and terms lose their direct reference to the material items they are supposed to represent. They are transfigured into metaphysical entities whose meaning oscillates at the leisure of the user, between contiguity with the concrete (but not coincidence with it) and an approximation to the abstract by defect. Thus communities, societies, economies, money, needs and exchange are but hazy metaphysical multiples of themselves. They can signify the here and now of the price of this commodity or of my need for it, as well as the numerous possibilities of all possible degrees of metaphysical vagueness I can contrive (including marginal price and satisfaction). The trick is possible because of the presence of Adam Smith's vicarious emotional content, of Cuoco's 'prevailing taste', and of Mill's choice, instead of perfect, natural and spontaneous creativity.

In other words, this is possible precisely because the individual is not – ever – using all his/her/its potentialities. One can need a commodity and yet have or not have it, depending on whether one's 'commercial man' endowments have procured enough money to purchase it. If we can part with emotions and enjoy them vicariously, we can much more easily part with bodily needs and desires, as is demonstrated by the depressing spectacle of worldwide deprivation that capitalism as we know it shows, and that is dealt with only as a metaphysical entity, for which we can passionately care (for passions are vicarious), not care at all, and even fight and/or demonstrate in favour of and against.

Life being metaphysics, and things and concepts being expressible in the wide range of undefinable degrees we find between the unreachable two of concrete and abstract, this is possible. One can undergo lack of food, but that lack is subject to a wide range of subtle distinctions of intensity and causation. Your undergoing it is a discussion of it instead of a feeling of hunger. After all, a ravishing hunger is only for the rich and the powerful, or, currently, for the visible media-wise. All of them fight for their own and the others' hunger, while common people go on starving passively, or being undernourished, or overnourished, talking and being talked about it with words that never can reach their objective, thus depriving them of the truth and actuality of their state.

2.3 Capitalist metaphysics

Although many may want to take issue with each of the interpretations of the Classical political economists that have been put forward so far, there is little contemporary interest in interpreting the overall picture. The reason, as introduced in Section 2.1, is that the implications are too radical (absurd, in Smith's language). Such an idea is logically wrong, but correct in its outcome when operating in capitalism as we know it: what we discuss is highly subversive with regard to the various pillars on which capitalism as we know it rests. Not wanting to see it is, obviously, no solution and rests on the bet that the inertia we have seen inbuilt in capitalist systems will hold. In this and the following chapters, we will show, however, that this belief is the most anti-realistic stance an observer of reality can take.

The most evident thing that strikes the eye of the economist is the discrepancy, indeed the apparent incompatibility, between standard microeconomic theory and Classical political economy. The Classical authors do not explicitly care to be precise or clear about the theoretical possibility of what standard microeconomic theory calls perfect competition, for they are unwilling to use it in practice. They in fact intended to refer to historical facts, which are conditioned by the variously interpreted inertia Smith calls the invisible hand, which we have taken as a symbol of all the types of historical, social and economic inertia. That is why Dr Mandeville's work is irritating for Adam Smith. It was, like microeconomics, a merely theoretical argument that showed the inner logic of what he proposed, and that he could not accept. His metaphysics, as well as that of all the other Classical political economists, is as highly imperfect as mainstream economics.

Classical political economists are continuously seeking to refer to the items of reality as they perceive it. This is precisely the problem: to do so, they are compelled to isolate relevant elements in order to summarize and generalize, and produce a description that, in a loop, holds only in that it is expressed in the very same overall logic, and language, of the general intellectuality of the world they are studying. The implications of this move are enormous, and also numerous. We deal with some of them in the rest of this book, leaving others to future endeavours.

The next question we must pose now is whether the difference between Classical and mainstream theories is actually binding to our purposes, or rather reveals a solely formal device. If, in fact, we look at modern economics more closely and carefully, we notice that, in the literature, as soon as the apparently uncompromising – and unreal – tenets of perfect competition configuration are stated, the tone suddenly changes and becomes accommodating. Bit by bit, elements of reality are brought in, starting with imperfect competition, to end up with macroeconomics. The same procedure is applied to welfare economics and to the theoretical study of economic policy and applied economics. The whole thing, as Cuoco proposed, is in other words expressed with the language of 'always tending' to 'political arithmetic', well represented by the use of calculus or by its supposed alternatives, for example, chaos theories.

Nor should we be put off by the internal incoherencies of the whole construction, as beautifully shown, for instance, by the 'Two Cambridges' controversy over the measurement of capital. At the peak of the diatribe, Paul Samuelson acknowledged defeat and made it clear that J. B. Clark's notion of capital was a 'fairy tale' that could not be defended in any theoretical way and had no counterpart in reality (1962). Yet, it was a 'useful parable' that described the truth – capitalism – by analogy. Perfectly coherently with what we have already discussed and what we shall further develop in the remainder of this book, this statement gained Samuelson and the mainstream a greatly deserved and greatly unjustified dominance, from that day when defeat was acknowledged, onwards.

The question comes down to the fact that theory and reality in the metaphysics of capitalism, as properly perceived by the Classical political economists, tend to overlap on many grounds. Terms and concepts tend to shade into real objects and vice versa, both in Classical and in mainstream theorizations, owing to their being metaphysical entities within a metaphysics (an intellectuality) that is openly acknowledged by the participants, whether they know economics or not. This is a vulgar Hegelian type of environment, in which real oppositions are unthinkable, and dialectical contradictions rule. Very Hegel-like, real oppositions are replaced

– in their inherent radicalism and in the entailed strong emotions (which, as Smith has made clear, are metaphysical and not concrete objects, and for precious few people, if they exist at all) – by the subtle cruelty of what actually happens.

Passive and active substances participate Hegel-wise in the action of power, which in actual reality and in banal terms is just straightforward organized violence (Micocci, 2012). To Hegel (2008a), this is what history is about and what makes states what they are (Hegel, 2008b; we will repeatedly come back to the work of Hegel through Marx). Organized violence replaces the direct action of economic, social and political interactions. What disappears, and is thereby decreed to be 'absurd' and incongruous with what is going on, cannot therefore be items that ontologically belong to the status quo. For a powerful instance, inefficient firms, or underdeveloped nations, do not disappear. They must wait for the next dialectical action to be reabsorbed into a new combination of the same old things.

To state it plainly: diffused, continuous cruelty replaces perfect competition and even many forms of natural (spontaneous) and occasional violence. What matters is the impression that is obtained, for such an impression is only vicariously perceivable and can be easily taken in by everybody. It belongs to those who can be talked about through the general intellectual logic: the rich and powerful in Smith's own time, to whom we can add, these days – thanks to the mass media – the poor and destitute, whose feelings are different in intensity, form and perception. The remainder of this chapter will discuss how this was present at the intuitive level in Marx the critic of Hegelian dialectics, i.e. the anarchist Marx.

Naturally, one could express all these things with another idiom, but, to the chagrin of the mainstream economists, who hate philosophy, there are good reasons to stick to the Hegelian critique. First and foremost, whether mainstream economists like it or not, Hegelian dialectical processes can be found in all the intellectual processes of capitalism as we know it.[14] Hegel's capacity to distil the bourgeois mentality into a 'high' form through philosophy has had unpredictable consequences, well analysed by two eminent philosophers of the twentieth century: Ernst Cassirer, who was writing during the fascist period in Europe, and Nicolao Merker, a contemporary Italian philosopher who has recently felt the need to counteract present-day populism, the flip side of the neo-liberal coin.

Cassirer (1961) and Merker (2009), in various different ways, charge Hegel with building the intellectual framework that leads to populism and fascism. Fascism itself, unfortunately, is not a passing fashion in the history of Catholic Europe and Latin America. It is, instead, a determining characteristic of capitalism as we know it. As argued in Micocci (2012), as a result of its 'moderate' features, fascism is the only position acceptable and the only policy path that is open to those who feel repelled by radical thought and want to stick to, and protect, the metaphysics of capitalism as we know it.[15] This last, in fact, as already noticed several times, cannot conceive of revolutionary breaks, ruptures with disappearance, i.e. Kantian real opposition (more creative developments further on).

Marx himself, before he could come into his own as a philosopher and political economist, had to come to terms with Hegel's philosophy, especially his logic, philosophy of right and theory of the state. We shall start with Marx (1986), written in his youthful 1846–7 period, for it puts together political economy and philosophy by attacking Proudhon precisely on the grounds of producing economic nonsense by means of a badly disguised and badly digested Hegelian metaphysics. The fundamental momentum of Marx's anti-Hegelian stance can be easily perceived in this work, and its importance as an expositive device can be easily guessed.

It is well worth starting from the end of Marx's *The Poverty of Philosophy* (1986), for its very conclusions summarize the main issues at stake here. We shall use here, for the quotations in English, McLellan's *Selected Writings* (Marx, 2005; the only text available at the time of writing), although there, Marx's works are selected and abridged in order to transform him into a Marxist of the mainstream kind. Reference to the complete Italian edition (Marx, 1986) are, therefore, added.

> The working class, in the course of its development, will substitute for the old civil society an association which will exclude class and their antagonism, and there will be no more political power properly so called, since political power is precisely the official expression of antagonism in civil society.
>
> (Marx, 2005, p. 232, 1986, p. 121)

In fact, class struggle between the bourgeoisie and the proletariat:

> carried to its highest expression is a total revolution. Indeed, is it at all surprising that a society founded on the opposition of classes should culminate in a brutal contradiction, the shock of body against body, as its final denouement?
>
> (ibid.; emphasis in the original and 1986)

The above means that a real opposition, if not 'brought into its higher expression', degenerates into the cruelty of a dialectical contradiction with its violence. 'Do not say that social movement excludes political movement. There is never a political movement which is not at the same time social' (2005, p. 32, 1986, p. 121).

In short, revolution can only be a rupture with disappearance. Attempts to bring class struggle to the (inappropriate) level of a dialectical contradiction causes organized physical cruelty of the violent kind. The whole point can only be the abolition of political power, for political power is the same as civil society, which entails a continuous dialectical (and cruel) class antagonism. Society as an intellectual device must be replaced by a spontaneous sociality of a material, natural kind. Only thus can we understand the need for a critique of political economy.

Now, the interpretation of Marx's criticisms of Proudhon's *La philosophie de la misère* can easily be followed in their logic. We need to concentrate, as is only too obvious, on Chapter 2, aptly titled 'The metaphysics of political economy': 'We shall now have to talk metaphysics while talking political economy' (2005, p. 215, 1986, p. 64). Proudhon is in fact another Dr Quesnay, the Quesnay of the metaphysics of political economy (ibid.). Famously, Marx states here that:

Economists express the relations of bourgeois production, the division of labour, credit, money, etc., as fixed, immutable, eternal categories. [. . .] Economists explain how production takes place in the above mentioned relations, but what they do not explain is how these relations themselves are produced, that is, the historical movement which gave them birth. [. . .] The economists' material is the active, energetic life of man; M.Proudhon's material is the dogmas of the economists. But the moment we cease to pursue the historical movement of production relations, of which the categories are but the theoretical expression, the moment we see in these categories no more than ideas, spontaneous thoughts, independent of real relations, we are forced to attribute the origin of these thoughts to the movement of pure reason. How does pure, eternal, impersonal reason give rise to these thoughts? How does it proceed in order to produce them?

(2005, p. 216–17, 1986, p. 65)

Marx continues to answer these very relevant questions, which are the same we are posing in this book, noticing that Proudhon's answer is 'intrepidly' Hegelian (p. 66), and proceeds by somersaults following the vulgar Hegelian triad. This is the only language that such a pure reason that can be separated from the individual can speak (ibid.). 'Instead of the ordinary individual with his ordinary manner of speaking and thinking, we have nothing but this ordinary manner in itself – without the individual' (2005, p. 217, 1986, p. 65).

Everything is reduced to a flawed logical category. Thus, the metaphysicians:

in making these abstractions, think that they are making analyses and [. . .] the more they detach themselves from things, imagine themselves to be getting all the nearer to the point of penetrating their core – these metaphysicians in turn are right in saying that things here below are embroideries of which the logical categories constitute the canvas.

(2005, p. 217, 1986, p. 66)

So one has only to make an abstraction of every of every character distinctive of different movements to attain movement in the abstract condition – purely formal movement, the purely logical formula of movement. If one finds in logical categories the substance of all things, one imagines one has transformed in the logical formula of movement the absolute method, which not only explains all things, but also implies the movement of things [. . .] All things being reduced to a logical category, and every movement, every act of production, to method, it follows naturally that every aggregate of products and production of objects and movement, can be reduced to a form of applied metaphysics.

(2005, p. 218, 1986, p. 67)

Marx continues discussing the dialectical movement of all this and concludes that, by applying such a method to the categories of political economy, you get the metaphysics we have seen, with the proviso that Hegel (and, we shall see, all the other Classical and mainstream political economists; see Micocci, 2002) is so misapplied as to be methodologically disfigured. But the economic categories are historical and transient.

All the above is well summarized, as follows: 'Hegel has no problems to formulate. He has only dialectics. M. Proudhon has nothing of Hegel's dialectics but the language' (2005, p. 22, 1986, p. 71).

With his 'Fifth Observation', Marx notices that the dialectics boils down to pure morality. His 'Sixth Observation' observes how the consequence of this is the positing of an absolute reason, the reason of the 'person–society', of humanity, i.e. human reason (this is similar to what we call here dominant intellectuality). Hence ('Seventh Observation'), the only natural institutions are those of capitalism. There used to be history, but it is no more. We have thus rendered the core meaning of Marx's booklet.

The whole matter has been variously dealt with in the twentieth century by the minority tradition of the anti-Hegelian Marxists (Colletti, 1969a, 1969b, 1972, 1973, 1974, 1975, 1979; Della Volpe 1945, 1949, 1963, 1967, 1978, 1980; see also Micocci, 2002, 2008/2010, 2012; Rosenthal, 1998). In this and similar literature, it is demonstrated that Marx's criticism of Proudhon was not an isolated episode, but just a manifestation of his long-term anti-Hegelian commitment. This has been a constant preoccupation in Marx that is not secondary to our argument.[16] We go on now exploring some more of the Young Marx.

To clear the field from the beginning, it is worth commencing by means of a most explicit statement. In the 1844 *Economic and Philosophical Manuscripts*, Marx first proposes the idea of alienation as alienation from the self, from others and from nature. But:

Estrangement appears not only in the fact that the means of *my* life belong to *another* and that *my* desire is the inaccessible possession of *another*, but also in the fact that all things are *other* from themselves, that my activity is *other* than itself, and that finally – and this goes for the capitalist too – an *inhuman* power rules over everything.

(1992, p. 366; emphasis in the original)

We can move backwards and discover that we no longer need God's mediation to discover nature, for the starting point is the 'theoretically and practically sensuous consciousness *of man and nature* as *essential beings*. It is the *positive self-consciousness* of man' (p. 357). In fact, you can eat, drink, buy books, love, go to the theatre, theorize, etc. (he has a long list) the less the more your capital grows: 'the more you *have the greater is* your alienated *life and humanity*' (p. 361). 'All passions and activities are lost in greed' (ibid.).

By abolishing private property, communism abolishes self-estrangement (p. 348) and – this is fundamental: 'This communism as fully developed naturalism, equals humanism' (ibid.). Marx then moves on to the core question of the present volume:

Man's first object – man – is nature, sense perception; and the particular sensuous human powers, since they can find objective realization only in *natural* objects, can find self-knowledge only in the science of nature in general. The element of thought itself, the element of the vital expression of thought – *language* – is sensuous nature.

(pp. 355–6; emphasis in the original)

That is why the worker is 'estranged' (see e.g. pp. 322–34 in the *First Manuscript*, 1992).

The matter is clear and straightforward. We can only understand political economy as the language of an artificial estrangement from nature and, hence, from the self and from others. The best way for the structure and language of political economy to do so is to present some typical features that make it necessarily similar to a vulgar Hegelian logic and progression. This applies not only because this is what Marx has at hand, through Feuerbach's criticism. More generally, Hegelian logic is the most appropriate epitome of a general mentality that is estranged from nature, about which, as noted in the preceding section, the other political economists would only agree, if we could ask them. They describe the alienated man within his alienated environment as if this were normal and above all universal: a Hegelian Universal.

In the *Third Manuscript*, Marx is unequivocal:

For the present, let us observe that Hegel adopts the standpoint of modern political economy. He sees *labour* as the *essence*, the self-confirming essence, of man [. . .]. Labour is *man's coming to be for himself* within *alienation* or as an *alienated man*.

(p. 386; emphasis in the original)

Hegel thinks that his is an absolute philosophy and is, therefore, led to invert the idea of self-consciousness. However 'Man is directly a *natural being*' (p. 389; emphasis in the original), equipped with natural powers and drives, and objects that are 'independent of him' (ibid.). He can only 'express his life' in sensuous real objects; hence, nature and sense are outside man (p. 390). Man suffers and is a passionate being, but he is limited, being different from animals and plants (p. 391) by the fact that his natural endowments also have 'origin in history' (ibid.). This last is a conscious process: 'History is the true natural history of man' (p. 391).

Marx continues by introducing issues that he deals with in his critique of Hegel's *Philosophy of Right*. We can only follow him on this ground if we want to complete our argument. We need a materialistic approach based on sensuousness and history. The study of sensuousness is the realm of Hume, as we shall see in the next chapter, and of Hume's Epicurean arguments.

It cannot be denied that Marx is not saying anything very different to the other Classical political economists. There is a logic outside the individuals that can only be undergone and embraced, and identified with the logic of things human.

Such logic is constantly perceived to be universal, whereas it is wholly dependent on historical circumstances. Feelings and emotions are a hindrance to it and, therefore, they are considered, by those who accept it, as remnants of a past of wilderness and fierce '*homo homini lupus*', but if what we have is historically determined, its end is inevitable. This is what the other Classical political economists seem to resist in various degrees, by noticing that there is an inertia in things social to which they attribute different degrees of resilience. Marx instead sees changeability as the path to going back to nature: as we shall see in the remainder of this book, this is the realm of freedom, where anything is possible.

The logic of vulgar Hegelianism best renders what is going on in political economy. The question remains whether such logic applies to economic and philosophical theorization only, or also to actual capitalist things, behaviours and institutions. We shall see that this latter hypothesis (already discussed in Micocci, 2002, 2008/2010) is realistic. So far, we have noticed that all the theorizations of Classical political economy can be described as Hegelian, or, more precisely, as generally moderate (see Micocci 2012), but that they all, unlike Hegel, start their disquisitions from material reality. We are already a considerable step forward. Marx takes us to a discussion of the state, furthering our progress.

The discussion by Marx of Hegel's theory of rights and of the state is a characteristic strength of the work of Galvano Della Volpe (see especially his 1978, 1980, and Micocci, 2002) and of his disciple Colletti (before he gave up on Marxism). Here, we will reconsider their arguments and those of Micocci (2008/2010) by adhering more closely to Marx.

Let us start from the following statement in Marx's *Critique of Hegel's Doctrine of the State* (1992, p. 63):

> Thus empirical reality is accepted as it is; it is even declared to be rational. However, it is not rational by virtue of its own reason, but because the empirical fact in its empirical existence has a meaning other than itself. The fact which serves as a starting point is not seen as such but as a mystical result.[17]

What Marx is seeking to show critically is that the bases of the existing states are taken to be naturally connected to the existing social arrangements by means of the flawed method of Hegel, which is similar, in its results, to that of the Classical political economists: 'the political state cannot exist without the natural basis of the family and the artificial basis of civil society [. . .] and yet the condition is posited as the conditioned, the determinator as the determined, the producer as the product' (ibid.). 'Logic does not provide a proof of the state but the state provides a proof of logic' (p. 73). There is almost an identification between the concept, its logic and the actual object of reality, precisely like in the theorizations of the Classical political economists. 'The abstraction of the *state as such* was not born until the modern world because the abstraction of private life was not created until modern times. The abstraction of the *political state* is a modern product' (p. 90; emphasis in the original).

As the whole point of the exercise is to create an *allegory*, to confer on some empirically existing thing or other the *significance* of the realized Idea, it is obvious that these vessels will have fulfilled their function as soon as they have become a determinate incarnation of a moment of the life of the Idea. Hence, the Universal appears everywhere as a determinate particular, while the individual never achieves its true universality.

(p. 99; emphasis in the original)

Man is, for instance, identified with its predicate (class, or entrepreneurship, or proletarian poverty and dejection). 'The same subject is given different *meanings*, but the meaning is not that of self-determination, but of an *allegory* foisted on to it' (p. 149; emphasis in the original).

The meaning of class distinctions in civil society in the political sphere is derived from the political sphere itself, but the opposite is also equally true. This uncritical (mystical) view 'interprets an old view of the world in terms of a new one' (ibid.), producing a 'wretched hybrid', which is 'the key both to the riddle of modern constitutions [. . .] and of Hegelian philosophy' (ibid.). All is reduced to a mediation. But: 'Real extremes cannot be mediated precisely because they are real extremes. Nor do they require mediation, for their natures are wholly opposed. [. . .] This point needs to be developed further in a critique of Hegel's Logic' (p. 155). This cannot be misunderstood.

If this last concept is true, and the present author cannot see how it can be denied in Marx and, more importantly, in general, then there is no way in the world one can defend dialectical materialism as well as all the other economic and political theories that do not contemplate ruptures with disappearance (real extremes that cannot be mediated, in Marx's words). Without these last there cannot be revolution, but only mediation of the bourgeois kind, i.e., as we have seen, diffused and continuous cruelty rather than radical breaks. It is worth remembering that outbursts of spontaneous and natural violence can take place that do not imply cruelty in the capitalist sense. Thus, we can borrow a sentence from *The Jewish Question*: 'Political emancipation is at the same time the *dissolution* of the old society' (1992, p. 232; emphasis in the original). 'Only when real, individual man resumes the abstract citizen into himself [. . .] only then will human emancipation be completed' (ibid., p. 234).

We can conclude by a succinct statement from Marx's letter to Ruge that summarizes what has been said so far: '*the ruthless criticism of the existing order*, ruthless in that it will shrink neither from its own discoveries nor from conflicts with the powers to be' (1992, p. 207; emphasis in the original). But no ruthlessness can be applied without emancipation from the intellectuality and language of capitalism as we know it. In another 1844 work (Excerpts from James Mill's *Elements of Political Economy*), Marx says the following:

We are so estranged from our human essence that the direct language of man strikes us as an offence against the dignity of man, whereas the estranged language of objective values appears as the justified, self-confident and self-acknowledged dignity of man incarnate.

(1992, p. 277)

From this point on, we are tasked with the solution of this.

We need to start from the fact that, in capitalism, 'greed' seems to dominate by replacing all the other feelings, but things are not so straightforward. In *Capital*, Marx mentions the effects of alienation, i.e. the lack of feelings or their transubstantiation into greed, and the illogical kind of reasoning thereby ensuing in many different guises. Hence, in Book I, Chapter 1, 'the nature of such [human] wants, whether, for instance, they spring from the stomach or from fancy, makes no difference' (1978, p. 43).

> Robinson soon learns by experience, and having rescued a watch, ledger, and pen and ink from the wreck, commences, like a true-born Briton, to keep a set of books. His stock-book contains a list of the objects of utility that belong to him, of the operations necessary for their production, and lastly, of the labour-power that definite quantities of those objects have, on an average, cost him.
>
> (ibid., p. 81)

The same chapter also introduces the character of fetish of the commodities, but this is evidently a corollary of the main issue, which Marx observes and discusses like the other political economists: the creation of a metaphysics. This last must appear detached from the concrete, for actual objects are transcended into something other than themselves, but it must also steer clear of rigorous and abstract reasoning, or it would reveal its perverse intellectual and moral poverty, like Dr Mandeville's work. Most importantly, all this only exists in that there is an intrinsic inertia in all modes of production that keeps them from reaching perfection, and, hence, decaying fast, and leaves them indefinitely suspended in a hard-to-justify resilience, even when the state of decadence is reached.

History is crowded with analysts who have identified the political and economic resilience of nations with their capacity to whip up consensus and national excitement against all odds, from Polybius, to Erasmus, to Talcott Parsons (see Micocci, 2002, 2008/2010, 2012). In capitalism as we know it, and, hence, for us here, such arguments contribute to Smith's invisible hand, which Marx renders by basing it upon greed and alienation. As a consequence, social injustices (exploitation and the extraction of surplus value) are secondary, for, if greed rules, it implies (as we have argued) diffused cruelty rather than straightforward violence. Only the elimination of capitalism can eliminate them, for all this exists in a circular relationship with its intellectuality: elimination means a rupture with disappearance, a Kantian real opposition, as we have seen Marx make clear.

It is well worth saying it plainly once again: the roots of the cruelty are in the vulgar Hegelian dialectical attitude. This last, therefore, cannot cure the system, but can only continue helping it exert it, which the history of so-called Marxist class struggle has shown clearly enough. Communism is about anarchism, Marx tells us. Revolution is about breaking away from the limited and limiting dominant intellectuality. Words and speech (language), Marx is well aware, play a great part here. It remains to finish by showing that Marx remained consistent with his 'young' self throughout his life. Let us go on with *Capital*.

In *Capital*, Volume III, Chapter LI, 'the capitalists themselves [. . .] confront one another only as commodity-owners [. . .] social interrelations of production assert themselves only as an overwhelming natural law in relation to individual free will' (1978, p. 881), for there is a 'strictly regulating authority' and a 'social mechanism' with a hierarchy. We could go on and on, rereading all three volumes in this light.

The purpose of the present work is not, however, an exercise in the exegesis, however original, of old authors. We are giving old authors their dues in order to progress, hopefully, far beyond what they say.[18] It follows that, instead of continuing with a painstaking analysis of *Capital*, we can provisionally summarize the issue of Marx's anarchist coherence by examining his *Critique of the Gotha Programme* (1972), written in 1875, more than 30 years after his 'young' phase and 8 years before his death. The consideration of such a publication is meaningful because its purpose was political rather than theoretical, and yet it is the anarchist Marx that appears throughout.

In *Critique of the Gotha Programme*, Marx accuses the German Party of being thoroughly bourgeois in mentality and Lassallian in fact. Starting from Part I, we read that, emphatically, 'Labour *is not the source* of all wealth' (p. 8; emphasis in the original), for nature is as important, and 'a socialist programme cannot allow such bourgeois phrases'. 'The bourgeois have very good grounds for falsely ascribing *supernatural creative power* to labour' (p. 9; emphasis in the original), for precisely because labourers are natural beings they must be enslaved to 'the owners of the objective conditions of labour'. But there is more to come.

Marx criticizes the assertion that labour (a source of wealth and culture) 'is possible only in and through society' (p. 10): 'in fact, this proposition has at all times been made use of by the champions of the prevailing state of society' (ibid.). In fact, he concludes, all this serves the only purpose of accepting Lassalle's catchwords of the 'undiminished proceeds of labour' (p. 11), but his next point challenges precisely the notion of labour's proceeds, and of their 'fair' distribution (pp. 12–13).

Marx is driving precisely at the point we have seen earlier: the shape of revolutionary change. What he objects to is that the Germans confuse communist society with the society that emerges from capitalist society (p. 15). Distribution is not a revolutionary issue and is not independent of the mode of production (pp. 15–18). Continuing in his critique of the Lassallian bent of the Programme, Marx then notices that all of the above derives from an incapacity to distinguish the national and international levels of the struggle (point 5 of the Programme). This, he regrets, is one of the most serious problems.

No wonder then that the 'iron law of wages' (p. 22) is confused with actual wages and is, with a perfect nonsense, claimed to be amenable to abolition together with the wage system. It is evident here that the question that the Gotha document refuses to accept is that wages (capitalist relationships) are what must be abolished. As discussed earlier, concepts and objects shade into each other seamlessly until, from the original two, you have moved to a new one that dialectically comprises the former two and is different from (but not other to) them. In this case, a metonymy (with a slightly changed meaning) hides a desire not to make revolution.

One cannot be amazed if, as a consequence, according to the Programme, cooperatives are organized by the state and not by the spontaneous activity of the workers, to Marx's horror. The next step is, obviously and sadly, 'the free state' (p. 26). 'One does not get a flea-hop nearer to the problem by a thousandfold combination of the word people and the word state' (p. 27). There follows the 'revolutionary dictatorship of the proletariat', a passing phase in which the state is destroyed to create communism.[19] The natural conclusion is 'freedom of conscience', 'nothing but the toleration of all possible kinds of *religious freedom of conscience* [. . .] but one chooses not to transcend the "bourgeois" level' (p. 31).

The so-called Mature Marx and its relationship with the Young Marx have been hotly debated, without any outcome in terms of moving the mainstream Marxists from their positions. A little step forward has been taken recently by the thorough and commendable scholar Luca Basso (Basso, 2012). In his last volume (which completes a study of the Young Marx that had preceded it; Basso, 2008), Basso justly prefers the term 'last' (*ultimo*) to that of mature. Although obviously defending the continuity between the two, Basso acknowledges the relevance of the analogies between Marx and Bakunin concerning the issues of the state and the role of politics.[20]

Unfortunately, Basso, despite a considerable degree of originality, proves unwilling to take a radical stance and bends all of Marx's arguments to a moderate point of view that serves the purposes of the usual orthodox dialectical materialism. Thus, Basso very much insists on concentrating on fetishism rather than on the wider and more fruitful alienation. In addition, he insists on the 'opacity' of the real deriving from his claim that 'essence and phenomenon' are not identical (2012, p. 20). To him, this is the doing of value, which shows a face, hiding other aspects. Combined with fetishism, a general opaque nature of the social relationships is produced that become 'falsely intelligible'; reality 'deceives' man (p. 24).

Although he acknowledges Marx's understanding of political economy as metaphysics (p. 27), Basso seems unwilling to draw the due (radical) conclusions. He rather ascribes all the questions we have seen so far (which he does not mention directly, nor does he list them) to what he has called the opacity of the real. This is the more surprising in that Basso himself notices, and gives it the right emphasis, that Marx abandoned work on *Capital* in the last 10 years of his life (p. 71) to study the natural sciences, money and banks. He also emphasizes the importance of Marx's ethnological studies.

The problem with Basso's argument is clear when, on page 114, he explains the nature of workers' action as 'in common', which is to him related to the ethnological and agricultural studies of Marx (especially concerning Russia). Thus, although communism is about 'individual realization' (p. 125), action in common is the main character of workers' action, and workers' action is all that is needed to produce the traditional Marxist hypocrisy, which he subscribes to, about change and revolution. This is a serious hindrance to the understanding of a complex set of questions that, with characteristic academic honesty, he poses: the Marx–Bakunin analogy.

To Basso:

> *In realtà, in merito a determinate questioni esistono forti punti di contatto tra Marx e Bakunin. È vero che Marx rifiuta il coup de main, ma è anche vero che lo scopo marxiano consiste nel superamento dello stato [. . .] un'associazione di uomini liberi e uguali che non è uno stato. Al riguardo Marx adopera 'in positivo' il termine 'anarchia'.*
>
> (pp. 181–2)

Translation:

> Actually, concerning some questions there are contact points between Marx and Bakunin. It is true that Marx refuses the *coup de main*, but it is also true that Marx's goal is that of going beyond the state [. . .] an association of free and equal men that is not a state. In this respect, Marx uses 'in the positive' the term 'anarchy'.
>
> (trans. A. Micocci)

He continues, recalling how Marx started from a critique of Hegel's state, and mentioned 'the kingdom of liberty' in *Capital*, Volume III, but, to Basso, surprisingly for those of us who have read Marx but not for those used to orthodox Marxism, the Marx–Bakunin difference is that the former prefers 'transitions', the latter abrupt change.

There is an obvious, and traditional, refusal to see and consider the anti-Hegelian Marx. To this, Basso adds that other big Marxist mistake that states that the possibility of rupture with disappearance is 'simplistic': for some thoroughly unexplainable and unexplained reason, change must be complex and come through long and painful transitions. Surprisingly, however, and commendably, Basso does not shrink from mentioning Marx's *Critique of the Gotha Programme* (pp. 184–5), which, however, he reduces to a critique of Lassalle and of his influence on the party.

Thus, he summarizes on page 188, the whole point of the Marx–Bakunin analogy is the state. In Basso's Marx, the state must remain to help the mysterious doings of the period of transition. The state, with Lenin, changes in the process of helping the transition (in fact '*Non si può delineare la classe operaia al di fuori del movimento operaio*' ('you cannot outline the working class without the workers' movement'), p. 163), while subjugated to the 'revolutionary' needs of the working classes. There remains the problem, duly acknowledged by Basso

(p. 209), that the immediate disappearance of the state remains an open issue, and that the question seems to be, nobody knows why, that the direct action of the anarchists must be prevented and altogether blocked.

Fortunately, Basso reminds us that Marx did not want to, and could not even if he had wanted to, give prescriptions for the future. Such prescriptions would in fact run the risk of being separated from the actual, material facts (p. 210). Basso himself knows the point: '*Così si tratterà di domandarsi se il comunismo, oltre ad essere oltre lo stato, si ponga anche oltre la politica*' (p. 182; 'Thus we will have to ask whether communism, besides being beyond the state, is also beyond politics' (transl. A. Micocci)).

He has no answer to this and, following the Marxist tradition, he leaves it at that. If it were for the Marxists, we would never know whether Marx (or anybody else, for that matter) had an answer. Nor would we be allowed to try a rupture with disappearance. To them, a long exertion of a 'moderate' (see Micocci, 2012) cruelty is greatly preferred to a peaceful and harmless abrupt revolutionary change (a rupture with disappearance).

2.4 Liberty

Before being a set of material situations, capitalism as we know it is a mental and emotional state that exists in the words (about it) that can be exchanged, for it is supported by a common – and flawed, limited and limiting – logic. Authors from Smith to Marx argue the existence of a common alienation that transforms feelings and emotions into concepts that are given a life of their own, quasi-independent from their relationships with all of us and from their actual existence; indeed, for Smith, only the powerful few can afford sentiments, which is what they potentially do and not necessarily what they actually do.

Also, for Smith and from the simple observation of reality itself, society is not regulated by the laws of perfect economic competition, whose existence is akin to that of feelings and passions: some special circumstances are supposed to have them in potentia, but their actual use is only a theoretical possibility. On the contrary, actual societies and economies are ruled by forms of social inertia that contribute to their resilience by causing, and preserving, their incapacity ever to be market societies. This keeps crises from destroying capitalism as we know it.

Instead of a world where real oppositions cause occasional revolutions, we get a world in which only dialectical contradictions operate, and are mistaken for change and even for revolution. The outcome is a 'moderate' environment that can find all sorts of meanings in its inertia and, as a consequence, can also hang on to the past, keeping and/or reintroducing features of preceding modes of production in present-day reality. This is heaven for forms of moderate thinking, such as fascism, that despise the radical and individualistic features of liberal and communist revolutions and aspire to organic communities in which the individual is blurred and submitted to theoretically conceived ancestral, ethical or economic laws and behaviours.

All the above is incompatible with the liberal philosophy we have used to connect to the Classical approaches to market competition and capitalism. But, as we all know, Classical approaches have been superseded by Neoclassical theorization first, and then, well into the twentieth century, by the Keynesian–Neoclassical synthesis we call dominant, mainstream economics. All these post-Classical approaches have solved problems by ridding their discipline of philosophy through the imposition of their methodological 'neutrality' to politics, sociology, ethics, history and even contingent opinions.[21] This sweeping solution creates an important difficulty in our progressing with the discussion of the literature.

The way mainstream economics has evolved makes it a sterile subject for discussion. It has crystallized into a discipline perfectly rendered by handbooks, which in fact have replaced the study of the single authors who have contributed to it. Mainstream economics coincides with the formulas it has produced; Cuoco would likely approve of it. Such formulas have succeeded in putting the mathematics of continuous and differential calculus to good use and have even been able to bend chaos theory to the same logic, for instance à la Thom (1978), approaching the description of the irregular regularity of the phenomena by producing only one way to perceive them (see also Barkley Rosser, 2000, 1999, 1991).

In Chapter 1 of their deservedly successful textbook, Samuelson and Nordhaus (2002) inform us that economics is a fascinating subject, and that it can be useful to understand the economy, and even to invest one's own savings (p. 4). After giving a list of items that comprises institutions, technology, financial markets, income distribution, the economic cycle, monetary policy, exchanges among countries, growth and development and public policy, they settle for a Robbins-type definition (ibid.) of economics based on scarcity of resources and useful goods. The next step is to introduce efficiency in the Pareto sense (p. 5) and then to come to the micro–macro split.

They also inform us (ibid.) that economists use the scientific method, which to them means the observation of phenomena and the use of statistics to interpret them. The only dangers are the post hoc, *ceteris paribus* and composition error troubles. On page 7, we are treated to an edifying little speech: society must find the right equilibrium between the 'hard discipline' of the market and the compassion of public assistance. Cold minds should inform warm hearts of themselves. A just and flourishing society can only come about under these conditions.

All they are left to do then is to introduce the problems of economic organization (what, how and for whom we produce), and from there move on to some more definitions, meant to introduce the production possibilities' frontier curve, the first theoretical graph students are exposed to. Indeed, there are precious few graphs in economics, for they all take the same few basic shapes. Nonetheless, all economics textbooks are crammed full of them, for they give the chance to deliver the subtle explanations needed to differentiate them from one another. This is often mistaken for the difficult part of economics, whereas it is only the boring part. The next chapter of Samuelson and Nordhaus (2002) is about markets and the state.

The problem is that, however impartial the authors of textbooks seek to be, they deal with real, concrete objects and metaphysical concepts as if the former could be reduced to the latter. The impartial justice of economics throws everything and everybody together, in an enchanted world where theoretical concepts interact with actual people, altering the nature of material objects. Human beings transform themselves into labour power, in order to change iron and rubber into washing machines, to then be rewarded by monetary tokens that are supposed to give them the opportunity to 'satisfy' themselves in the market by buying as many things as their budget allows.

Scarcity of resources equally applies to iron ore and labour power, and needs and satisfaction are something one can peddle just like one's own (life)time. Labour power, in actual reality, is in fact life time, which has no price, nor any logical possibility ever to be associated with any monetary quantity, however big the satisfaction and utility delivered by money. There is nothing surprising here. It is just a form of what Marx had called alienation from the self, the others and nature. Only, mainstream economics and mainstream Marxism were devised long after Marx the anarchist had shown the presence of alienation, and in perfect and guilty ignorance of it.

The first result implied by everything said so far is the confirmation of what was announced in the introduction. A general metaphysics is produced that is deprived of an ontology. There is, in fact, an internal mechanism of functioning that hopelessly mixes up material items, (right or wrong) notions, and any relation between the two. Everything is replaced with its simulacrum conceived as between the abstract and the concrete, and capable of any action and interaction one can attribute to it. The point seems to be, not the action or interaction itself, but the possibility to inscribe such action or interaction within this general framework of potentiality rather than actuality.

Marx was perfectly correct in noticing the metaphysics of economics and the ensuing alienation. This has been argued in the preceding section but, inevitably, that momentous observation (which was repeated throughout Marx's own life and writings ad nauseam, to no avail) has proved perfectly useless, for it was inscribed by the Marxists within that very same dialectical framework that it was supposed to subvert. Everything was therefore distorted along that vulgar Hegelian bias that has erased revolution and intellectual freedom from the agenda of political economists, activists and common people alike. Materialism itself was prevented, and we are paying dearly for it now, not only with the dominance of mainstream economics and the practical absurdities ensuing (take the present crisis), but also with the unbearable boredom that surrounds us and that looks impossible to lift.

The plain truth that is there for everybody to see is that Hegelian or dialectical approaches are methodologically wrong (see Micocci, 2002, 2008/2010; Della Volpe, 1980; Colletti, 1974, 1975; Rosenthal, 1998), and that is precisely the reason why they work in practice (for better or for worse: crises and catastrophes of all sorts are necessary for capitalism to keep to its asymptotic trajectory towards its own completion, to pretend to approach its accomplishment in order never to reach it, lest it should perish). Actual capitalist reality is a vulgar Hegelian array of quasi-fascist practices, for this is the only way to avoid that very capitalist liberal revolution that is continuously hailed as a matter of fact, without any supporting empirical evidence. Nation-states deal with each other in the moderate way outlined and transform the spontaneity of market relationships (another unproven potentiality) into administrative and legal frameworks.[22]

Real oppositions, and more generally ruptures with disappearance, with the entailed need for toleration, are refused by the mean and evil trick being played of inverting the meaning, role and method of the idea of radical break. The possibility to do so descends directly from the claimed (and wrong) homogeneity of material objects, theoretical notions and mistaken logical syllogisms that is favoured by the vulgar Hegelian dialectics as the basis for the dominant intellectuality.[23] Words and discourses replace facts. Thus, the idea of an abrupt rupture can be (wrongly) associated with the idea of organized violence and suffering, whereas the actual (and identical) prolonged organized violence and suffering that take place all the time in reality are passed off as smooth, moderate and reasonable calculations of the least damage. This last aspect, with its character-istic evil, is perfectly reasonable in Smith's sense: it is what politics in capitalism as we know it is all about.

The outcome is a continuous, successful effort to oust radical arguments on the erroneous grounds of their being dangerous and imprudent. As a result, even the most obvious capitalist categories, such as, for instance, market competition, are replaced by their moderate, vulgar Hegelian counterparts that allow for no disappearance, thus mirroring the theory and practice of state intervention. This perverted process further justifies this whole, logically absurd spiral of moderate stupidity. Given the moderate nature of all these activities, well rendered by the mathematics of differential calculus, this process can wind up *ad libitum*. There is no actual end, but solely local sets of (mathematical) properties that look relevant only when looked at from within the capitalist (as we know it) perspective, to paraphrase Allen (1960).

There is no need to waste time here in order to demonstrate that this is valid for mainstream Marxist thinkers as well. These last use the very same general logical method to argue their critique of market competition. Like the mainstream economists, they wind up their moderate, logically wrong sets of syllogisms in the fortunate and providential environment of capitalism as we know it, where actual economic relationships behave according to the same flawed logic. Prole-tarians believe that they are selling their labour power when they are wasting away their lives; they believe they are unjustly rewarded when their wages do not keep pace with inflation; they think that they are fighting for their rights and their happiness when they participate in the quasi-fascist rounds of negotiations in which wages and rights are defined (for the Italian case, see Di Mario, 2015); if and when needed, they then go and die for their country in war, or beat their own comrades if clad in a police uniform.

Entrepreneurs can spend their whole lives working the whole year round, as long as they believe that there is a difference between dealing with work matters in suit and tie and in a swimming suit. We could go on and on: there is nothing in the life of capitalism as we know it that escapes the overall logic of the dominant metaphysics. All this can and does happen because there is no way to articulate any alternative in words (Micocci, 2008/2010).

It would appear very easy to infer from all this that what is at stake is the concept of liberty, or, reciprocally, the question of individual emancipation. Once again, this is nothing new, if you have read Marx, the anarchists and the liberals. Putting it this way, however, would be within the same logic as capitalism as we know it. It is not a matter of liberating ourselves, although this last is an undeniable part of this complex issue. What we are discussing here is wider. It is the liberation of chance itself from the dominant intellectual logic of capitalism.

If we are trapped in a metaphysics, we must break out of it. The only way to do so is to seek to return to actual reality (the material) by letting actual reality itself go on without interference. Capitalist metaphysics interferes in two main ways with the functioning of nature: first of all, by its very existence, for it poses itself as a self-contained bubble that must defend itself from the unpredictability of nature in general (from revolution, as we shall denote creative unpredictability from now on). Second, also in importance, by setting up this artificial bubble, capitalism poses itself as a hindrance to the functioning of nature, not only because of its non-natural logic and behaviour. In fact, despite and simultaneously because of its non-material and non-abstract nature, its metaphysics also has a powerful, direct bearing upon nature. Capitalism's artefacts and activities interact with material reality.

It is necessary to anticipate a few words about this issue here, for this type of argument is greatly discussed in our time within the dominant logic. Ecological imbalances and catastrophes are justly argued to be the outcome of capitalist activities, but we shall see that this is not because of what we are being told. In a few words (the next chapter will deal with this matter at length), there is no balance or equilibrium to be recovered in nature, for this typically static and moderate concept exists in capitalist intellectuality and capitalist economics and natural sciences, but not in nature.

If equilibrium in nature existed, we would never have the selective pressure that ensures the variability that is typical of evolution. On the contrary, as we shall see the next chapter, we can suppose nature to be in a state of continuous lack of equilibrium, with the consequent possibility of the existence of ruptures with disappearance. Of course, there should be no way to establish the likelihood of a rupture with disappearance, or the effect would be spoiled (or, conversely, that would mean that nature works only by means of regular, easy laws, as Darwin, 2013, hypothesizes). Nature needs to be – simply – unpredictable, to itself and to the observer. Things could go on in a routine for unpredictable lengths of time, to then undergo a sudden, or slow and progressive, revolution.

The above point is central for us. We need to do the opposite of what has been done so far. We must operate giving nature freedom to go on, without the interference of our metaphysics, and instead stick to our ontological search. We need to strip the items of reality of the disguise in which they are hidden by socially determined intellectual domination. All this must be done within the further complication caused by the material influence that the metaphysics itself has upon nature. The struggle to recover nature, therefore, coincides with the struggle to intellectually debunk institutionalized society. As such, it only can take place in the apparent form of an individual emancipation, while being in fact a release of chance, as we shall see in Chapters 3–5.

It will be argued in what follows that all the above is not new in Western philosophy. As well as by Marx, similar points were made by Epicurus and the tradition that is influenced by him. Particularly noteworthy for our task is David Hume, for he proved capable of giving a radical bent to the empiricist method championed by Francis Bacon.[24] Hume's argument is based on the importance of ridding ourselves of the conditioning imposed on us by society, which he symbolizes in the split between philosophers, who need to doubt what seems obvious and recurring, and common people, who can only live by basing themselves upon the necessity of recurrence and repetition.

If we look back at everything that has been said so far, we notice that one of the main characteristics of capitalism as we know it now and its metaphysics is the repetitious nature of its operations. Instead of having Schumpeterian ruptures (but see the following chapters for a sobered-up, sad, routine-fearing Schumpeter), we get endless iterations of what is already known. If what is peddled is metaphysical[25] and can only be rendered with words, then only stability can ensure the usability of the system. If objects and words change, the very features of what is being peddled might be altered or might disappear, rendering the whole thing a useless, continuous production of ephemeral notions and words deprived of a direction.

The above occurrence obviously does not exist in reality, and that is so because whatever changeability (both dialectical and not) exists in capitalism as we know it is tamed and redirected towards the preservation of the system, with its elementary, limited and limiting intellectuality. The trick to doing so is that words, given the unpredictable variability of nature (and, hence, of human whim), can only be vague containers of indefinite meanings. This quality makes them infinitely adaptable to whatever change takes place. They are simulacra of those potential material objects and immaterial feelings that are supposed (à la Smith) to be there as a matter of fact, but hardly exist. Rather, they are conveyed by means of word peddling to pretend that they reside in the doings of precious few symbolical human or natural items.

The reasoning so far pursued leads to a formulation of the problem of materialism connected with naturalism. However, as capitalism as we know it is made of a metaphysics that hides and disguises nature, and refuses to acknowledge both its freedom and its power, we cannot tell what kind of naturalism we are pursuing. We cannot even tell what kind of materialism we can devise, let alone pursue. All we can do is work in a negative way and rid ourselves of whatever we find to be the result of the dominant intellectual maieutics. Materialism and naturalism are the same thing as emancipation, at least as long as we work in the knowledge that there is a dominant intellectuality and a split between this last and actual nature, of which our actual selves are part.

The identification of nature and self is an easy hypothesis in these conditions. It rests upon the condition – acceptable for the present chapter – that we exist in that we are a product of natural relationships. At this level of approximation, we cannot say anything concerning the reality of what we perceive, which is, in fact, well beyond what we can achieve here. This volume's main purpose is to intervene on the economic, social and political side. By dismantling metaphysics, we can build a world without institutionalized features, and without the ensuing need for cruelty.

Our search is for concrete facts, not words. The latter are our object of criticism. The endless, iterative and meaningless set of illogical discourses that transcend everything into a metaphysics must be exposed and abolished. This is a rupture with disappearance: in short, a revolution. We must return human endeavours to the realm of the natural and unpredictable. We must transform them into what can be told without involving in any speech utterance an iterative preservation of the capitalist mentality, and, hence, of capitalism as we know it itself.

2.5 Political economy

One of the main consequences of the argument so far is that, in this environment, economic studies – which we should call, to pay homage to the established materialist tradition, political economy – are, and only can be, a historical subject. Very differently from the mainstream method, and from established dialectical materialism, there is no need to build any a priori theoretical framework of the types so far known. We need, rather, a theoretical method capable of detecting the presence of metaphysics.

We shall see in the course of the present book that we need to devise a continuously shifting framework, capable of capturing the existing limitations on the analysis of reality without imposing new ones, however elastic they are, as final. That is the meaning of a critique of political economy. One might want to argue whether this is what Marx actually had in mind when he proposed this felicitous expression, but this is not at stake here.

The main difference from the authors in the Classical tradition is that the present proposal is built upon a radical and libertarian argument. If the present state of things, with the entailed intellectual boredom, has a social (hence, economic and, in turn, intellectual) origin in the history of capitalism, then we must be firm in our endeavour. We must not shrink from venturing into those fields that are often referred to as the place for adventurers and for 'impractical' types of person. On the contrary, it is hoped that the present argument will prove 'practical' vis-à-vis the useless, iterative and conservative metaphysics produced by those who are after the useful and the feasible.[26] These last are precisely the preservers of the metaphysics of capitalism and the custodians of the continuous cruelty and injustice entailed.

As a historical subject, political economy would also lose its characteristics of being a tool for practical planning. Many would be horrified at this perspective, even among the non-economists, for at first sight it seems to endanger human survival. This last is, obviously, only an illusion. Simply, political economy would not be needed if the planning and organization of production were done in a libertarian environment. In such a place, in fact, there would simply be the planning and organizing of production, without the hindrance of political and economic considerations. These economic and political considerations pertain to the capitalist state of things. In other words, without capitalism, the planning and the organization of production would be easier, for they would have nothing to do with economic considerations.

It has already been clarified that what present-day language would call individual emancipation from capitalism is an illusion. The actual thing that must be pursued is the liberation of chance, i.e. the opening up to the unpredictability of nature. Only in this sense can political economy be a tool of emancipation. It must tell us what is wrong with the past and the present economic ideas, objects and relationships. That is why it must be a historical subject. We will develop these issues in the rest of the present book. It is important, however, to point out, as an introduction to what is coming, that political economy must be a destroyer of concepts rather than a builder of notions and frameworks.

Political economy must be made independent from the continuous exchange of vague words and syllogisms that capitalism as we know it is about. Its basic role must be that of discoverer, and uncoverer, of the guilty vagueness of theories and of practical objects and relations. There is no way a priori to tell how far this destructive work can and must go, but, if all that has been argued so far is sound, this type of job will be needed as long as institutionalized societies exist. Let us face reality: political economy, as Marx made clear, is an anarchist enterprise. Marxists should be told.

By emancipation, then, something wider than liberation from the capitalist mode of production is meant. Emancipation is to do with the whole of the life of human beings and, above all, it is highly unpredictable. If we knew what it was like, we would be unable to free ourselves from the present condition. This is a matter of creativity versus repetitiveness.

In Chapter 3, after having developed a general discussion concerning nature and economic and social life, we will come back to economics and political economy, a discussion to be fully developed in Chapter 4. We will further argue that economics and Marxist and heterodox approaches to political economy mean very little, for all they do is whip up a chain reaction of interrelated emotional and rational activities based upon the intrinsic and unredeemable intellectual vagueness that has been introduced here and that will be further developed. Economic activities come down to a discursive set of interrelated deceptions about actual reality that, however, work perfectly in being useful to the practices of capitalism as we know it.

In fact, as introduced here, all that is amenable to this repetitive exchange is metaphysics, and, as long as one fits within it, the game can go on at leisure. This is most evident of all in how money functions (see, for instance, Micocci, 2011a, 2011b; Rosenthal, 1998), the main role of which is that of being an indispensable token of loyalty to the capitalist system, whereby allegiance to the system, and therefore to the metaphysical game of continuous reciprocal recognition as *Homines Oeconomici*, is demonstrated and achieved. The consequences are as metaphysical as they are material, as shown, for a powerful instance, with plenty of blood-curdling horrors, by the present crisis, starting from the sub-prime episode up to the days of writing this chapter (and much further on, there is ample space for fear).

2.6 Conclusions

Starting from a discussion of the Classical approaches to political economy, in this chapter we have proposed a general theoretical background for the contention, already proposed on partially different bases in Micocci (2002, 2008/2010, 2012), that capitalism is a metaphysics. From this, we have started to develop a framework for analysing the faults of hitherto-known political economy, economics and capitalism itself, for these mirror each other in terms of their inner logical working. It has been argued, at the introductory level, that capitalism as we know it can be seen as a continuous, iterative re-proposing of known communicative items based on the vagueness of the expressive means used.

If it must be useful to change the world, political economy must, as a consequence, be modified into a historical subject capable of grasping the most important aspects of reality in general, accepting nature's most important character: its unpredictable changeability. This has been understood at the intuitive level by Marx, who also, it is argued in this chapter, saw the inevitable anarchist implications of this argument, *pace* the dialectical bent of mainstream Marxists. Also at stake here is, therefore, the meaning of revolution. This final issue must be returned to its meaning of openness to abrupt change, whether it actually comes about or not. This particular aspect also means liberation from the intrinsic and unavoidable iterative cruelty of capitalist relationships, best understood and used by fascist and quasi-fascist movements worldwide.

The study of political economy in this new framework is the same thing as the destruction of capitalism and of its continuous, vague, emotionally numbing communication of iteratively repeated references to meanings that are very hard to pin down to actual material things and/or feelings. This is, there is no hiding it, a call to come back to nature, returning the *Homo Oeconomicus* of capitalism to his/her natural self, so far concealed by a useless heap of metaphysical emptiness articulated in an endless array of words and speeches supposedly concerned with it.

It is time to see through this ever-growing outpouring of words. We must start that search for the material that was announced by Francis Bacon (and many others, from his time onwards), evolved into its 'sensist' philosophical discussion by the French philosophers of the eighteenth century, and was connected to its void of meaning by the Classical political economists. Marxist political economy of the mainstream dialectical kind and mainstream economics have uselessly detained us for the intervening period, right up to current times.

The core question is about the difference between language and silence. The former is capitalist, the latter revolutionary. This is not to mean that language itself is not natural to humankind. To argue that is not within the scope and aim of the present volume, for it needs a type of knowledge very different from what is being discussed here. Let us stick with what we can do: discuss capitalism and its horrors and produce alternative, libertarian frameworks. The next chapter is about nature in general and the liberation of chance.

Notes

1 All theoretical frameworks (see especially ch. 3) are bound to be superseded by others, if the unpredictability of reality we will keep arguing about throughout the book is accepted.

2 Transforming it into parodies of itself, like the Bolsheviks, Chinese and for that matter all so-called revolutions (Micocci, 2012).

3 Khalil (2005) goes some way towards what we will argue next by noticing that, in Smith (2009), the idea of society/state comes from the invisible hand that coordinates individual situations, and not from the rational acceptance of a contract, as in Classical liberalism. In any case, this makes the discussion of the so-called 'Adam Smith's problem' quite irrelevant. For this last, see, for instance, Macfie (1967), Heilbroner (1982) and Skinner (1992).

4 I should thank Brunella Antomarini here, with the usual emphatic disclaimers.

5 This from the consumer's side. It does not imply that property and resources are equally well distributed; on the contrary. Keynes was probably much influenced by this, but precious few Marxists ever paid attention to it.

6 Offer (2012) sees the importance of the question of the opinions of others, but does not enter the difficult field we take up here.

7 'The interests of the rich and the poor [. . .] not opposed to each other' (Say, 1863, p. LIX).

8 As Say famously defended in (1936).

9 The means to do so being necessarily, as we shall soon see, the criticism of Hegelian dialectics and its abandonment.

10 Maybe this explains the foolish fear that present-day superpowers have of poorer, usually Muslim, countries.

11 This is not at all a very restrictive condition in the framework of the *Homo Oeconomicus*, as we shall see in due course, because individuals can only do what they only can do, being entirely homogeneous and predictable.

12 This is not to deny, however, that Mill's proposals are noble and worthy of attention; on the contrary.

13 Mill's political economy was written quickly, around 1845–8. The ideas put forward there, as can be noticed, are taken back in 'On liberty' (1986).

14 See Micocci (2002, 2008/2010, 2012). See also Rosenthal (1998).

15 It should be clear by now that the moderates are the vast majority in capitalism as we know it and cannot comunicate with, or understand, radical thought.

16 This discussion is necessary to fend off the dominance of mainstream Marxism, with its dialectical materialism and its Leninist belief that Marx was all over exploitation and proletarian riots.

17 Here, Marx is famously echoing Feuerbach's criticism of Hegel's logic and its hypostatizations. See Della Volpe (1980) and Micocci (2002).

18 I have to say this because we live in an age in which it seems that, in academia, little else is allowed besides the recycling of old authors. Of course, this also is a consequence of everything I will say in this book, and I have argued in my preceding works.

19 The Leninist 'withering away of the state' implies the dictatorship of the party that represents the proletariat, a perfectly bourgeois concept, Marx would say.

20 It is very sad that Marxists keep referring to single authors to mean anarchism. It is time they should be able to use that word.
21 Which, incidentally, rescued mainstream economics, isolating it from the stupidity of neo- liberal ideas. See Micocci (2012).
22 This is argued at length in Micocci (2008/2010, 2012), where it is shown that even diehard liberals such as Hayek, Mises and Sylos Labini take shelter in this type of arguments, and even celebrate the nation-state and the need to believe in it (especially Mises and Hayek).
23 Here, I am summarizing and reworking the argument of Micocci (2002, 2008/2010) and its development in Micocci (2012).
24 For a treatment of Bacon, see Micocci (2008/2010).
25 That is, it is perceived as such independently from its material, metaphysical or abstract nature.
26 In Micocci (2012), I produced an argument on the absurdity of pursuing the useful and the practical. This is precisely what the metaphysics of capitalism is about.

References

Allen, R. G. D. (1960) *Mathematical Analysis for Economists*, MacMillan, London.

Barkley Rosser, J. (1991) *From Catastrophe to Chaos: A general theory of economic discontinuities*, Kluwer, Newell, MA.

Barkley Rosser, J. (1999) 'On the complexities of complex economic dynamics', *Journal of Economic Perspectives*, 13, 4, 169–92.

Barkley Rosser, J. (2000) 'Aspects of dialectics and non-linear dynamics', *Cambridge Journal of Economics*, 24, 311–24.

Basso, L. (2008) *Socialità e Isolamento: La Singolarità in Marx* [*Sociality and Isolation: Singularity in Marx*], Carocci, Rome.

Basso, L. (2012) *Agire in Comune Antropologia e Politica nell'Ultimo Marx* [*Acting Together: Anthropology and politics in the late Marx*], Ombre Corte, Verona, Italy.

Cassirer, E. (1961) *The Myth of the State*, Yale University Press, New Haven, CT.

Colletti, L. (1969a) *Ideologia e Società* [*Ideology and Society*], Laterza, Bari, Italy.

Colletti, L. (1969b) *Il Marxismo e Hegel* [*Marxism and Hegel*], Laterza, Bari, Italy.

Colletti, L. (1972) *From Rousseau to Lenin*, NLB, London.

Colletti, L. (1973) *Marxism and Hegel*, NLB, London.

Colletti, L. (1974) 'A political and philosophical interview', *New Left Review*, 86, 34–52.

Colletti, L. (1975) 'Marxism and the dialectics', *New Left Review*, 93, 3–30.

Colletti, L. (1979) *Tra Marxismo e No* [*In Between Marxism and Not*], Laterza, Bari, Italy.

Cuoco, V. (1991) *Statistica della Repubblica Italiana* [*Statistics of the Italian Republic*], Archivio Guido Izzi, Rome.

Darwin, C. (2013) *The Origin of Species*, Signet Classics, London.

Della Volpe, G. (1945) *La Teoria Marxista dell'Emancipazione Umana, Saggio sulla Trasmutazione Marxista dei Valori* [*A Marxist Theory of Human Emancipation. Essay on the Marxist transformation of values*], Ferrara, Messina, Italy.

Della Volpe, G. (1949) *Per la Teoria di un Umanesimo Positivo. Studi e Documenti sulla Dialettica Materialistica* [*For a Theory of a Positive Humanism. Studies and papers on dialectics*], C.Zuffi Editore, Bologna, Italy.

Della Volpe, G. (1963) *La Libertà Comunista. Sulla Dialettica* [*Communist Liberty. On dialectics*], Edizioni Avanti!, Milan, Italy.

Della Volpe, G. (1967) *Critica dell'Ideologia Contemporanea* [*Critique of Contemporary Ideology*], Editori Riuniti, Rome.

Della Volpe, G. (1978) *Rousseau and Marx*, Lawrence & Wishart, London.

Della Volpe, G. (1980) *Logic as a Positive Science*, NLB, London.

Di Mario, F. (2015) 'The Monti Cabinet reform of the welfare state: Metaphysics of inequality', *International Journal of Applied Economics & Econometrics*, 23, 3, 68–98.

Hegel, G. W. F. (2008a) *Scienza della Logica* [*Science of Logic*], Laterza, Bari, Italy.

Hegel, G. W. F. (2008b) *Outlines of the Philosophy of Right*, Oxford University Press, Oxford, UK.

Hegel, G. W. F. (2008c) *La Fenomenologia dello Spirito* (Phenomenology of the Spirit), Einaudi, Turin, Italy.

Heilbroner, R. (1982) 'The socialization of the individual in Adam Smith', *History of Political Economy*, 17, 427–39.

Khalil, E. L. (2005) 'An anatomy of authority: Adam Smith as political theorist', *Cambridge Journal of Economics*, 29, 1, 57–71.

Macfie, A. L. (1967) *The Individual in Society: Papers on Adam Smith*, Allen & Unwin, London.

Marx, K. (1972) *Critique of the Gotha Programme*, Foreign Language Press, Peking.

Marx, K. (1975) 'Preface to the Critique of Political Economy', in Marx, K., and Engels, F., *Selected Works*, p. 182, Progress Publishers, Moscow.

Marx, K. (1978) *Capital*, vols I–III, Progress Publishers, Moscow.

Marx, K. (1986) *Miseria della Filosofia* [*The Poverty of Philosophy*], Editori Riuniti, Rome.

Marx, K. (1992) *Early Writings*, Penguin Books, London.

Marx, K. (2005) *Selected Writings*, ed. D. McLellan, Oxford University Press, Oxford, UK.

Marx, K., and Engels, F. (1985) *The German Ideology*, Lawrence & Wishart, London.

Merker, N. (2009) *Filosofie del Populismo* [*Philosophies of Populism*], Laterza, Bari, Italy.

Micocci, A. (2002) *Anti-Hegelian Reading of Economic Theory*, Mellen Press, Lampeter, UK.

Micocci, A. (2008/2010) *The Metaphysics of Capitalism*, Lexington, Lanham, MD.

Micocci, A. (2011a) 'The preponderance of finance and the present crisis', *Studies in Political Economy*, 87, 49–64.

Micocci, A. (2011b) 'Marx and the Crisis: A necessary theoretical premise', *International Journal of Political Economy*, special issue on Marx and the Crisis, 40, 3, 72–87.

Micocci, A. (2012) *Moderation and Revolution*, Lexington, Lanham, MD.

Mill, J. S. (1986) *Utilitarianism*, Fontana Press, Glasgow, UK.

Mill, J. S. (1998) *Principles of Political Economy*, Oxford University Press, Oxford, UK.

Offer, A. (2012) 'Sympathy and the invisible hand: From Adam Smith to market liberalism', *Economic Thought*, 1, 2, 1–14.

Ricardo, D. (1962) *The Principles of Political Economy and Taxation*, Dent, London.

Rosenthal, J. (1998) *The Myth of Dialectics*, MacMillan, London.

Samuelson, P. A. (1962) 'Parable and realism in capital theory: The surrogate production function', *Review of Economic Studies*, 29, 3, 193–206.

Samuelson, P. A., and Nordhaus, W. D. (2002) *Economia* [*Economics*], McGraw-Hill, Milan, Italy.

Say, J. B. (1863) *A Treatise on Political Economy*, Lippincott, Philadelphia, PA.

Say, J. B. (1936) *Letters to Thomas Robert Malthus on Political Economy and Stagnations of Commerce*, George Harding's Bookshop, London.

Skinner, A. S. (1992) 'Adam Smith: Ethics and self-love', in Jones, P., and Skinner, A. S. (eds), *Adam Smith Reviewed*, pp. 142–67, Edinburgh University Press, Edinburgh.

Smith, A. (1999) *The Wealth of Nations*, 2 vols, Penguin Classics, London.

Smith, A. (2009) *The Theory of Moral Sentiments*, Penguin Classics, London.

Thom, R. (1978) *Structural Stability and Morphogenesis: An outline of a general theory of models*, Benjamin/Cummings, Reading, MA.

3 Nature and liberty

3.1 Introduction

In the preceding chapter, we have argued that capitalist metaphysics – the general intellectuality of capitalist understanding, its actual intercourses and its scientific disciplines – transcends what is physical and material, thus losing the possibility of an ontology. Instead of starting from actual reality, capitalist understanding regulates its world by basing itself upon a moderate, dialectical logic that is iteratively applied to all fields. There is no ontological difference between social arrangements and natural reality: both function as if a general equilibrium existed and were attainable. Things as different as ecology, psychology and economics are thus collapsed together methodologically. Only the subject matter and the terminology used change. Herein lies another problem that will accompany us in this book.

The metaphysics of capitalism requires that words are laden with a set of tasks that are as vague as possible, and yet their supposed meanings are pursued as closely as possible in everyday life. The likeness of this aspect to infinitesimal calculus has been pointed out in the previous chapter. In the human and natural sciences, as well as in everyday life, words are attributed a never-to-be-fully attained truth value. This is supposed to be potentially there constantly: hence the need to root it out, any time it appears to be missing. Words must simultaneously signify objects and thoughts and are the only tool that can be used to understand the concrete, despite the occasional correspondence, or lack of correspondence, to truth, or reality, as economists prefer to say. They can, and must, correspond to what the metaphysics of capitalism proposes as reality, or they would have no meaning: no use in such metaphysics itself.

In capitalism, words therefore both signify, and constitute, an appearance of reality. This is why, as introduced in the preceding chapter, the metaphysics of capitalism lacks the necessary logical rigour and is perfectly out of touch with material reality. Those sceptical of the above theoretical argument can consider the issue from the point of view of Marx's triple alienation from the self, the others and nature (which can be argued both from a Feuerbachian, theoretical point of view, or from a Classical political economy, empirical historical perspective). If words signify anything, they signify the rational activities of the capitalist (flawed) metaphysics. Their direct relationship with actual, material things and logically sound rational activities can only be inadvertent and occasional.

When a direct link with reality is achieved,[1] the magical spell of exclusively moderate intellectual mediations upon which capitalist metaphysics is based is challenged. In fact, nature, which comprises time and therefore history, and therefore social and economic reality and the human and natural sciences, is unpredictable: not inconceivable but unconceived, as we will see in Chapter 5. This argument has been introduced in the preceding chapter with the argument for the undeniable possibility that reality in general presents, besides dialectical relationships, real Kantian oppositions and, more generally, ruptures with disappearances. There are obvious and undeniable empirical instances of such possibilities: the disappearances of the dinosaurs or of the Aztec culture are among the many examples one can put forward.

By admitting the possibility of ruptures with disappearance, we do two momentous things: first, by recovering a radically sceptical attitude, we build the possibility of revolution. This is nothing new in the Western philosophical tradition, as we shall show in this chapter and in the next. Second, we can argue that the excessive reliance of capitalist metaphysics on words and speech is extremely problematic and complicates what Hume and Locke would call 'human understanding'. Its only use is social: by repressing individuality and understanding, and, hence, a conscious and autonomous relationship with the other human beings and nature, it serves to hold capitalist society together as a flawed metaphysics. This explains, in part, the inertia and resilience of the capitalist institutionalized societies introduced in Chapter 2. It will be shown repeatedly in the course of the book that speech also performs a psychological role, replacing natural drives with their rationalized enacting and/or talking about them.

In the present chapter, we build upon the logical possibility that nature is prone to revolutions and begin to argue such a point by means of resorting to the European tradition of sceptical and Epicurean thought. A selection of such arguments will therefore be offered to the reader, held together by a reliance on the anarchist Marx that was introduced in Chapter 2 and that will be further argued and enriched. This is, unfortunately, necessary and urgent, in that the Hegelian reading of Marx as an anti-revolutionary socialist rather than as a communist anarchist is overwhelming and presents itself in a wide variety of sophisticated versions.

It is evident that the issue of the presence of the material world is central to the present argument. Despite all the efforts that are made in capitalism as we know it to keep nature out of any intellectual endeavour, producing a milieu in which material actions are unfailingly transcended (mediated) into intellectual items amenable to storytelling in words, nature is still admitted to be the ontological constituent of reality. The tension in human individuals that is produced by this schizophrenia takes well-known and typical psychological forms, the most normal being the sexual connotation of mass political actions and ideas, à la Wilhelm Reich. We will keep seeing, throughout the book, that this contributes to the fascistic tendency of the capitalist world.

The more general question of the character of nature itself and of its holding the possibility of catastrophes is, from the present perspective, and indeed in general, obviously rather difficult. How can we study it, and understand it, if our expressive means are geared precisely to deny this very fundamental characteristic of nature? The first part of the answer is quite obvious: silence is the key need we have when studying the material. In this case, silence means empirical observation deprived of the constraining armour of capitalist intellectuality (the metaphysics). The problem, therefore, is, on the one hand, that our main priority is intellectual emancipation from the metaphysics of capitalism. On the other hand, however, we also need to describe and tell in words what we learn, in order to be able to use it together with our fellow human beings.

Emancipation as silence and the necessity of description are strictly linked, but are not amenable to a straightforward solution. It will be argued throughout the book that precisely this lack of cosy and tranquillizing solutions marks the scientific approach that is pursued here. There is a fundamental difference between nature's unpredictability and the (capitalist) political, economic and psychological need to pretend that reality in general is predictable. To complicate the issue, as we shall see in what follows, nature often gives the impression that it can be moulded by humans into the desired form. Plants and animals lend themselves to the ordering activity that is the main premise of human productive tasks. Families, and phyla, seem to neatly fit the differences and similarities between live creatures. Farming appears to tame nature and instil order, but this is only an illusion, easily dispelled by a closer look and, theatrically, by the occasional natural catastrophe.

We will argue, in this chapter and in the next, that the criticism of science and the associated doubts that were put forward in the eighteenth century are valid and useful. We will also submit, in this chapter and in the whole book, that natural freedom and human freedom are closely linked: indeed, they are one and the same thing. We obtain emancipation from the metaphysics of capitalism by returning our understanding of chance to its actual free action. We must break out of the regularity that the capitalist self-seclusion from nature produces. This is easy and needs no organized violence and no taking of the Winter Palace or the Bastille. Yet, it is a revolution from capitalism. In other words, intellectual emancipation can, without humiliating and/or hurting anybody through mass action, erase capitalism from history for good.

Section 3.2 starts with Marx, because we have the unfortunate and boring duty to confute the anti-revolutionary nature of various Marxisms. We shall move from that to describing the features of the issue of regularity in the capitalism–nature relationship, thus starting to sketch the basic features of human individuality.

Section 3.3 is about nature and liberty. It discusses French sensism and the British empiricism of the eighteenth century, in order to prepare for its radical, Epicurean version put forward by David Hume (discussed in Chapter 4) and the issue of predictability in nature and in society. This theoretical discussion is central to the general argument, because it introduces the role of words and speech.

Section 3.4 continues the discussion of words and speech with the goal of beginning to return the general argument to economic issues. Words are described as the imposition of metaphysical regularity and, hence, as the main mechanism to avoid radical arguments and to prevent the direct observation of nature.

The conclusions will summarize the argument, sticking to the topic of liberty as chance, i.e. materialism as individual emancipation. This will introduce the questions of political economy of Chapter 4.

3.2 Capitalism, regularity, isolation

It is convenient to start the discussion of this section by continuing our exploration of Marx the anarchist. After having considered instances from the beginning and the end of his life work in the preceding chapter, it is appropriate here to look at statements from the 1865–70 period: 'Wages, price and profit' (1865, in Marx, 1975) and *The Civil War in France* (around 1870–71; Marx, 1977). Whereas Engels took care of the subsequent fortune of the latter work, it was Eleanor Marx who published the former, in London, in 1898.

Both works have enjoyed a considerable success up to the present day. For instance 'Wages, price and profit', translated for the first time in Italy by Palmiro Togliatti in 1932, has had many subsequent editions. It is widely considered by Marxists to be useful for its lucid explanation of the issue of capitalist exploitation of the workers, thus providing a solid basis for political agitation and trade-union activities. By means of using a few quotations, we shall show this not to be the case.

Like all of Marx's works, these two are also characterized by wide, humanitarian concerns that are very explicit and often repeated. After having made clear in Section 4 ('Supply and demand', Marx and Engels, 1975) that the level of wages is not to be ascribed to the play of supply and demand, for these only determine the 'normal', routine fluctuations of prices, as any mainstream economist would confirm, Marx claims that the central problem is value and its achievement, but what is the value of human labour? 'The exchangeable value of all commodities are only *social functions* of those things, and have nothing at all to do with their *natural* qualities [. . .] What is the common *social substance* of all commodities? It is *labour*' (1975, p. 201; emphasis in the original, also in all the following quotations).

Social wants require '*crystallized social labour*' (ibid., p. 202). This means non-natural labour. This is what Marxists seek not to notice.[2] As a result of the above said fluctuations, value and price (crystallized social labour) do not often coincide in what Smith calls the '*natural price*'. Marx ominously concludes the section as follows: 'Scientific truth is always paradox, if judged by everyday experience, which catches only the delusive appearance of things' (ibid., p. 207).

In fact, that is how he continues in the next section (VII, 'Labouring power'):

> All of you feel sure that what they daily sell is their Labour; that, therefore, Labour has a Price, and that, the price of a commodity being only the monetary expression of its value, there must certainly exist such a thing as

the *value of Labour*. However, there exists no such thing as the *value of Labour* in the common acceptance of the word.

(ibid., p. 207)

He proceeds further by saying that, as it is crystallized social labour we are talking about, we cannot say what the value of a 10-hour working day is other than by a tautology: it is worth 10-hour labour. The problem is that the working man is not selling labour, but rather his own 'labour power', i.e., Marx notices, what Hobbes in *Leviathan* (2008b) calls 'the use of his power'.

What follows is so simple and clear that most Marxists, immersed as they are in the metaphysics of capitalism rather than in the study of the concrete, are perfectly blind to it. The worker in capitalism is divorced from his primitive union with his tools, nature and the other human beings. This is the triple alienation we have seen in Chapter 2. 'The labouring power of a man exists only in his living individuality' (ibid., p. 208). Man, by selling his labour power, is annihilating precisely that individuality. What could the price/value of that be? Only in the metaphysics of capitalism, where everything is dialectically transcended and mediated, and hence not directly natural, can one think of a price/value for this atrocity, but participating in this type of intercourse would be participating in insanity.

'The cry for an *equality of wages* rests, therefore, upon a mistake, is an *insane* wish never to be fulfilled [all men being individually different, AM]' (ibid., p. 208). But he goes further than that:

> To clamour for *equal or even equitable retribution* on the basis of the wage system is the same as clamour for *freedom* on the basis of the slavery system. What you think just or equitable is out of the question. [. . .] The *value of labouring power* is determined by the *value of the necessities* required to [. . .] perpetuate the labouring power.
>
> (ibid., pp. 208–9)

Only one conclusion is possible, and Marx does not hesitate in pursuing it.

Class struggle is not the means whereby the working class can emancipate itself from this insane world in which monetary value is attributed to human life, and justice is sought in assessing its quantity and its fair distribution by denying individuality. Class struggle is only the way not to lose out to the capitalist desire to over-exploit the workers, for this would weaken the movement by weakening the people who are in it and prevent higher goals.

> The workers ought not to forget that they are fighting with effects, but not with the causes of those effects; that they are retarding the downward movement, but not changing its direction; that they are applying palliatives, not curing the malady.
>
> (ibid., pp. 225–6)

It follows that:

> Trade Unions work well as centres of resistance against the encroachment of capital [. . .] They fail generally by limiting themselves to a guerrilla war against the effects of the existing system [. . .] instead of using their organized forces [. . .] for the final emancipation of the working class, that is to say, the ultimate abolition of the wage system.
>
> (ibid., p. 226)

Quite a thing to say while addressing the Socialist International! But, in those days, a few radical things were still possible, an eventuality that the intellectual collaboration between most Marxists and the capitalist system has completely erased from the intellectual horizon these days. In Marx's time, words could still be used, at least in part, in a more general and precise sense than they are used now.[3] Expressions such as 'the ultimate abolition of the wage system' still unequivocally signified revolution as individual emancipation from the insane confusion between human life, value/price and politics. Marx himself was aware both that the abolition of the wage system required the abolition of the state, and of the existence of the danger that this very simple concept would be transferred, in the metaphysics of capitalism, to the realm of the obscure past when revolutions happened, or to the distant future.

Marx's work on the Paris Commune (1977) makes clear in a repetitious way that the Commune is not remarkable only because its institutions had started to think about simple things such as the abolition of the state and of the private ownership of the means of production. Additionally, the Commune actually sought to do such things, with various degrees of success. From this perspective, one that is easily arrived at by actually reading this work of Marx, the following words sound terribly desperate: 'After every revolution marking a progressive phase in the class struggle [he is referring to the Middle Ages – French revolution – bourgeois power passage, AM], the purely repressive character of the State power stands out in bolder and bolder relief' (1977, p. 51). Imperialism follows suit (p. 53); that is why the Commune abolished the army. The power of the nation-state had to be abolished (p. 55). But:

> It is generally the fate of completely new historical creations to be mistaken for the counterpart of older and even defunct forms of social life, to which they bear a certain likeness. Thus, this new Commune, which breaks the state power, has been mistaken for a reproduction of the medieval Communes [. . .] the substratum of [. . .] State power.
>
> (p. 55)

Here, the limiting power of capitalist words and speech, which will accompany us for the rest of the book, is made clear by Marx in a way that cannot be mistaken. Hence, the following even more desperate bitterness. The Commune has been mistaken for the old fight against centralization: nobody outside it (but we should not forget that we do not know about those inside) could think about, and observe, the concrete facts. 'The Commune, they exclaim, intends to abolish property, the basis of all civilization! [. . .] But this is Communism, "impossible" Communism! [. . .] what else, gentlemen, would it be but Communism, "possible" Communism?' (ibid., pp. 57–8).

Although there can be no doubt that Marx knew Hume, Berkeley, Locke and Hobbes, whom we shall discuss in this chapter and in the next in order to organize what is proposed in Marx at the intuitive level, it would be well beyond the scope of the present book to prove how far Marx's work was influenced by, let alone consonant with, theirs. We can nonetheless show, which we will do from the next section onwards, that their thought revolved around – and is crucial to – the central issues we have found in Marx. Their contributions help shed light on phenomena that are far from new, for they indeed are basic, historical, constituent parts of that insane thing called capitalism. We must, therefore, concentrate on capitalism's intellectual structure, the flawed metaphysics that alienates us from ourselves, our fellow human beings and nature and permits so much evil.

To argue that the majority of Marxists willingly misinterpreted Marx's words for political purposes would be unfair and an inadequate explanation. Of course, there is no denying their good faith and the enormity of the task of a conscious misreading of an *oeuvre* as large as Marx's by so many generations of scholars and activists.[4] There must and can be a cultural, social and political explanation, which is the Marxists' belonging to the metaphysics of capitalism with its vulgar Hegelian, dialectical mediating attitude, which is also the Marxist majority's intellectual attitude.

If that is so, then the detailed explanation of the Marxist misunderstanding of Marx must mainly lie in the misuse of words and speech that is being progressively presented here. The degree of alienation from humanity, the self and nature at its basis allows Marxists and non-Marxists not to notice (which could also be, at least in part, ascribed to a hierarchy of priorities in their analysis, for instance, bent to give primacy to the issue of exploitation) and, more importantly, not to perceive the 'insane' atrocity of the world Marx is describing, and also his outrage at it. Whereas Marx is sympathetically feeling the human losses capitalism perpetrates, his interpreters coldly look at them as a set of phenomena that can be disregarded in their urgent human individual drama. They concentrate, unlike Marx, on the collective nature of the phenomena, seen as part of a supposed historical regularity, visible or to be ascertained. Like Catholics, they take for granted that we are in the world to suffer.

What is the difference between actual capitalist exploitation of the labouring class as a complete destruction of their individuality, and the Marxist vulgata's detached observation of it, in the belief that the conditions for revolution are not there yet, and a fair wage is the realistic and just thing to propose? The present author cannot see any, but this seems not to matter, here and in general. Let us, then, at least seek to make sense of it, in the hope that it could help overcome this iniquity.

The general discussion so far developed implies that, in capitalism as we know it, the relationship of words to facts is a secondary issue. Words matter for themselves because they are pure capitalist metaphysics. They hang somewhere between their concrete reference in reality and a logically sound (i.e. for a first approximation, useful here, not only dialectical) usage of their meaning. This last feature, in capitalism as we know it, is vague, generic and elastic. It comes to depend on the framework in which it is inscribed for its clarity and precision (e.g. a mainstream economic argument, or a Marxist political economy one, or a practical political issue). This is why, on most occasions, we can disregard and impotently observe actual atrocities. They are not strictly material in meaning. That is why, also, we need to add meaning to them by means of appropriate adjectives, invectives and cause–effect analyses, as if the destruction of human individuals needed that rational passage to be perceived and make our hair stand on end. This criticism is not moralistic; on the contrary.

The necessity for ethics and morality is, in fact, only felt in social, economic and political life and comes precisely from this alienated and alienating – and unfortunately only – way of expressing things, natural in general and human in particular. By requiring adjectives and explanations of why what is described is insane and atrocious to then finally spark a non-formal word reaction, it also requires a generalized sharing of what is meant in that circumstance and for that purpose. Those who undergo the observed trouble must lose their individuality and become victims. In other words, a community of reference (the observers, as well as the observed) is needed that is capable of tuning in to what is being described and collectively gives little weight to the degree of relationship to the concrete that is meant.[5] Society must be intellectually, and as a consequence emotionally, homogeneous. To communicate to the metaphysics of capitalism you must belong to it.[6]

Anticipating a theme we will discuss in more depth in the rest of the book, it follows from the above that revolutionary thought is unthinkable in the metaphysics of capitalism. Ruptures with disappearances are only conceived as deeds of the past (e.g. during the transition from feudalism to capitalism) or utopias for the far-distant future. As a consequence, revolutionary authors, too, either belong to the past or are not recognized, or both, as in the case of Marx we just examined. It is, then, worthwhile going briefly back to Adam Smith and John Stuart Mill, to check whether we can detect similar mistakes to those made about Marx in the interpretation of their work. It is important to signal, as a premise, that the Marxist misinterpretation of Marx described above is shared in all its structures and characteristics by all types of non-Marxist and anti-Marxist, or they would not be able to argue their agnostic or oppositional position. The same holds valid for Smith, Mill and anybody else.

It is easy to show that Adam Smith is a clear instance of a revolutionary thinker of the same type as Marx. Despite his evident politically conservative desires and beliefs, which we shall come back to in Chapter 4 while discussing economics, as anticipated in Chapter 2, he does three revolutionary things:

1   He refers straightforwardly to the material.
2   He discusses chance and gives it a prominent role.

3   He notices, and projects into the future, especially in *The Wealth of Nations* (1999), the evident ruptures with disappearance that mark the transition to capitalism by means of the industrial revolution.

Smith's discussions of Point 2 are in Smith (1980, 2001), which also deal with language, and which are better left to the next section. Here, we will limit ourselves to pointing out some simple and well-known instances that support Points 1 and 3.

In the case of Smith, of course, we cannot talk of pleasure similar to that taken by Marx in the thought of a completely new world to come that breaks all relationships with the old. This is precisely the difference that marks a nineteenth-century thinker from one of the eighteenth. Nonetheless, despite Smith's desire for the permanence of important features of the feudal world for the invisible hand to function (Smith, 2009; Micocci, 2014b; Di Mario and Micocci, 2015), in Smith (1999), we find an admiring description of the fundamental ruptures with disappearance that we find in the arrival of the capitalist mode of production. First and foremost is the existence of the 'commercial man', the individual who manages his self within society and the economy, following their mechanisms.

In fact, famously, 'our dinner' does not come from the benevolence of the butcher, baker and brewer (1999, p. 119). Not even a beggar would 'choose to depend chiefly upon the benevolence of his fellow citizens' (ibid.). The greater part of a beggar's occasional wants are in fact 'supplied in the same manner as those of other people, by treaty, by barter, and by purchase' (ibid.). From this 'trucking disposition', the division of labour famously originates (ibid.). In fact, in Smith, the true rupture with former modes of production is in the full chance for the human 'trucking disposition' to freely deploy its potential. This is so because, like in Marx, individuals are different from each other, but, more explicitly than in Marx, who usually limits himself to allow for equal potential, they are born equal.

As seen in Chapter 2, 'The difference between the most dissimilar characters, between a philosopher and a common street porter, for example, seems to arise not so much from nature as from habit, customs and education' (ibid., p. 120). It is the division of labour that makes men different, enhancing or playing down their talents. In a market society, one can choose which way to live one's life. In fact, in it, owing to such individual economic liberty, one's 'respective talents' are brought into a 'common stock, where every man may purchase whatever part of the produce of other men's talents he has occasion for' (ibid., p. 121). In such a world, there is no chance for exploitation, or the mechanism would not work (class struggle sees to that: see Book I, pp. 165–70). Like in Marx, we witness a very radical and utopian argument that got lost in the present-day metaphysics of mainstream and heterodox capitalist economic theories, as we will show in Chapter 4.

However, the central point is that Smith can do all this because of Point 1 above. His subject matter is empirical reality. He studied the concrete men, women, institutions and their encroaching relationships he witnessed by observing the material. From a present-day point of view this is hard to believe, and Smith is put together with Marx in the group of those Classical political economists who used a 'historical–philosophical approach' (see, for instance, Sylos Labini, 2004). Although, at this point in our reasoning, we can only approve of Smith's method, we must notice that it leaves a momentous problem open, which we will deal with in the next section and also later on (see also Micocci, 2014a): how does he know that he has identified, and grasped, the material? How does he know he has reached that 'silence position' of complete detachment from the conditioning of society we introduced earlier on?

From the point of view of Smith's internal coherence, we could simply say that he had no intention to detach himself from a society and economy he approved of. This is very different from, and more defendable than, the position of the various dominant Marxisms and of mainstream economics, for they pretend to be about transforming reality. Unlike them, Smith does not build a theoretical model upon a logically flawed (vulgar Hegelian) set of premises about human nature, the role of history and the usefulness of limiting the set of economic objects to those amenable to treatment by the methodology used. Smith simply takes what he sees as a matter of fact and analyses and judges it, always and consistently seeking to isolate the social, economic and political characteristics. As Hume suggested in fact,[7] human society is the only place where cause–effect connections and repetitiveness (predictability) have a chance to work.

Smith does not mortgage history and nature as Hegel mistakenly does.[8] He simply makes a political statement from which he infers the due consequences. His historical reality is what he is talking about. We will see in Chapter 4 how his invisible hand, which we introduced in Chapter 2, is much sounder than anything devised by mainstream economists and opposed by Marxist political economists. We will indeed confirm that it does not correspond to what is given that name these days (see also Micocci, 2014b; Di Mario and Micocci, 2015).

Smith sees the inevitable monopolistic tendency of capitalist free initiative:

> Their interest [merchants' and manufacturers', AM] is [. . .] directly opposite of that of the great body of the people. As it is in the interest of the freemen of a corporation to hinder the rest of the inhabitants from employing any workmen but themselves, so it is in the interest of the merchants and manufacturers of every country to secure to themselves the monopoly of the home market. [. . .] Hence the high duties and prohibitions upon all those foreign manufactures.
>
> (Smith, 1999, IV, Vol. 2, pp. 72–3)

It took the mainstream several decades to grasp this truth, along with Chamberlin and Robinson, for it clashed with their metaphysics of market competition, which took imperfect competition as an exception rather than an inevitable tendency.

As a consequence, Smith was famously aware of what Marx and Engels would notice many decades later: that the division of labour had terrible consequences for the labouring class (ibid., V, 1, pp. 368–9). That is why barbarous societies were to be feared (see also Chapter 2): the ingeniousness of their populations could not be matched by the 'torpor of mind' of civilized societies. These last were protected only by their technological level, that is to say, by the amount of capital needed to undertake a war against them. This is a very radical indictment of the connection between creativity, innovation and technology that, for opposite reasons, both mainstream and Marxist practitioners continue to take for granted. This disturbs no one, for it clashes with material reality but not with the prevailing metaphysics.

The case for John Stuart Mill is more complicated, for he is not as radical as Smith and Marx, especially in his understanding of the role of society and politics. As introduced in Chapter 2, Mill relies on 'community' (which he often calls society, e.g., 1998, pp. 6–8),[9] thus surrendering to the flawed logic of capitalism (Micocci, 2002, 2008/2010, 2012). For our purposes, it suffices to come back to the following programmatic statement in Book II of his *Principles of Political Economy* (1998):

> The laws and conditions of the production of wealth partake of the character of physical truths. [. . .] Whatever mankind produce, must be produced in the modes, and under the conditions, imposed by the constitution of natural things, and by the inherent properties of their own bodily and mental structure.
>
> (p. 5)

'Future extension of our knowledge of the laws of nature' may change 'productiveness.'

> But howsoever we may succeed in making for ourselves more space within the limits set by the constitutions of things, we know that there must be limits. We cannot alter the ultimate properties either of matter or mind, but only can employ those properties more or less successfully.
>
> (ibid., p. 6)

Material reality rules over everything, including human capacities. That is why in Mill there is an inevitable tendency to a final stationary state in economic activities, determined by the limits imposed on them by nature (1998, Book IV, ch. 6). Hence the inevitable end of the antagonistic tendencies of capitalism and the need for brotherly collaboration after that day (ibid.).

Not only does Mill show some of the radical features we have announced, which present day liberals have simply forgotten. He also presents us with the preponderance of nature: the centrality of the concrete. This is a fundamental starting point for our materialistic investigation. Nature, time and the concrete are, for our purposes here, the same thing; naturally, one can always think that the three of them might be separated and made distinct by some as yet unknown forces, but, like Adam Smith, we must start from somewhere: this is the most satisfactory starting point at this stage in the book.

We can start drawing up the lines of the argument, identifying the main themes in order to go beyond what Classical political economists have said. We are dealing here with the complex – and as yet quite unexplored (at least in the social sciences, as we shall see in more depth next chapter) – issue of the relationship between individuals, societies and communication as a part of natural history, to use an old term. More precisely, we are studying how far the capitalist mode of production succeeds in alienating itself from nature by isolating and using only those objects and relationships that are amenable not only to mediation but also to repetition (iterativeness). We are comparing the endless, unpredictable and destructive power of nature with the conservative attempt to live in seclusion from it through capitalism.

If there is a general, ontological unity of everything material, then capitalism has a problem in attempting to (intellectually) build and preserve such seclusion. It can only resort either to supernatural powers, which have so far proved not to exist, or to bending, changing and perverting the natural endowment of humans, nature in general (which in our days is called, to that purpose, the environment) and time itself. This is possible up to a point: nature and time, unlike humans, can be bent only as far as they bend themselves. Beyond a certain point, we have a crisis, after which the outcome can only be death/disappearance: a crippled and time-limited life if the original natural combination cannot be reverted back to, or a sudden return to the original situation.

The metaphysics of capitalism, by its inability to produce radical, clear-cut concepts and statements, deceives those who reason in speech instead of observing reality in silence. The achievements of science and technology are a fact hailed as:

(a) the possibility to actually bend nature to humankind's will;
(b) even sillier, the possibility to mend by the same means the mistakes produced by pursuing (a).

This silly belief in technology is typically found in mainstream economics and Marxist political economy and is thus fully shared by ecological protesters of all brands. All of them, in fact, bovinely base their activities at least upon (b), which requires (a) to exist (see Micocci, 2015).

There is almost no need to add that this type of mentality implies that the possibility of scientific revolutions à la Kuhn (1969) must be ruled out. Science, as well as nature, must necessarily resemble Walrasian equilibrium, with its pompous succession of attempts to reach equilibrium, and a supernatural (i.e. not supernatural, but capitalistically metaphysical – neither material nor abstract) crier who, in the suitable forms and ways, cries the necessary information for everybody to satisfy their needs by fair sharing of the resources available. In the natural world, appropriately renamed and reimagined as a capitalist metaphysical entity (the environment), the same happens. Plants and minerals act as if pushed by a rational set of laws.[10]

Rainforests or deserts are imagined by capitalist science as timeless places that enjoy a perfect equilibrium. Like in every capitalist story, that requires the presence of morality/ethics. The (dialectical) alteration of the holy equilibrium is in fact, in the prevailing narrative, an evil (evil here, as usual in capitalism, means subversive) action, even when it is not caused by humans. Little matter whether, in case of human action, the one who perpetrates the misdeed is pushed by the search for profit or by misguided attempts to improve upon natural laws.

The reason for this is that natural laws (the supernatural Walrasian crier) are a mediating, dialectical spirit that proceeds like Hegelian history. In it, true disappearances (Hegel's butcher's desk) are no moral problem, for they concern what does not pertain to the smooth dialectical proceeding of the whole. This last is what must be preserved. Only human action can be an act of will, following or hindering the direction of the Spirit. Subversion is allowed, only to be repressed. Revolution is unthinkable.

3.3 Humans and nature

As for the metaphysics of capitalism, evolution is not the coming of ruptures with disappearance, but the unperturbing elimination of inadequate items; the problem for the morally laden capitalist understanding of nature is that it has no need for mercy and sympathy. Any loss that cannot be mended is disregarded, for it is attributed to the supernatural and unchangeable judgement of the butcher's desk. Morality and ethics can turn their attention to checking the evil doings of those natural and human deeds that attempt the smooth working of the dialectics of the system. Natural evolution happens; only it is deprived of the liberty of chance. It is instead compelled to persistently follow the only cause–effect logic understandable to the metaphysics of capitalism.[11]

In a world where chance is not free, we can potentially fit in place the parts of any puzzle we are presented with. We will explore the social sciences from the next section onwards. However, let us dwell a little on natural history here, for it helps us introduce the philosophical issues we will need to discuss later. In science, we need something analogous to the capitalist use of words and concepts introduced earlier on: measurement. With measurement, concepts (data) are produced that lose their direct connection with the concrete object they refer to. In doing so, in the needs of capitalist intellectuality and, hence, in science, they gain primacy over that very object. This is valid for common speech too. A metaphysics of forever imprecise and yet precisely measured and measurable things is thus produced.

Measurement is in need of continuous refinements, which the continuous changeability of reality eludes all the time. This is not to do with the liberty of chance: rather, it is an expression of the iterativeness of capitalist logic and of the preponderance of the intellectual mechanisms of infinitesimal calculus, whereby, aping Schrödinger's formula, one is perpetually condemned to ever approach precision and objects without reaching them. Despite all this, science works for its practical purposes because its mechanisms (which may not work, or may be changeable) depend upon laws that bind the behaviour of animate and inanimate things. Engineering is, therefore, possible, because measurements are useful to practical purposes, especially if they are fairly stable.

As a consequence, by setting up a measurement system for a contained area (Lawson's enclosures in economics, and what natural scientists call experiments, or environments), anything characterized by the possible attribution of given parameters can be measured. For a fashionable instance, once you have measured the relationship between the trees and the lesser plants that characterize a forest area, you can measure all other forest or jungle areas, *mutatis mutandis*. The supernatural crier – the laws that rule the regularity (iterative behaviour) of the whole – allows this.

For an outrageous instance, by means of the various agronomic measures that are used in agriculture, one can study natural systems. The implication is clear. One assumes that there is no substantial difference, and no external or unforeseen disturbance, let alone a rupture with disappearance. The laws of equilibrium rule. Little wonder, then, that rainforests are supposed to be systems in immutable equilibrium, if left to their own devices. Little wonder that such equilibrium, if altered, can be restored by human intervention. Little wonder that the alteration is necessarily a human-induced thing: sometimes a case of straightforward evil (e.g., exploitation of the forest's resources), other times an indirect effect, or a mistake.[12]

By this same principle, agriculture can be ecological, i.e. in equilibrium with nature, reductively renamed the environment. The parameters whereby such equilibrium is judged are the outcome of capitalist intellectuality and of its perception of time. Thus, whereas the management of salty irrigation water in the ancient fertile crescent (the cradle of civilization) is, by the vast majority, judged to be an instance of an 'eternal' (sustainable) technique, the decrease in the long-term organic fertility of European and North American soil (e.g., in the Corn Belt) that is hidden by the increased productivity induced by chemical fertilization is disregarded, except by the usual, occasional impotent minority. But what is the length of time required to tell us that a technique is good? Nobody can tell. Judgement is left to the empty rhetoric of words, speech and numbers.

To further complicate the issue, there is the undeniable fact that, up to a point, nature bends itself to human exploitation. Agronomic calculations do produce amazing harvests. Genetics does contribute to that same result, and not only with questionable monsters such as hybrid plants and genetically modified organisms. Both in industrial and traditional agriculture, cultivated plants as well as wild weeds seem to collaborate towards forming those cosy and reassuring country landscapes that everybody affects to love. You can be fairly sure, when planting your seeds or seedlings in the well-ordered rows you have prepared for them, that they will follow the rules you have set for their development. They respond to your chemical or organic fertilizer the way you expect them to, and so do parasites and weeds to your efforts to eliminate or reduce their effects.

Domestic animals big and small do not protest when confined in their paddock or cage. They grow, or produce milk or eggs, following the programme the vet has provided, responding as expected to the calculations of their food and exercise requirements. Occasional cases of sterility, hysteria or disease let the farmer know when artificial constraint has gone too far. Some, like water buffalos, even seem to throw off some of their wilder, more aggressive traits. Finally, they offer their heads to the butcher, easily and tamely if they come from confined breeding, after some resistance if they have been bred free range. Other animals, like dogs, oversee the smooth functioning of this fairy tale.

At a superficial look from outside, the key seems to be the imposition of regularity and order. The more you regulate and organize it, the more agriculture pays you back with results unequalled by less efficient farmers. It is well worth noticing that similar types of observation were made by ancient writers, from Hesiod onwards. Nature seems to adapt itself to serve humankind. Even such subversive writers as Chernishevsky could celebrate the achievements of modern agriculture as 'artistic feats' (see Pardjanadze and Micocci, 2000). Sereni (1996) could write a celebrated history of agriculture based on ancient paintings.

Is this realistic? From the materialistic point of view we are seeking to build here, this is not the correct question. Rather, we should wonder whether we are looking at the right objects, and, more importantly, whether the regularities, laws and connections that produce the landscape and the very idea of agriculture exist. Resorting to the list of equally undeniable facts of nature reverting to its old ways and not caring for man (e.g. cattle, horses, dogs and cats returning to wilderness; genetically new plants having retro-mutations or new mutations; geological disasters caused by agriculture; human over-, under- or bad nourishment; disappearance of waters or increase in their salinity; appearance of entirely new parasites; and so on) would only be a palliative argument.

What is more relevant, and is done in the subsequent part of this chapter, is to verify the soundness of the cause–effect relationship that makes us see agriculture as simultaneously (for some) the effect of the harmony between humankind and the 'environment' and the cause of some of the most frightening natural phenomena that affect the Earth and humankind. The materialistic method that is being worked out here must necessarily rely upon this type of doubt: while we do not know how far agriculture is unnatural, we cannot and must not deny that a form of collaboration between nature and humans, with an apparent temporary subservience of some plants and animals to humans, is possible. What is not possible is to pass that as the rule, and pass measurement for scientific statements.

An alternative way to summarize what has been said about nature and agriculture is by noticing that the most striking characteristic of the humanity–nature relationship typical of agriculture is the regularity ensuing from the imposition of collectiveness. It seems that, if we put our seeds and trees together in a regular fashion, or if we constrain our animals in a contained closeness, they adapt to the situation by taking on homogeneous features. The only plants that do not conform to the pattern, for an instance that everyone must have noticed, are those in the rows at the edge of the field, i.e. those relatively open to nature in general. It is further observable that agricultural plants and animals are kept, both in traditional and in industrial agriculture, in a much closer proximity than they would be if they were in wilderness, that is operating autonomously. This amazing homogeneity quickly vanishes when the plants and animals are abandoned and left to their own individual destiny.

Indeed, without such homogeneity, humans would not be able to plan their survival. Although present-day homogeneity can be attributed in part to genetic manipulation, this only applies to modern varieties derived from intensive manipulation. Old varieties of plants and animals were rather non-homogeneous by modern standards; hence the need to teach the art of choosing the good animal and the good plant for reproduction in the old agricultural schools, in order to achieve homogeneity. Can this be proved by means of the parameters of modern science? Not fully and satisfactorily, or there would be no controversy over what kinds of agricultural technique are best.

As for instinct, or migration (allegedly a consequence of the former), official science can only invent a term and hope that nobody asks what it means. This is usually done by adding a description of the phenomenon to the term. Again, take instinct in zoology, or gravitation in physics. We know how they work, how to use them. We even know when they are lost or do not work, but not what they are. In the case of animals and perhaps plants, we should add the fundamental importance of what Epicurus and other ancient and modern philosophers identified as prolepsis. The best-known case is that of hens, which lose their instinct to become broody and sit on their eggs if they are born in incubators, but regain it, in the next generation, if they are incubated in the natural way by a hen or any other suitable bird.[13]

In other words, there is an amazing, non-scientific relationship between order and regularity and tameness and homogeneity. Organization imposed by humans seems to do the trick, in nature, in agriculture and, which we all know, in human societies. Although no scientific soundness can be claimed for this observation (we can only notice that it is evident, under all latitudes, to all observers), it certainly casts a powerful shadow on the widespread claim that human beings have always lived in societies built precisely upon the imposition of regularity and order from above. In fact, nobody can deny that such a way of living produces the possibility of identifying a society, i.e. a population, by the time-enduring homogeneity of its characteristics. However, if humans are part of nature, and nature is as a whole unpredictable, this is obviously only one possible way of living, which, in all likelihood, individuals can leave in order to regain their individual differences. The possibility that humans are not natural creatures can be easily disregarded, and in fact it is not contemplated by science or even by most religions.

In any case, the puzzling readiness of nature to submit in certain minor ways to the needs of human societies is a powerful help to the cause of capitalism, and of human societies in general, in pursuing their goal in seclusion from nature. So, we need to reconsider this problem by looking at it from another, wider perspective. We need to distinguish between the single manifestations of nature and nature as a whole. This is, again, nothing new in Western culture, for it goes back to Parmenides and the question of Being. We can, then, refer it to the history of philosophy and turn to see whether similar phenomena happen to human beings in society.

In the dialectical world of capitalist intellectuality, some might want to argue that humans are natural but have some peculiar characteristics: speech and collectiveness. Although arguing against this unprovable argument would take us too far without adding anything relevant to our philosophical and epistemological discussion, it is well worth noticing the following. If humans are by nature a speech-endowed collective animal, then a set of explicated rules is needed to organize society, or speech would lose its main purpose. In a dialectical environment, a Walrasian general equilibrium is perfect for this task, for it reduces the need for a tyrannical authority by allowing for a crier and by setting prices as the main indicator of human intercourses. That, put simply, would mean, for example, that Marx is wrong. Such a world would not be 'insane', atrocious and evil, but natural.

We are facing the momentous alternative between nature and society. The only way to criticize society is by posing oneself outside it, from a naturalistic point of view that needs radical philosophical arguments to be proposed, because the only way to organize it is by attempting to directly observe the material. This corresponds to the irreconcilable difference between the autonomous individual and organized societies. Either you have one or the other. No dialectical mediation is possible between these two poles, to the chagrin of the Marxist majority. Now, we can turn to examine the salient features of human collectiveness, with its order and organization.

Both liberal and Marxist theories appear to accept the idea that the social dimension of humankind is inevitable. From the present point of view, even if that were true, it would be preferable to argue that the social dimension is caused by the physical properties of nature, which no individual can fully and continuously overcome. The doubt remains that the instance of agriculture might indicate that nature can only occasionally and for limited purposes tolerate an ordered and regulated collective gathering of a few animal and botanical species. The question, therefore, of the individual–society relationship and of the bonds – and the limits – imposed by language and speech, is far from solved.

As the collective and social aspects of liberal and Marxist theories are well established and discussed and simply unsolved, and as we have programmatically accepted doubt in our methodology, we can turn to discussing a useful paradox that goes unnoticed if you acritically accept present-day liberalism and Marxism. There is, at present, a revival of theories and scholars linked to the so-called Italian '*operaismo*', a brand of majority Marxism that well epitomizes the reactionary features of the orthodox interpretation of Marx. After participating in the 1977 wave of protests in Italy, many of those associated with these theories have soared to prominent professional and political positions. From these, they are seeking to rewrite the history of that period.

In order to conjugate their affection to the intellectual features of capitalist society and their 'exploitation first – protest second' interpretation of Marxism, they need to show that Marx is not the writer we have been reading in the present volume. When they cannot resort to the long-standing apparatus of dialectical and historical materialism, they simply invent, grafting capitalist ideas on to Marx. The most astonishing case is represented by the idea of 'general intellect', which allows them to throw everything back to class struggle as the tool to preserve, rather than destroy, capitalism by dialectical interaction between masters and workers meant as political organization of the reciprocal collective interests.[14] Such a type of analysis also allows them, as we shall see presently, to overcome the numerical shrinking of the working class caused by the Western processes of de-industrialization. Nature is erased.

Virno (2007) claims that the idea of general intellect, i.e. 'mass intellectuality' (2007, p. 6), is:

> the depository of cognitive competencies that cannot be objectified in machinery. Mass intellectuality is the prominent form in which the general intellect is manifest today. What is at stake is not the scientific erudition of the individual labourer. Rather, only (but this only is everything) the more generic attitudes of the mind come to the fore as productive resources; these are the faculty of language, the disposition to learn, memory, the capacity to abstract and relate, and the inclination towards self-reflexivity. General intellect needs to be understood literally as intellect in general: the faculty of thought, rather than the works produced by thought.
>
> (ibid.)

There are three main problems with what Virno says: first, this definition not only does not say anything, but it also deliberately restricts the range of human thought and capacities; second, even if we tried to give it some content, it simply identifies Adam Smith's 'numbness of mind' generated by the division of labour; third, simply and obviously given the first two points, none of it is in Marx, especially in the pages of *Grundrisse* Virno refers to (Marx, 1973). Rather, we find the rationale for this idea in Hegel. Let us see each point, one by one.

In the first place, Virno identifies the 'faculty of thought' with a limited set of functions: the faculty of language, the disposition to learn, memory, the capacity to abstract and relate, and self-reflexivity. Even admitting that these were the only sources for thought to be defined and to operate, there is, in the way Virno puts it, the evident echo of the catholic anthropology that fakes wonder at the capacity of human beings to praise God and to convince people that only arid rationality following given definitions is valid. Of course, he simply does not know whether only these things constitute thought; nor does he know whether concentrating only on these faculties would kill other faculties we might have (in all probability, he hopes this is so, or political organization would be difficult); third, he values them highly, for no reason; finally, how do we know that animals and plants do not do all this? Simply because they do not converse with us?

Virno's definition says nothing about humankind that cannot be heard all the time, on all sorts of occasions, expressed by all sorts of people. That is why there is good reason to suspect that he has simply selected, among human faculties, those that are amenable to political treatment in the most banal Leninist sense. Language is needed for us to learn and memorize the abstract (in the common Marxist sense) categories that show relationships that, being Hegelian Universals, are also the objects of your self-reflexivity. In fact, he means 'intellect in general': a social object.

Second – and unforgivably, unless you are a Hegelian or a Christian – he identifies the activities of the mind with what can be used as 'productive resources'. He is telling us that the act of thinking only matters if it is socially shared, inscribed in the only human activity worth discussing, i.e. labouring for economic purposes. This obviously entails societies' existence and must make sense only in that they are productive in an economic sense: they create value. This is precisely (see Section 3.1) what Marx opposed, and what he sought to destroy as 'insane'. It is, in fact, that world Adam Smith praises, in which the deception of the invisible hand transforms the lower classes into users of their own labour power by alienating it to productive purposes that will increase the wealth of the nation, but there is a powerful condition.

Adam Smith was well aware of the human losses implied by the productive activities of alienated labour:

> The understandings of the greater part of men are necessarily formed by their ordinary employment. The man whose life is spent in performing a few simple operations [. . .] has no occasion to exert his understanding or to exercise his invention. [. . .] He naturally loses, therefore, the habits of such exertion, and generally becomes as stupid and ignorant as it is possible for a human creature to become [. . .] incapable of conceiving any generous, noble, or tender sentiment.
>
> (Smith, 1999, V, I, pp. 368–9)

Such a man cannot make proper political judgement. He needs, Lenin would be quick to infer, the guidance of the party, but a Christian would reply that his sheep-like behaviour will take him to Heaven.

Commentators usually hurry to connect these words of Smith with the assembly line and with menial jobs. Smith did not mean any of that, for he felt nostalgia for pre-division-of-labour man. Jobs that require 'a few simple operations' make you stupid, but which job does not require this? If all, or even most, jobs required unrestrained creativity, efficiency would be impossible, for reasons that are too evident to be discussed. This concerns all levels and types of work, manual and intellectual. Those jobs that require creativity must be as few as possible and bear as indirectly as possible on the productive system. Schumpeterian revolutionary innovation is unbearable to the smooth, iterative working of the capitalist system (Micocci, 2008/2010, 2014a; Schumpeter, 1987). Virno is confusing general intellect with generalized lack of it, or willingly proposing that the vast majority of us be 'as stupid and ignorant' as possible – a quite different thing from Marx's emancipation.

In fact, nothing of what he says can be found in the *Grundrisse* pages he refers to (Marx, 1973, Notebook VII, 1858 fragment on fixed capital):

> The full development of capital [. . .] the mode of production corresponding to it [takes place] when the means of labour has not only taken the economic form of fixed capital, but has also been suspended in its immediate form, and

> when fixed capital appears as a machine [. . .] and the entire production process as not subsumed under the direct skilfulness of the worker, but rather as the technological application of science [. . .] direct labour [is] reduced to a mere moment of this process.
>
> (p. 699)

The worker undergoes the effects of a technical/scientific appearance. He does not participate in it! Science and technology and labour are 'a combination which appears as a natural fruit of social labour (although it is a historical product)' (p. 700).

Marx continues by arguing that this scientific characteristic (that might dissolve capital) is based on fixed capital, which 'appears as a reduction of individual labour to the level of helplessness in face of the communality [. . .] represented by and concentrated in capital', but also takes the form of circulating capital, which further alienates labour 'in the form of money' (ibid.), mediating between different workers (p. 701). Machinery replaces the worker, making operations more and more mechanical (p. 704); 'capital absorbs labour into itself' (ibid.).

> The human being comes to relate more as watchman and regulator to the production process itself. [. . .] He steps to the side of the production process instead of being its chief actor. [. . .] *it is, in a word, the development of the social individual which appears as the great foundation-stone of production and of wealth*. The *theft* of alien labour time, on which the present wealth is based, appears a miserable foundation in face of this new one, created by large scale industry.
>
> (p. 705; emphasis in the original in all *Grundrisse* quotations)

But this, to Marx, makes the creation of wealth independent from labour time, challenging capitalism. This latter must, therefore, also control disposable time '*outside that needed in direct production*' (p. 706), for '*the products of human industry*' and of '*human participation in nature*', the '*power of knowledge*' become with fixed capital a 'direct force of production', determining 'to what degree, hence, the conditions of the process of social life itself have come under the control of the general intellect and been transformed in accordance with it' (p. 706). 'The development of fixed capital indicates [. . .] the degree of development of wealth generally, or of capital' (p. 707). The general intellect is the product of capital and of its enforced sociality.

If and when capital becomes unable to appropriate the increasing quantity of disposable time, transforming it into surplus labour, then the workers will have a chance to subvert capitalism, making disposable time grow for all (p. 708). This is the opposite of the revelling in their own technical and communicative skills that Virno proposes, echoing Lenin. It is, instead, an evidently Hegelian idea: the worker, by participating in the satisfaction of social needs (Hegel, 2008, V, B) finds and realizes himself in this forced reciprocity. This 'universal substance' speaks a universal language in the customs and laws of a population, thus fully realizing 'each single individuality, despite this looking like a contradiction' (p. 239). In fact 'the existence of the Spirit consists in language' (ibid., VI, C, p. 430), that is, self-conscience. If language communicates, 'it understands itself and is understood by the others'. There is no need for individual emancipation in Hegel, just like in Virno, and of course in most types of Marxism.

Virno's mistake, and its unconcerned reception by the public, is a clear example of words and speech being a perfect tool to deliver the metaphysics of capitalism (in this case, in its most directly Hegelian form), to which, as a consequence, no one objects by raising the issue of its relation to both material reality and the words and speech of its main theoretical reference, Karl Marx. In other words, Virno is perfectly right in emphasizing the Hegelian social role of language as annihilation of individuality and of anything that is not social and does not belong to the metaphysics of capitalism. The problem we must solve now is whether what appears clear in capitalism is also relevant more generally. We will do so by appealing to the European materialist tradition started by Epicurus and continued by Francis Bacon (Micocci, 2008/2010) in the next section.

3.4 Nature out there: liberty

The relationship between individuals, society and nature, and how it is communicated, is a strictly materialistic problem. Concentrating on the material world about us helps us to penetrate its ontological nature and see its internal differences – if there are any. But the communication and society elements are, from our analysis so far, a hindrance that prevents a direct grasp of the material, the concrete. As already noticed, this is not a new problem: it goes all the way back to Parmenides and Heraclitus and, more usefully for us here, to Epicurus. Its modern analysis starts with Francis Bacon (see Micocci, 2002, 2008/2010, 2012).

Bacon, however, is often referred to as a contributor to the experimental method. He is considered to be a man who studied reality by means of empirical research. Defining the empirical is precisely the type of difficulty we face in economics and the other social sciences. It has the appearance of an invented term (a word) that does not correspond to anything in nature, but that is vague and malleable enough to be adapted to current use in everyday engineering measurement, i.e. what passes for routine scientific research these days. The empirical is nothing but a proxy for measurement that cannot be used as such across the board because, in empirical research, there are also qualitative analyses. Naturally, as all economists know, qualitative analyses are just another form of measurement.

Thus, natural and human studies of reality are supplied with a term, the empirical, which opens up two endless fields for further work. On the one hand, there is the question of methodology, and, on the other, that of selecting the significant empirical material. Some, however, might wish to argue that this latter, by leaving this or that item out, distorts the interpretation of empirical facts. Such dispute takes place, even at this very first level, no longer in reality but through the various proxies that have been deemed correct in its representation, just like in the actual empirical studies themselves.

If that were the only problem, the solution would be closer at hand than it actually is. Instead, empirical objects and methodologies are powerfully rendered more distant from the concrete by the fact that they are devised, not out of the concrete itself, but out of discourses about it. In being devised, they are transcended into metaphysical objects in our usual flawed sense. Although this happens in general, in capitalism, which only conceives of metaphysical items, this passage is less detectable but inevitably more thoroughly present. That is not all. The presence of prolepsis, or even the suspicion that it may exist, is a cause of further distortion and doubt.

Finally, the apparent inevitability of language necessarily reduces everything to regularities. If a degree of iterativeness were not supposed to be present, we would not know how to name phenomena, because we would feel we could not identify them. As a consequence, phenomena that are not regular, or not sufficiently and provably regular, are disregarded or attributed a regularity whose main purpose is to make them an object of communication. Agriculture in relation to nature in general is a typical case in point. We do not know exactly what goes on, but we act as if we did and produce endless narratives of facts, the existence of which is far from demonstrable.

For practical purposes, this whole absurdity works. Chemists produce new compounds; farmers reap harvests; rockets are sent to outer space. Sometimes, some are tempted to wonder whether this brings about losses, and whether such losses outweigh the gains. This last aspect is not logical from a humanitarian point of view, as Marx taught us for the 'insane' case of the exertion, use and evaluation of human labour. Economists, who are under fire for being the most creative inventors of non-existing items that they insert in their mathematical models, thus retain their place among the most revered scientists, and indeed their much-derided models often work. This marks the fundamental passage for us between the natural and the social sciences.

In the former, a degree of uncertainty is admitted, even within the metaphysics of capitalism (see Micocci, 2005). The latter only discuss regularities, as we will argue in what follows through discussion of the work of the French sensists and the British scepticals, and in Chapter 4. The consequences for economics and political economy are enormous, as we will see in Chapter 4.

Having announced a discussion of sceptical and Epicurean works, it might come as a surprise that we start from the work of Epictetus, a Stoic of the early Roman Empire. This is coherent with our purposes because we use Giacomo Leopardi's[15] Italian translation and 'vulgarization' of the *Manuale* (*Handbook*; Epictetus, 2009).

Let us start from a comment Leopardi makes in his '*Preambolo del Volgarizzatore*'. He claims that the philosophical practices taught in the booklet are better suited to the 'weak' modern man, for Epictetus's philosophy seems tailored to the 'weakness of man' (2009, p. 9). This is all the more necessary given the '*imbecillità naturale e irreparabile dei viventi*' (p. 10; 'the natural and irreparable imbecility of living beings', trans. A. Micocci). We cannot, and should not, be looking for happiness, but should rather take what comes without being upset by it. As in the Marx of the last section and of the preceding chapter, we should not be bothered by the effects, but look to the causes, and this only can be done if we are as far as possible unperturbed, and strong in our weakness.

In Leopardi's translation, Epictetus starts by warning us that there are two types of thing: those within our power (opinion, mind, soul, motions, appetites, aversion, everything that can be 'acted') and those that are not in our power (the body, our belongings, reputation, magistrates, everything we cannot operate/act ourselves). One should not pursue wealth, for one may not get it, and in any case this will cause the loss of the fortitude of your mind (p. 16): '*Pertanto ciascuna apparenza che ti occorrerà nella vita, innanzi ad ogni altra cosa avvezzati a dire: questa è un'apparenza, non è punto quello che mostra di essere*' (ibid.; 'Therefore, get into the habit of saying, this is just an appearance, it is not what it appears to be about each appearance you will witness in life', trans. A. Micocci).

Apparenza means subjective representation (φαντασία), which – crucially – depends on our assent to it to be comprehended in the sense of catalepsis. In other words, we must avoid taking things without questioning them, in the sense we have been proposing so far and we shall further refine in the rest of the book.

Not only words, but objects themselves, depend for their existence, and influence on us, upon our assent to them. By refusing it, we can both overcome and defeat their influence on us and proceed to a further, deeper analysis. This is fundamental and strengthens our argument here by showing that we are dealing with a need felt in general by the ancients and moderns alike.

In fact, Leopardi's Epictetus continues: '*Gli uomini sono agitati e turbati, non dalle cose, ma dalle opinione che eglino hanno delle cose. Per modo di esempio, la morte non è punto amara [. . .] ma l'opinione che si ha della morte, quello è l'amaro*' (p. 19; 'Men are agitated and upset not by things, but by their opinions about things. For instance, death is not bitter at all [. . .] but the opinion we have of death, that is what is bitter', trans. A. Micocci).

It is very interesting to notice that he continues by saying that our troubles with the relative feelings are nobody's fault but our own (ibid.). The '*addottrinato*' (the philosopher, in Hume's language we will see), however, does not blame himself or others for his own being upset, for this is simply inevitable. '*Quando tu vedi alcuno che pianga per morte [. . .] lontananza [. . .] o perdita della roba, guarda che l'apparenza non ti trasporti [. . .] questi è tribolato e afflitto, non dell'accaduto [. . .] ma del concetto che egli ha dell'accaduto*' (pp. 24–5; 'When you see someone weeping over a death [. . .] or separation [. . .] or loss of possessions, you should not be misguided by appearance [. . .] such person is burdened not by what happened [. . .] but by the concept he has of what has taken place', trans. A. Micocci).

Inevitably, the recommendation Epictetus has to offer is the following: '*Tacciasi il più del tempo, o dicasi quel tanto che la necessità richiede, con brevità. Solo qualche rara volta [. . .] discendasi a favellare distesamente; ma non di cotali materie ordinarie [. . .]*' (p. 38; 'Keep quiet most of the time, or just say what is required by necessity, and do it briefly. Only rarely [. . .] indulge in long discourses; but not on mundane matters', trans. A. Micocci).

Also, Epictetus will not ask you to concentrate on Crisippus's textbooks, for, '*che è poi veramente quel che io desidero? Intendere la natura e seguirla*' (p. 47; 'What is it that I truly desire? To understand nature and follow it', trans. A. Micocci). In fact there is no point in interpreting and over-interpreting the great authors, for, even if you become an expert, it would be convenient to blush when you are asked about them, '*quando io non possa mostrare i fatti concordi e somiglievoli alle parole*' (p. 48; 'when you cannot demonstrate the facts which support, and resemble, the words').

Epictetus concludes his booklet by observing that the sequence of philosophical work must start from 'practical moral propositions' and lead to their demonstration, and their confirmation, this final part being the discussion of whether the demonstration has any fault. Instead, we usually go the other way around, starting from what is true and false and moving backwards to the first step. Hence, if for instance we want to prove that we should not lie, we end up, by working the other way around, lying every day (p. 50).

The French sensist philosophers (we will consider d'Holbach and La Mettrie here) present a common set of problems: they are too general and devoted to a hardly defined 'reason', they do not trouble themselves to explore how the senses should lead our investigation about the world, and they seem to want to make very radical points from which they recoil immediately. Also, but this is a problem we will find mirrored in the British empiricists, they cannot bring themselves to admit to the influence of Epicurus over their ideas. Although this is understandable, for the accusation of Epicureanism was a philosophical infamy, it cannot be easily forgiven in d'Holbach, who has the admirable courage to launch a frontal attack on Christian religion.

D'Holbach (1985; the English translation used here is from www.ftarchives.net/holbach/good/gcontents.htm) offers, in fact, a very straightforward plea to the reader to come to admit that religion is an unreasonable idea, and so too is the very idea of God. What interests us here is the fact that he establishes a very interesting connection between reason in the sense of common sense, nature and spontaneity. As at the very beginning of D'Holbach (1985), he states that 'common sense' (*buon senso* in my Italian translation, *le bon sens* in French) is something that humankind does not usually make use of, especially concerning the problems that are commonly judged to be the most essential (p. 3). *Le bon sens* is that part of our capacity of judgement that is sufficient to know the simplest truths, to refute the most manifest absurdities, to be struck by the most evident contradictions (ibid.).

D'Holbach's primary target is the idea of God, which a natural reasoning would not contrive. It takes a complex process to get there (1, 12, p. 17). The consequence, just as we saw for institutionalized social life, is the development of a sadomasochistic behaviour in individuals and the masses, which originates both in autonomous and mass processes of wrong thinking (ibid., p. 6). We must tear our eyes away from the sky and turn them to the earth, at a political level too (p. 7). Unlike Hume and the present argument, however, d'Holbach believes (43, p. 34) that nature is made of precise and fixed laws. 'The universe is always in order. [. . .] The bodies, causes and beings, which this world contains, necessarily act in the manner in which we see them act, whether we approve or disapprove of their effects' (44, p. 35).

However:

> Earthquakes, volcanoes, inundations, pestilences, and famines are effects as necessary, or as much in the order of nature, as the fall of the heavy bodies, the course of rivers, the periodical motions of the seas, the blowing of the winds, the fruitful rains, and the favourable effects, for which men praise God, and thank him for his goodness.
>
> (ibid.)

D'Holbach's natural order includes catastrophes, unlike that of the metaphysics of capitalism that always looks for a cause–effect of an ethical, or at least supernatural, type.

An important consequence is that animals might well be, rather than less intelligent than humankind, more capable of grasping nature, for their intellectual faculties, unlike ours, do not make them unhappy (94, p. 83):

> Doesn't this instinct, of which thou speakest with contempt, often serve them better than thy wonderful faculties? Is not their peaceful ignorance more advantageous to them, than those extravagant meditations and worthless researches, which render them unhappy, and for which thy zeal urges them to even massacre the beings of their noble species?
>
> (94, p. 83)[16]

Intellect and reasoning, if not firmly grounded without mediation on nature, lead humankind to bloody aberrations that animals are incapable of.

'Will men ever renounce their foolish pretensions? Will they never acknowledge that nature is not made for them? Will they never see that nature has placed equality among all beings she has produced?' (99, p. 90). Here is the essence of materialism, for d'Holbach and for all materialists. D'Holbach reacts to the objection that, 'materialism makes of man a mere machine' (105, p. 94), by noticing that the superiority of the spirit derives from two illusions (ibid.): that we do not know about this spirit (some think it exists, typically the religious approaches), and that we presume to know what the mechanisms that operate our body are. 'But the most simple movements of our bodies are to every man, who studies them, as inexplicable as thought' (ibid., p. 95).

La Mettrie is less concerned by religion than d'Holbach, and is more of a natural scientist. However, his thought is very incoherent, and it is hard to disentangle his ideas from the maze of contradictory statements and sudden reversals. Let us start from his *Discourse preliminaire* of 1751, for it was produced as a preamble to the collection of his philosophical works. In it, La Mettrie seeks to justify his materialism by defending it against accusations of subversive consequences in society (1996). His argument is that philosophy does in fact often appear subversive, but only to the eyes of the non-philosopher. Luckily, non-philosophers do not as a matter of fact need philosophy: it follows that the danger of subversion is only formal, a diatribe among materialistic and conservative philosophers.

Interestingly (1996, p. 148), philosophy of the materialistic kind is submitted to nature, in a mother–daughter relationship. Morality is not related to nature, and, hence, it has no philosophical justification (ibid.). It is an 'arbitrary fruit' of politics (ibid.). Philosophy 'is absolutely irreconcilable with morality, religion and politics' (p. 149), which are its enemies in society, but, despite this, philosophy does not break the ties of society (p. 159) in practice, but only in theory (p. 151). Society is even strengthened by its theoretical threat (ibid.). In fact, proper reasoning has never produced a sect or a subversive organization (p. 152), and common people are supremely uninterested in it. Why not leave the philosophers alone, then?

The above reasoning might be the self-serving apology it appears to be, but it contains various similarities with the general framework of the metaphysics of capitalism worth noting. Politics, the economy and society follow a logic that is unnatural and flawed and breeds a type of human that is oblivious to nature and to sound logical reasoning based on the material. The two are enemies; La Mettrie seeks to reconcile them, which is impossible for us after Marx (our anarchist Marx). He does not ask himself, in fact, how society, politics and the economy, by preventing a direct relationship with the concrete, alienate individuals in Marx's three ways.

Let us then see what kind of relationship between individuals and nature we find in La Mettrie. In his *Histoire naturelle de l'âme* (1745, revised as *Traitè de l'Ame* in 1751), La Mettrie states:

> He who would learn the properties of the soul must first seek those which clearly show themselves in the body, whose active principle the soul is.
> This reflection leads naturally to the thought that there are no surer guides than the senses. They are my philosophers.
>
> (La Mettrie, 1996, ch. 1, p. 43)

The soul is the 'motor principle' of the body: the consequences are momentous.

The one that most directly interests us here is (ch. 6) that we have a 'conventional language' (spoken) that does not 'express our sensitivity best' (p. 50). To do so, we need a 'language of feeling' (p. 63), made of sounds rather than words. The most obvious implication of this distinction is the general similarity (which we have also noticed, and will notice again, in Adam Smith) between the animal and human kinds, most evident in the sense system (ibid.). In fact (ch. 10), 'My soul manifests constantly, not thought, which is accidental to it whatever the Cartesians may say, but activity and sensitivity' (ibid., ch. 10, p. 65).

This is clarified in Chapter 11 (I am using the Italian text, 1992, here, for the 1996 text stops at Chapter 10), which deals with instinct. First of all, instinct enables us to avoid useless training in performing necessary operations (1992, p. 105). Also, our soul does not completely rule our bodies (p. 107), for certain operations are purely instinctive, but there are differences between animals, and between animals and men. The former have 'few ideas' (ibid.), and so few terms to express them. Hence, our capacity to express ourselves differs from that of animals, simply because it is more 'verbose' (p. 108). Letters, words, ideas and everything are arbitrary, in humans as well as animals (ibid.). Human superiority lies simply in the apparent capacity to store and use more ideas.

The general, important point is that instinct is at the base of knowledge. It makes us react in predetermined patterns to what stimulates us. Inevitably, knowledge is material-based, or this whole reasoning would not hold. The senses matter a lot, and the mystery of how wrong we can go in putting together what they supply to us lies in words.

In Chapter 14, La Mettrie resorts to his medical studies for a further refinement of the argument that the soul can think about nothing when it is not supported by the feelings of the senses. The origins of evil are therefore inexplicable to him (1992, p. 140). He goes on to supply the reader with a number of stories, to pertinently conclude that savage men are never bored by their wild life, so similar to that of animals (1992, p. 159). Even when they are delivered to our type of civilization, they feel no regret about their past and don't remember a moment of boredom. Their lack of language, evident in those wild children who were so much talked about at the time, is no intellectual limitation.

In '*L'homme machine*' (1747), he clearly says that the original man could be judged intelligent only by looking at his facial expression of attentiveness, for he could not talk in speech. 'Words, languages, laws, sciences and arts came, and thanks to them the rough diamond of our minds was finally polished. Man was trained like no animal; he became an author in the same way as he became a porter' (1996, p. 13).

Our education reduces itself to sounds and words, but who was the first to talk? In all likelihood, men helped each other to do so, led by the most intelligent among them.[17] Yet, at the base of knowledge (1996, p. 14), is similarity between figures. Our whole knowledge is 'a mass of words and figures' (ibid., p. 14).

However, is it imagination that comes first and connects what it contrives with words and terms (ibid.)? If this is so, he concludes, why should we divide our intellectual from our sensory faculties? The separation is just the perverted outcome of the use of 'grand words' (ibid., p. 15) such as 'spirituality, immateriality, etc.' (ibid.), that are used without any attention to their actual meaning (like in religion). Measurement (p. 15) is natural to the mind, which does it automatically as part of its activity of grasping reality, and not as a separate function. Unfortunately, however, La Mettrie ('*L'homme plante*', 1748) believes that nature presents no gaps. It is akin to a mathematically continuous function (1996, p. 86).

In Aphorism XXVI of the System of Epicurus, La Mettrie tells us that we must look around ourselves, which is a beautiful task in itself, but we must not wish to understand everything by a superfluous curiosity, i.e. when our mind is not supported by the senses (1996, p. 97, XXVI). At least in this respect he was coherent. We cannot be contented with his work, just like we could not be contented with d'Holbach's. Let us move across the Channel, therefore. To make this crossing, we need a means of transportation and a cultural mediator. We find them in a few basic observations Rousseau makes in his *Discourse on Inequality* (1754, in Rousseau, 1992).

The time has in fact come to pose the fundamental question that we need to move from the first, analytical part of this book to its second, propositional, emancipating part. Rousseau put it in a form that is still perfectly valid for our purposes here and, sadly, for our times in general. He notices that:

> It is by no means a light undertaking to distinguish properly between what is original and what is artificial in the actual nature of man, or to form a true idea of a state which no longer exists, perhaps never did exist, and probably will never exist.
>
> (1992, p. 44)

He then asks, 'What experiments would have to be made, to discover the natural man? And how are those experiments to be made in a state of society?' (ibid., pp. 44–5).

Rousseau answers by saying that neither the philosophers nor the sovereign could do anything about it. He continues about the difficulty of discussing natural rights and concludes (p. 89) that man's innate respect for his fellow humans is similar to that of the animals and is based on sensitivity. Now he can face the actual theme of the *Discourse*, which he does in the pages that follow. For us here, instead, we have at last posed, in a clearer-cut, and as a consequence more radical and frightening, way, the question that the work of the anarchist Marx seems to revolve around. Can we free ourselves from the unnatural ties placed on us by society, and how, and is a return to the natural possible? We shall see at the end of the present book that this formulation, however useful and suggestive here, is not correct, nor is it a viable option to solve the problem of individual emancipation.

It is sufficient, however, to keep to our present reasoning and to follow Rousseau, who will lead us to the sceptical, British Epicureans. Rousseau connects language with socialization of an institutionalized kind based on economic exchanges. In this, he is on common ground with Adam Smith, as we will soon see. However, in Rousseau, humans are intrinsically good and become evil only in society, whereas, in Smith's *Wealth of Nations*, humans are physically and mentally handicapped by the division of labour and, in his *Theory of Moral Sentiments*, are 'deceived' in some things by the regime.

In the first place, Rousseau notices that, given the enormous quantity of uses that are made of the gift of speech, we must suppose that, after the first 'invention' of languages (p. 111) 'thousands of centuries' must have been necessary to make them as complex and sophisticated as they are now (ibid.). Only, he warns us on page 112, we must be very careful not to transport the ideas we get in society to the state of nature. Thus (p. 113), we cannot solve the vicious circle of whether thought is necessary to have language, or vice versa. The important consequence for our reasoning here is that 'abstract' ideas (p. 116) can only be 'seen' by the use of words. Such philosophical practice was not for the primitive man.

He wonders, as a consequence, whether it was the creation of society that helped languages, or the other way around. Society does not need instinct, but needs a 'cultivated reason' instead (p. 119); this inverts the concept of virtue. In the natural state, the virtuous individual abandons himself to instinct. In society, he avoids all instincts and natural impulses. But Mandeville is wrong in accepting society's virtue (pp. 122–3), for the impulse of piety, which helps all social intercourse, is natural. A cultivated, civilized man can shut his eyes to a murder, which a savage cannot, for he must spring to the aid of the victim. Hence, marital love is an artificial feeling, developed and cultivated by (social) women for their own (social) interest (p. 126).

Adultery is thus created by the idea of marriage, and endless suffering from the idea of domination, both of which would be incomprehensible to the natural man. The most important pillar of civilized society is, however, private property, which, of course, is as unjustifiable as marriage and domination.[18] The price to be paid for civilization is the loss of the capacity to interact with nature, which further pushed towards the development of society as the only option for human survival (p. 137). The very moment a man first needed the help of another man, and saw that it was useful to have provisions for two, equality disappeared, private property appeared and work became necessary, producing slavery and misery (p. 141; which connects us to the anarchist Marx).

Finally, for us here, the creation of one society made it indispensable to have all the other societies (p. 149). Trade and conventions replaced natural compassion (ibid.). Hence the wars, murders and retaliations we know about (ibid.). So many evils from the birth of languages! Can they be compensated for by the advantages? Certainly not: either you have society or not. Any compromise between the two basic options means to be in option one, language and civilization. This is a crucial point: we are starting to see what Marx only had an intuition of, that the 'insane' world we live in can only be completely wiped out, for any other solution would leave its main pillars in place without one inch of progress.

The contrast between individuals, society and nature, when controlled by language, can only resolve itself in favour of institutionalized society, eliminating individuals and nature. However materially apparent the result of this isolation could be, it only represents an illusion, for perfect isolation from nature is impossible. You can perhaps seal out the weather, germs, weeds or anything else, but you cannot take nature away from yourself, unless, that is, humankind is not part of nature. This final question is the big question all these authors pose and is best exemplified by Rousseau's doubt. That is what we must explore: we cannot find the natural man, but perhaps we can rid the civilized man of his social crust. This is emancipation (Micocci, 2014a).

3.5 Human understanding

In a paper written, apparently, in 1752, i.e. before he became acquainted with Hume and his work, Adam Smith (1980) puts forward ideas that help us move on to the discussion of Hume in the next chapter. The actual main reference in Smith's argument is Berkeley, whose work we will also consider in this section. This paper, and the next we will consider, marks Smith as a firm opponent of what Holland and Oliveira (2013) call 'system thinking'. Unfortunately, Holland and Oliveira's interpretation strips Smith of his radical features, because the aim of these two authors is to concentrate on economic method without criticizing economics as a whole. In the rest of this chapter, we will prepare the conditions to see, in the next, why this is wrong.

After reviewing the functioning of the various senses, Smith concentrates upon sight, and makes very interesting observations.

> The objects of sight, as Dr. Berkley finely observes, constitute a sort of language which the Author of Nature addresses to our eyes, and by which he informs us of many things, which it is of the utmost importance for us to know. As, in common language, the words or sounds bear no resemblance to the things they denote, so, in this other language, the visible objects bear no sort of resemblance to the tangible objects they represent, and of whose relative situation [. . .] they inform us.
>
> (1980, p. 156)

However, Smith is very critical of Berkeley's comparison, for he has no time for subtleties.

> The language which nature addresses to our eyes, has evidently a fitness of representation, and aptitude for signifying the precise things which it denotes, much superior to that of any of the artificial languages which human art and ingenuity have ever been able to invent.
>
> (p. 158)

Smith is seeking to argue that instinct, or a sort of Epicurean prolepsis, is at work, and that we must learn to appreciate the attitude to reality of animals, savage children or people cured of blindness. In so doing, he comes close to important points made in the nineteenth century by the Russian Nihilists on different, anti-Hegelian grounds (see Pardjanadze and Micocci, 2000; Micocci, 2002): 'Painting [. . .] endeavours to imitate those objects; yet it never has been equal to imitate the perspective of Nature' (p. 160). 'In this language of nature, it may be said the analogies are more perfect [. . .] The rules are fewer, and those rules admit of no exception' (p. 161). 'That, antecedent to all experience, the young of at least the greater part of animals possess some instinctive perception [. . .] seems abundantly evident' (ibid.). 'Children [. . .] I am disposed to believe that even they may have some instinctive perception of this kind' (p. 163).

He continues by noticing that not all senses are necessary, for worms live well without some. Most of life's endeavours require no language and no system of thought, at least in the natural state. It is, then, well worth turning to his 'Considerations concerning the first formation of languages' (2001).

In that work, Smith is mainly concerned with a comparison between modern (mainly English) and ancient languages (mainly Latin and Greek). This obviously limits the momentum of what he says, at least for our purposes here. He begins by noticing that words denoting the concrete, e.g. green or blue, were necessarily invented before the relatively abstract notions of greenness and blueness, for these last need 'a much greater effort of abstraction' (2001, p. 206). In fact: 'The invention, therefore, even of the simplest noun's adjective, must have required more metaphysics than we are apt to be aware of' (p. 207). However, interestingly:

> Numbers, considered in general, without relation to any particular set of objects numbered, is one of the most abstract and metaphysical ideas, which the mind of man is capable of forming; and, consequently, is not an idea, which would readily occur to rude mortals, who were just beginning to form a language.
>
> (p. 214)

Abstract and rigorously logical notions are nothing to do with language.

In fact, for Smith, languages have the bad habit of getting more and more uselessly prolix and complex as they develop from the ancient simplicity. Instead of *pluit*, the 'simple event is artificially split and divided' (p. 215–16). A 'sort of grammatical circumlocution' is produced 'of which the significancy is founded upon a certain metaphysical analysis of the component part of the idea expressed by the word *pluit*' (ibid.).

> It is in this manner that language becomes more simple in its rudiments and principles, just in proportion as it grows more complex in its composition, and the same thing has happened in it, which commonly happens to mechanical engines.
>
> (p. 223)

When first invented, machines are extremely elaborate; further refinements make them simpler:

> But this simplification of languages [. . .] has by no means similar effects with the correspondent simplification of machines. The simplification of machines renders them more and more perfect, but the simplification of the rudiments of languages renders them more and more imperfect, and less proper for many of the purposes of language.
>
> (p. 224)

There are three main reasons. First, simplification makes languages more prolix, expressing with many words what ancient languages could say with one: 'how much the beauty of any expression depends on its conciseness, is well known to those who have any experience in composition' (ibid.). Second, languages become less agreeable to the ear. Third, this 'restrains us from disposing such sounds as we have, in the manner that might be most agreeable' (ibid.).

Latin and Greek declensions guaranteed a concise way of expression that was signalled by the endings of the words. Modern languages are prolix, monstrous and, it seems one can infer, perfectly incapable of grasping and rendering all those things that all the authors discussed in this section have pointed out as fundamental. Scientific work is prevented, just like poetry and beauty of expression. Not only can modern languages not represent reality other than by boring circumlocutions, but they do not even lend themselves to the consolation of beauty of expression (however useless, as the Russian Nihilists observed; see Pardjanadze and Micocci, 2000).

To summarize, language complicates reality and misleads us. It is a historical deed, but that does not guarantee that it is just and inevitable, let alone natural. Rather, it corresponds to the need to transcend and mediate reality that is felt when you live in society. Only such a type of endeavour would, in fact, be consonant with, and capable of expressing, the convoluted, illogical and artificial rules and facts of social and economic life. All this implies important psychological consequences. The social man is not spontaneous and represses instincts. As a consequence, if he is a natural creature, he necessarily suffers the oppression that is imposed on him and that he accepts, and even assists with the imposition.

There is no denying that all the considerations developed so far pose the problem of evil. On the one hand, all these authors and their arguments push us towards hypothesizing that humans would be naturally good. Posed in this form, this is not a very convincing argument, for it admits of no positive proof. However, assuming that humans are natural, which present-day science would not deny, we can certainly argue that institutionalized societies are the main cause of the evil actions of man. Capitalism, as Marx notices, is a case of an 'insane' political and economic form. But it does not take much analysis to notice that injustice and prevarication have been present in all societies of all eras, as testified by the 'deception' of Adam Smith's invisible hand and by Xenophon (Senofonte, 1991, 1997) for ancient times, as we will see in the next chapter.

Although the problem of evil as identified here is a different thing from ethics and morality, as La Mettrie correctly notices, it does pose problems that, some feel, call for the discussion of the divine will. Thus, it is not inappropriate to continue this discussion with Bishop Berkeley's approach to what we have called materialism and what we can call from now on, with Locke and Hume, human understanding. There is, in fact, no better or more concise expression for what we have been discussing so far.

The importance of Berkeley in the eighteenth century, testified to, for instance, by Smith's own referring to him all the time, has been progressively undermined by his religious solution to the problems he so originally posed. In fact, if the materialistic reasoning pursued so far is correct, God does not exist, not only as such: it cannot exist even in the mind. Second, a divine intervention of the monotheistic type is a mistake analogous to that made by the majority of Marxists: a historical object is raised to be a Universal and appealed to in order to solve problems that are strictly material, i.e. natural. Yet, there are some aspects of Berkeley's work that are well worth considering.

The most exciting part of Berkeley's thought is the idea that reality is in one's mind. It is a very extreme way of posing the nature–intellect–individuality problem, and it is very useful here. His (2004) starts by stating that 'the illiterate bulk of mankind' (p. 37) is not only untroubled by reality, but is not even inclined to scepticism. In fact, they rely on their senses. Only to philosophers do things appear obscure and troubling, but such 'difficulties which have hitherto amused philosophers, and blocked up the way to knowledge, are entirely owning to ourselves' (ibid., p. 38). The problem lies with 'the nature and abuse of language'. 'Abstract' ideas in fact depend upon language, which bestows them with an existence that 'brutes', who have no need for words, do not need to consider (p. 42). Normal communication does not need such abstract ideas.

Preceding Cassirer (1961), Reich (1970) and the contemporary managers of people's minds in politics and in marketing (see Micocci, 2002), Berkeley says that creating concepts by crystallizing in words supposedly abstract meanings (La Mettrie's 'grand words') 'is not the chief and only use of language, as is commonly supposed' (2004, p. 48). Raising passions ('fear, love, hatred, admiration, disdain and the like') upon the perception of certain words is the other end. Such passions coincide with precisely those feelings that, since ancient times (see, for instance, Aristotle, Livy or Polybius, in Micocci, 2002), have been managed by institutionalized societies to hold themselves together, overcoming the centrifugal forces of human individuality. By this, however, Berkeley thinks he has proved the impossibility of abstract ideas. He can thus work, being sure 'to get clear of all controversies purely verbal' (2004, p. 49).

He is practical enough to know that he cannot completely do without words (p. 50); thus, all one can do is seek to rid oneself of the encumbrance of words that 'blind judgement and divide attention' (ibid.):

> There are ideas actually imprinted in the senses, or else such as are perceived by attending to the passions and operations of the mind, or lastly ideas formed by help of memory and imagination [deriving from operating in the first two ways].
>
> (p. 53)

But it all takes place in the mind, which works on what the senses convey, on the passions and on a form of prolepsis à la Epicurus, but abstract notions are the cause of silly ideas such as there being a difference between the existence of sensible objects and their being perceived. 'It is indeed an opinion strongly prevailing amongst men, that houses, mountains, rivers, and in a word all sensible objects have an existence natural or real, distinct from their being perceived by the understanding' (p. 54). This is a beautifully radical way to pose the problem.

However, senses are not sufficient, for 'they do not inform us that things exist without the mind' (p. 59). It is the Spirit that counts to Berkeley, therefore, and it cannot be otherwise, or God would not have an avenue to enter our understanding. 'Now the set of rules [. . .] wherein the mind [. . .] excites in us the idea of sense, are called *laws of nature*: and these we learn by experience' (p. 63; emphasis in the original). 'This gives us a sort of foresight, which enables us to regulate our actions for the benefit of life' (ibid.). 'The ideas imprinted on the senses by the Author of Nature are called *real things*: and those excited in the imagination being less regular, vivid and constant, are more properly termed *ideas* [. . .] which they copy and represent' (p. 64; emphasis in the original). And yet, 'Whatever we see, feel, hear, or anywise conceive and understand, remains as secure as ever, and as real as ever' (p. 65).

Berkeley clearly sees that, 'language is suited to the received opinions, that are not always the truest' (p. 71), and that society conditions our understanding, but there are higher things, and they are out of society:

> The connection of ideas does not imply the relation of *cause* and *effect, but only a mark* or sign *with the thing* signified. [. . .] Hence it is evident, that those things which under the notion of a cause cooperating or concurring to the production of effects, are altogether inexplicable [. . .] may be very naturally explained [. . .] when they are considered only as marks or signs for our information.
>
> (p. 77; emphasis in the original)

The conclusion is that the idea of matter ('material substance') has been a great tool for atheists of all kinds and for their 'monstrous' ideas, which are, as a consequence, plain wrong, or at least impossible to prove. The solution is divine, lest we move from monstrous atheism to an even worse threat, anarchism.

Berkeley also considers as an example the idea of gravity (p. 91), which can be described but not explained. In any case (p. 93), we cannot posit and demonstrate regularity and laws in nature, for that would imply that we know that God operates uniformly, which is impossible to prove.[19] Again, anyone who does so is considering signs rather than causes. The same applies to the demonstrations of mathematical theorems (p. 99). In short, our senses perceive what God has created, but the perception of how reality works is of man's own making (p. 109). The *Dialogues* (in 2004) add nothing to this general reasoning. If we substitute for God the idea of nature, we reduce all this to the issue of liberty as chance, which is part of what we want to develop here and is best proposed first by Hume.

We cannot trust our senses, but we can get rid of whatever obfuscates them, i.e. the strict and limiting connection between language and institutionalized society. That does not guarantee that at the end of the process we can safely trust them, but at least we will potentially be able to freely produce straightforward, logical thoughts, on the condition that we let material reality be free to be whatever it is, regardless of what we believe it to be, and to follow chance without any imposed artificial regularity. This last point, we have seen, is not only intellectual, for it is materially possible up to a point, like in the case of agriculture or of the psychologically distorted social man.

Berkeley, whom, from our point of view, we might call a materialist, in his works considered here, explicitly and vehemently attacks materialists and materialistic arguments, meaning Epicureans and atheists in general. We cannot move on without a brief consideration of two more non-materialist materialists of the time: Hobbes and Locke. Their lack of effectiveness derives from their fear of admitting Epicurean themes in their work, and from their shyness in proposing a fully divine argument. In this last sense, Berkeley is much more radical and, hence, useful. Let us start from the less exciting of the pair, Hobbes.

We could call Hobbes a materialist, if only he did not attribute to nature 'immutable' laws that also govern the behaviour of man, which we know well, and about which, anyway, he is here to enlighten us. This type of mistake compels us to place him among those empiricists who were fairly common at the time and who greatly influenced present-time empiricism in the social sciences. This is a pity, for he starts his *Leviathan* (2008b) with the senses and their relationship with thought. This could be a beautifully naturalistic way, were it not for the following initial proviso: '*NATURE* [. . .] is by the art of man [. . .] imitated' (2008b; emphasis in the original). As a consequence, 'that great *LEVIATHAN* called a *Commonwealth* or *STATE*' is created (ibid.), 'which is but an artificial man' (ibid.).

Unlike in Adam Smith, his comparison of man and animals necessarily reduces itself to the claim that 'the imagination that is raised in man [. . .] by words, or other voluntary signs, is that we generally call *understanding*; and is common to man and beast' (p. 15; emphasis in the original), but man's understanding is enhanced and made more powerful by 'speech'. In other words, Hobbes agrees with all the other authors we have considered on the artificial connection between society/civilization, speech and knowledge. Only, by the fact that dogs and horses understand words, and by the alleged capacity of man to artificially reproduce nature, he seeks to claim that society is the only way for man to live, because of his well-known conception of the natural life as '*homo homini lupus*' (see, e.g., 2008b, p. 66, 82–6).

Surprisingly, the war of man against man (2008b, p. 82–6) springs precisely from that substantial equality between men that Smith also notices, but which in Hobbes leads to the inevitability of society being a non-libertarian place, in order to preserve liberty. This last is 'the absence of opposition [. . .] external impediments to motion' (2008b, p. 139). Like in mainstream economics and unlike in Smith, man's equality rather means homogeneity. Hence, the well-known maxim, 'Do not do to another, which you wouldest not have done to thyself' (p. 104), which to him seems a perfect way to mix up the laws of man and the laws of nature, so that, by just following it, you follow both without wasting time in reasoning about it. Anyway, 'The laws of nature are immutable and eternal, for injustice, ingratitude, arrogance, pride, iniquity, acception of persons, and the rest, can never be made lawful' (p. 105).

Even though science and knowledge come from the senses, as he confirms in *Human Nature* (2008a, p. 41), we notice in Hobbes the typically contemporary attempt to transform everything into a metaphysics, hidden behind the attempt, in *Leviathan* (2008b), to proceed '*more geometrico*' (geometry having been bestowed on us by God, 2008b, p. 23). Despite, for him, the material being what reality is made of, and the soul itself being material, he typically mixes up the idea of the material with its mediated and transcended understanding and, as a consequence, with supposedly natural endowments of man, which are equally mediated and transcended into metaphysical entities hung between the concrete and the abstract.

In such a mean and constrained world as Hobbes's society, we need not pose the problem of language in the same way as we did for the other authors. In fact, if the natural man is evil, and such evil brings about the need to have iron laws that forbid iniquity and the rest, language can only be perfectly functional to the whole construction, which is natural in the sense of being an imitation of nature. Hence, knowledge is only what language can tell, because there is no tension whatsoever between natural impulses and the repression of those impulses by society. The only tension comes from our natural iniquity clashing with the prohibitions imposed by the law, but that is, if not fully natural, so useful as to deserve to be borne with serenity.

Hobbes's assumption that man is intrinsically evil is weaker than our supposition of a hypothetical goodness, because, if it falls, Hobbes's whole construction falls with it. From our point of view, and in general for the tradition of thought we are referring to in this book, we do not pose that man is good as a basic condition; we simply say that man's instincts are likely to be benign for the very simple reason that society, in particular capitalist society, is 'insane' and appears to be the cause of most – if not all – of the evils we see. Thus, the intrinsic goodness of man's instincts is only a reasonable second-order hypothesis, and its fall does not cause the fall of the observation that society is insane. The status of this last observation, which is not based on ethics and morality, is what we need to explore in this book. Of course, we cannot say whether or not we can ever discover the true nature of humans.

It follows that the main issue for us now is the exploration of the empirical. This is complicated by Berkeley's hypothesis that it could be all in our minds. Let us then turn to our last, not actually materialist, empiricist, John Locke. In the next chapter, we will narrow down our perspective to political economy, starting from the philosophical work of David Hume, with its Epicurean scepticism.

The general impression one gets from Locke's *An Essay Concerning Human Understanding* (2008) is that he seeks at all costs to avoid radical statements. The work is, as a matter of fact, a plea for an empiricism based on the senses. Yet, there are but few things we can use to our purposes, and these are not new, for they had been said by former thinkers, for instance Francis Bacon (Micocci, 2002, 2008/2010).

Locke starts by warning not to affect general knowledge (2008, p. 14). In fact, he has declined to deal with questions of essence, motions of the Spirit, and whether things depend on matter, for these are all 'Speculations' (p. 13). Also, he is very much opposed to the possibility of prolepsis (p. 17) of the kind 'stamped in soul' (ibid.). Our innate faculties are sufficient to determine knowledge (ibid.). A minor type of prolepsis is allowed, however: not innate ideas, but 'Affections of the body' (p. 83) that take place before children 'come to the world'. The ideas of warmth and hunger, which according to him we get in the womb, are typical. Given that it is difficult to discern the origin and extent of prolepsis, we can avoid worrying about this distinction.

Children, in any case, get their knowledge in the form of speech, which only can convey abstract ideas (p. 23). 'The senses at first let in particular *Ideas*, and furnish the yet empty Cabinet: And the Mind by degrees growing familiar with some of them, they are lodged in the Memory, and Names got to them' (ibid.; emphasis in the original). Like Hobbes, Locke knows the whole sequence whereby nature helps humans use the senses and organize knowledge. Chance has no place, and even less the mere possibility that things may not follow the rules dictated by Locke. Anyway, 'most of the *ideas* we have, depending only on our Senses, and derived by them to the Understanding, I call SENSATION' (p. 55; emphasis in the original).

The mind 'furnishes the Understanding with Ideas of its own operations' (ibid.). Ideas come in four ways: First, by one sense only; second, by more than one sense; third, from reflection only; fourth, by both sensation and reflection (p. 65). But (we are moving much further forward, to ch. XXX, p. 232), 'real ideas' are those that have a foundation in nature, and they conform to the 'real being' or the 'Archetypes'. There also are fantastical or chimerical ideas, which are the opposite. Locke then proposes a classification of ideas (ch. XXXIII, p. 242) based on their complexity. From there, he moves on to language.

Language (Book III, ch. I) has been provided by God to help society by providing a 'common tie' (p. 254). Words (ibid., ch. II, p. 256) are the 'signs of men's ideas'; in other words, although ideas might well be original and very different, as explained before, yet they can be traded socially. A man's idea can be expressed and conveyed to other men. This is helped by the 'common acceptation of a language' (p. 258). This means that each man has a right to make up his own ideas, but these can hardly be communicated, for 'obscurity and confusion' (p. 258) is produced if we signify those ideas of our own that are not accepted and shared in language, i.e. in society. There also is the opposite possibility, i.e. that words are accepted without knowing their meaning, 'no otherwise than Parrots do' (p. 259).

Although Locke goes on discussing the types of term, it is clear that to him only human relationships that can be socially shared are meaningful. Only political and economic relationships seem to count in life. If there is something else outside, it matters only when it can be communicated by means of the accepted language. No wonder Locke is among the philosophers revered by the ideologists of capitalism: he is supplying a justification for capitalism's metaphysics. Especially useful to this purpose is his acknowledgement that, 'the signification of Words, in all Languages [. . .], must unavoidably be of great uncertainty, to Men of the same Language and Country' (ch. IX, p. 312).

As a consequence, 'Men must also take care to apply their words, as near as may be, to such Ideas as common use has annexed them to' (ch. XI, p. 323). Also, words should be constantly used in the same sense. This would avoid many voluminous disputes. Book IV starts by saying that knowledge is the perception of the connection and agreement, or the disconnection and disagreement, of any of our ideas (p. 332). Many mistakes come simply from using words and ideas in different senses (p. 390).

Finally, in Book IV, Chapter XVII, he warns us against reducing our intellectual endeavours to sterile syllogisms. Logical proofs must be attained. What is the use of syllogisms, then? 'To an ingenuous Searcher after Truth, who has no other aim, but to find it, there is no need of any such Form' (p. 438). Syllogisms only serve to help the thinker relax by finding a logic in what he does. It is unfortunate that Francis Bacon (see Micocci, 2002, 2008/2010) had said similar things, much better and with an eye to the possible social and cultural sources of illusions, with his *idola*. The feeling that there are readers who know Epicurus, like in Hobbes, puts Locke in a constant fear, and thus he avoids saying anything that might make manifest the connections between what he says and it.

We have found out, after this fairly erudite discussion, that materialism in the sense of 'human understanding' is powerfully limited by the presence of society, because this needs a language that reduces everything to a banal metaphysics without ontology, i.e. an absurdity. This is especially so when we notice, with Marx, that our society is undeniably insane because of its triple alienation. There remains the problem of how to regain intellectual independence, i.e. the problem of emancipation. This is tied to the management of empirical evidence. We need Hume to finish with this type of thinker and move on to original conclusions. That will take us back to economics and political economy.

3.6 Conclusions

We have introduced here a discussion of materialism in the form of human understanding. This is necessary in that, as argued in the preceding chapter, capitalism is a paradox: a metaphysics without ontology, based on empty discussions of logically flawed syllogisms. Also, this has brought to our notice that nineteenth-century thinkers, as important and widely discussed as Marx, are the object of evident misunderstandings: the clear-cut, radical part of their thought is not acknowledged by readers and analysts, however shrewd, experienced and politically sensitive.

Acknowledgement of Marx's own radicality (his communist anarchism) had to be completed with the discussion of the role of human understanding, i.e. the way the individual–society–language connection limits our understanding of nature and of the concrete in general. It is well worth repeating that not 'understanding' nature and the concrete in general is just another way to signify Marx's own triple alienation, determined by capitalism.[20] As we do not find radical approaches to the needed issues in the twentieth century and the beginning of the twenty-first (as exemplified by the case of 'general intellect'), to find radical statements, we had to go back in time a couple of centuries, when the metaphysics of capitalism was not as developed as now. Eighteenth-century thinkers could see what was coming, and yet could express themselves fairly radically, despite the widespread failure to acknowledge the presence of Epicurean themes that makes itself felt at all levels, as pointed out.

We have noticed that the French sensists d'Holbach and La Mettrie, if bridged by Rousseau's *Discourse on Inequality*, are compatible with, and complementary to, the British empiricists. In this respect, it is worth emphasizing that the most useful thinkers of this last group, that is to say the two most radical among them, are Adam Smith and George Berkeley. It is also worth underlining that being radical carries no political connotations: we have repeatedly pointed out Smith's reactionary ideas and Bishop Berkeley's divine argument.

Despite this evident progress with respect to current approaches to the question of materialism, we are still far from either a satisfactory methodological approach or a secure path to individual emancipation from the massification induced by capitalist reality, its non-radical criticisms and their supporting theories. As to the former, we need first of all to understand the relationship between the senses and rational analysis. This can be achieved, as we shall see in the next chapter, starting from the radical scepticism of David Hume, from which we can move on to a reconsideration of economics and political economy comprising majority Marxist approaches.

The role of language in all this, as evident from the discussion of the present chapter, is fundamental. Language, and, as we shall see in the next chapters, its underlying logic, is a social production, if not in historical terms (which is hard to prove), at least in its effects. There is a correspondence between the logic of society and its economy and language: this is a very crucial aspect of the metaphysics of capitalism and, in inevitably different forms, of all the constraining aspects of organized societies in all eras. The issues of liberty and of individual freedom and originality require an anarchist mentality. Pro- and anti-capitalist thinkers have sought to deny this, but there is no escaping it.

The consequences of all this are momentous and will be developed in what follows. The main issue of capitalism as we know it is the question of anarchism and of the consequences of the passive acceptance of organized societies and of the 'insane' logic of economic exchanges, both theoretical and practical. To borrow and develop the reasoning of La Mettrie in his introduction to his collected philosophical works that we have seen, although it is understandable that workers, as well as the privileged classes, might not want, for opposite reasons, to face the issue this way, it is difficult to forgive scholars. One of the most painful paradoxes of the metaphysics of capitalism is, in fact, that true preachers of the violence that is explicit or implicit in capitalist relationships are tolerated and even openly praised, or at least discussed (take Lenin, or Karl Schmitt, or neo-liberal apologists), whereas opponents of capitalism's organized violence and, like the present author, even of violence in general, are either accused of too much erudition/technicality, or of violence. In fact, one of the consequences of the metaphysics of capitalism and of its stunted language is that radical thinking is associated with violence, and institutionalized violence is borne serenely.

Thus, whereas revolution as organized, violent mass subversion is widely practised, endorsed and discussed (and praised or opposed), and nobody is disgusted by the suffering entailed, or by the prevarication and harnessing of the fighting masses, non-violent arguments are censored as violent or ignored. As shown in the present chapter, the civilized man in Rousseau's sense, having repressed his instincts, can witness unperturbed both the normal and continuous insanity of capitalist reality and its most horrid occasional bouts of open and unrestrained violence, while simultaneously condemning radical arguments (e.g., for our thinkers, their Epicurean features). Lenin, Guevara and Castro can easily replace Epicurus and Marx, as long as a ritual, cold-hearted moral distance is kept, not from natural violence, but from metaphysical, language-expressed 'violence'.

The high moral ground is ritual in capitalism. That is why it is so needed. It serves as Aristotelian catharsis. What we need, to stop this hypocrisy and its materially unbearable consequences, are logically sound radical arguments. The next chapters will propose some.

Notes

1 There are two ways to do that, as we shall see: by intellectual means or by material deeds (e.g. agriculture).
2 On the one hand, they admit its historical character. On the other, they join all the other social scientists in pretending that its ontological status is the same through the ages, for natural labour is a mythical idea, supposedly better left to the Garden of Eden.
3 Although, as we shall see in Section 3.3, the British empiricists in the eighteenth century had already started to entertain serious doubts about the science–words relationship, following the observation of Francis Bacon (see Micocci, 2008/10).
4 That would also belie Marx's certainty that all human individuals are potentially different, which is at the basis of the present book as well, and that homogenization is the doing of politics and society.
5 We will have more occasions to show the types of interaction that take place between the metaphysics and material reality.
6 We will meet the fascistic features of this need also, later on.
7 We will discuss that in Chapter 4.
8 Although Hegel light-heartedly relies on Smith. For a sympathetic (to Hegel) treatment of this aspect, see Herzog (2013).
9 See Micocci (2012) for the fascistic features of the society–community confusion.
10 The idea of mechanism is banished from scientific and common speech, for it implies no conscious, superior inner or outer logic. In fact, it depends on laws existing that are challenged only by uncertainty or mistakes.
11 Which, of course, never admits of not being able to construe a cause–effect connection. Time, in a benevolent dialectics with human efforts, will grant success in the future if it is not forthcoming in the present.
12 Natural catastrophes are conspicuously missing, or confined to statistical lack of relevance.
13 Darwin noticed similar phenomena in artificial races of hens, long before the present author and his university teachers of natural and agricultural disciplines (2013, p. 251).
14 In so doing, they simply endorse Adam Smith (1999, vol. I, pp. 165–70).
15 Leopardi was greatly influenced by the French sensists, whom we shall discuss after Epictetus. See Micocci (2000) and Biscuso and Gallo (1999).
16 This type of thought greatly influenced Leopardi.
17 Rousseau too supposed that speech came at a later stage of human development, as we shall see when talking about Adam Smith later on.
18 This does not prevent him from claiming, in *Emile*, that children must be educated to private property.
19 The same holds if we replace God with nature.
20 It is well beyond the scope and aim of this volume to explore in depth how much of the triple alienation was present in pre-capitalist societies. It is clear from the discussion of Classical authors that this is a relevant issue, better left to a specialized work.

References

Berkeley, G. (2004) *Principles of Human Knowledge and Three Dialogues*, Penguin, London.

Biscuso, M., and Gallo, F. (1999) *Leopardi Antitaliano [Anti-Italian Leopardi]*, Manifestolibri, Rome.

Cassirer, E. (1961) *The Myth of the State*, Yale University Press, New Haven, CT.

Darwin, C. (2013) *The Origin of Species*, Signet Classics, London.

D'Holbach, P. T. (1985) *Il Buon Senso [Common Sense]*, Garzanti, Milan, Italy.

Di Mario, F., and Micocci, A. (2015) 'Smith's invisible hand. Controversy is needed', *ESHET Conference*, Rome, 15–18 May.

Epictetus (2009) *Manuale Volgarizzato da Giacomo Leopardi [Handbook, Adapted by Giacomo Leopardi]*, SE, Milan, Italy.

Hegel, G. W. F. (2008) *La Fenomenologia dello Spirito [Phenomenology of Spirit]*, Einaudi, Turin, Italy.

Herzog, L. (2013) *Inventing the Market Smith, Hegel and Political Theory*, Oxford University Press, Oxford, UK.

Hobbes, T. (2008a) *Human Nature and De Corpore Politico*, Oxford University Press, Oxford, UK.

Hobbes, T. (2008b) *Leviathan*, Oxford University Press, Oxford, UK.

Holland, S., and Oliveira, T. C. (2013) 'Missing links: Hume, Smith, Kant and economic methodology', *Economic Thought*, 2, 2, 46–72.

Kuhn, T. (1969) *La Struttura delle Rivoluzioni Scientifiche [The Structure of Scientific Revolutions]*, Einaudi, Turin, Italy.

La Mettrie, J. O. (1992) *Opere Filosofiche [Philosophical Works]*, Laterza, Bari, Italy.

La Mettrie, J. O. (1996) *Machine Man and Other Writings*, ed. A. Thomson, Cambridge University Press, Cambridge, UK.

Locke, J. (2008) *An Essay Concerning Human Understanding*, Oxford University Press, Oxford, UK.

Marx, K. (1973) *Grundrisse*, Penguin, London.

Marx, K. (1975) 'Preface to the Critique of Political Economy', in Marx, K., and Engels, F., *Selected Works*, p. 182, Progress Publishers, Moscow.

Marx, K. (1977) *The Civil War in France*, Progress Publishers, Moscow.

Micocci, A. (2000) 'Leopardi Antitaliano [Anti-Italian Leopardi]', *Il Cannocchiale Rivista di Studi Filosofici*, 3, 199–209.

Micocci, A. (2002) *Anti-Hegelian Reading of Economic Theory*, Mellen Press, Lampeter, UK.

Micocci, A. (2005) 'Uncertainty in market economies', *International Review of Sociology*, 15, 1, 39–45.

Micocci, A. (2008/2010) *The Metaphysics of Capitalism*, Lexington, Lanham, MD.

Micocci, A. (2012) *Moderation and Revolution*, Lexington, Lanham, MD.

Micocci, A. (2014a) 'Unusual Humean issues in materialistic political economy', *Journal of Philosophical Economics*, 7, 2, 22–6.

Micocci, A. (2014b) 'Smith's invisible hands in neoliberal times', paper presented at IIPPE Conference, Naples, Italy.

Micocci, A. (2015) 'Traditional issues need novel thinking', in Figus, A. (ed.), *Land and Water Will Save Us from the Crisis: The role of universities*, pp. 131–54, Eurilink, Rome.

Mill, J. S. (1998) *Principles of Political Economy*, Oxford University Press, Oxford, UK.

Pardjanadze, N., and Micocci, A. (2000) 'I Nichilisti Russi [The Russian Nihilists]', *Il Cannocchiale Rivista di Studi Filosofici*, 2, 183–202.

Reich, W. (1970) *The Mass Psychology of Fascism*, Farrar, Straus & Giroux, New York.

Rousseau, J.-J. (1992) *The Social Contract and Discourses*, Everyman Library, J. M. Dent, London, C. E. Tuttle, Rutland, VT.

Schumpeter, J. A. (1987) *Capitalism, Socialism and Democracy*, Unwin, London.

Senofonte (1991) *Economico* [*Economic*], Rizzoli, Milan, Italy.

Senofonte (1997) *Ciropedia* [*Cyruspaedia*], Newton, Milan, Italy.

Sereni, E. (1996) *Storia del Paesaggio Agrario Italiano* [*History of Italian Agrarian Landscape*], Laterza, Bari, Italy.

Smith, A. (1980) *Essays on Philosophical Subjects*, eds J. C. Bryce and W. P. D. Wightman, Clarendon Press, Oxford, UK.

Smith, A. (1999) *The Wealth of Nations*, 2 vols, Penguin Classics, London.

Smith, A. (2001) *Lectures on Rhetoric and Belles Lettres*, ed. J. C. Bryce, Clarendon Press, Oxford, UK.

Smith, A. (2009) *The Theory of Moral Sentiments*, Penguin Classics, London.

Sylos Labini, P. (2004) *Torniamo ai Classici* [*Let Us Go Back to the Classics*], Laterza, Bari, Italy.

Virno, P. (2007) 'General intellect', *Historical Materialism*, 15, 3, 3–8.

4 Economic discipline

4.1 Introduction

In what follows, we will explain how economic discourse disciplines capitalism. If we must go beyond capitalism, this entails the need to devise a method of freeing chance, which capitalism binds to itself. We will, therefore, further develop the consequences of the metaphysics of capitalism, keeping our attention on its overall logic, language and speech, starting from some philosophical themes we find in Hume. At the end of this chapter, we will have completed the description of the functioning structure of the metaphysics of capitalism and be ready for the outline of the alternative materialistic method based on silence, the unfolding of which will be the main task of Chapter 5.

We will see that all current criticisms of economics and political economy, whatever their philosophical and methodological arguments, are inadequate. They do not concentrate on the big, typical, logical problems of economic theories and of capitalism itself. They offer to mend rather than destroy and replace economic theories. This is part of the generalized lack of creatively radical thinking that characterizes the metaphysics of capitalism and its flawed dialectics.

We will go back to Smith's invisible hand for a number of new considerations that shed light on the need capitalism has never to fully develop to survive. Marx will, instead, help us penetrate the mystery of the present-day preponderance of finance and its relationship to capitalist (lack of) development in general, and to the particular issues related to the liberation of chance. Such themes produce a rupture with present-day economic theories that cannot – and indeed must not – be healed. All the other criticisms of economics and the ideas we will propose in the present chapter and in the next depend upon these basic questions.

Nothing new and relevant concerning economic ideas can be achieved, in other words, unless we take a radically materialistic stance that frees us from the fetters of capitalist metaphysics and the discipline it enforces. Within this is the importance of Hume, with his extreme sceptical, Stoic and Epicurean ideas. His approach nicely dovetails with Berkeley and the other eighteenth-century thinkers we saw in the last chapter, and complements the radically straightforward questions that Marx the anarchist and Smith put forward. Freeing chance is what Hume, for us here, is about. This is the fundamental achievement all materialists owe to him. His uncompromising uncertainty opens the path for materialism to fulfil its task of emancipating us from the strictures of capitalist intellectuality and its seclusion from the unpredictable freedom of movement of nature.

In fact, we will keep arguing, the purpose of materialism is that of filling the intellectual and practical/political gap between human understanding and material reality that capitalism has built. By disciplining capitalism through their reciprocal intellectual cause–effect relation with it, economic theories, orthodox and dissenting, help preserve and even continually increase the limits of human understanding. This whole process is practised, enunciated, studied and criticized through the capitalist, language-based maieutics. Such language-based maieutics, with its simultaneous approximation and continuous striving for a precision that is impossible to attain, must be discarded and abolished. The economic discipline of capitalism can, despite its complexity, be described as an iterated words-and-speech ritual that only can talk of itself to itself, or it would evolve into its full potentialities and present the problem of the stationary state and of revolution.

The economic working of capitalism does not in fact aim to achieve a market society, and even less a democracy, but only to foster what is possible: the empty rhetoric of free economic initiative and private property. These two matters are precisely what capitalism already has, together with the required inequalities that Adam Smith signalled as the fundamental rationale for free private initiative to contribute to the wealth of nations. A market of perfect competition – provided it could ever be achieved – would instead mean, with its fairness to everybody and its static economic nature, the end of the system. Thus, whereas at the microeconomic level firms shield themselves from competition instead of facing it (Micocci, 2002), at the macroeconomic level, the capitalist system needs to keep its injustices, its class rigidities and its lack of competitive markets. The best way to obtain this is to exploit the inconclusive and incoherent nature of the rituals of economic words and speech. Capitalist discipline is the outcome of its intellectual confusion and its need for iteration instead of novelty.

The endless subtleties of the heterodox criticisms of economic theories that the metaphysics of capitalism supplies originate in this basic mechanism, as do the subtleties of Marxist theories, both in their lack of effectiveness in criticizing bourgeois economics and in their evasiveness in even trying to outline (let alone make!) revolution. In contrast, the strength of mainstream economics, and its dominance, comes from its relatively radical approach, as we will see: from its refusing material reality and refusing to appreciate its historical nature. These are what make it the most appropriate and most coherent interpreter of the metaphysics of capitalism, its flawed logic and its approximate and repetitive language. With a typically capitalist move, mainstream economics, in its sublime absurdity, appears theoretical and daring precisely because it is neither the former nor the latter, nor can it be referred to reality with any precision; hence the endless need for it to seek to be (mathematically) precise, in this way resembling the logic of capitalist language we are studying.

The present-day preponderance of finance, and the unsolvable crises it induces, is the logical and inevitable outcome of the intellectual idea of profit as a monetary entity that preternaturally proceeds from the triply alienated behaviour of the 'commercial man' and from the iterativeness of capitalist economic activities at the macroeconomic level. Finance is the ultimate and highest paradise of economic monetary profit, for this last overcomes the physical limits of material production including services. The need remains for inequality and for the illusion that economic activities have to do with material survival. The retention of this misunderstanding is a most obvious instance of what capitalist words and speech can do to confuse and mix the abstract and the material through the flawed dialectical metaphysics that lies between them.

The task of materialism, and of a materialistic political economy, must at this stage be that of seeking to retrieve the direct link between individuals and the material, i.e. nature and history. Yet, at least in the present state of knowledge, there is no way to know whether we can ever actually grasp the material, or are bound to remain in the grip of a mental construction à la Berkeley. Hume's Epicurean and Stoic scepticism, very much in line with the radical approaches of Smith and Marx, helps us see how we can only, at this stage, work to emancipate ourselves from society's limited and limiting intellectuality, the dominant and pervasive metaphysics of capitalism. It is worth repeating that intellectual emancipation is revolution from capitalism, and it needs no organized violence, even less organization in general. It is an anarchist task. Any other way to seek to overcome capitalism is bound to fall back into the sticky web of its verbose and flawed metaphysics, with the organized violence that this entails.

Section 4.2 presents the relevant parts of the thought of David Hume. It also discusses Smith's invisible hand from a perspective wider than that adopted in Chapter 2 and introduces the limits of present-day criticisms of economics.

Section 4.3 continues the discussion of the cosy fiction of economic theories. It discusses some thoughts about human economic psychology put forward by, among others, Kahneman (2011) and Akerlof and Shiller (2009), and goes back to Marx's alienation.

Section 4.4 deals with present-day trends. Starting from the Humean issue of liberty as chance, it observes the way capitalism is condemned never to fully develop and to live in a state of intellectual and social inertia. The only sector that promises a formal dynamism is finance, which thus becomes preponderant, causing the crises we all see and preserving the required injustices.

The subsequent section, 4.5, is meant to put all this material together organically by using finance and Marx's *Capital* in order to prepare for the positive arguments of Chapter 5.

A materialistic political economy is a historical subject with no positive function. A non-capitalist society, and in particular a communist anarchist society in the tradition of Marx, does not need it for its organization and survival, because it is beyond politics. A materialistic political economy is only and solely a revo-lutionary method.

We will conclude by outlining the evil role of society and politics.

4.2 The discourse of economics[1]

In this section, we will discuss Hume, Smith's invisible hand and, indirectly, Mandeville, before then introducing the present-day criticism of contemporary economic theories. As in the preceding chapters, we will see that seeking to extricate scepticism, Stoicism and Epicureanism from one another in the authors we study is a pointless exercise. We will start by discussing Hume's 1751 *Principles of Morals* (2009), which is the least radical, in terms of the argument we are seeking to put forward, when compared with Hume's other works. This is not a problem, however. On the contrary: although we are looking for some clear ideas in Hume, we do not want to bestow on him a coherence of our own. Authors must be left free to convey, if that is the case, the flavour of their own doubts and, indeed, of their incoherencies and rethinking.

The other works that will be considered in the present section are his 1739–40 *Treatise of Human Nature* (2011), the 1748 *Enquiry Concerning Human Understanding* (2008) and the 1754 *Dialogue Concerning Natural Religion* (2006). In them, we will find, in their most straightforward and radical form, the arguments leading to the idea of liberty as chance, which we need in order to proceed with our materialistic argument. Only when armed with this, and with its complementary argument on society and politics as the source of regularity and inertia (and evil), can we look at economic theories, be they Smith's invisible hand, modern mainstream economics or conventional Marxist political economy.

The spectre of Mandeville (1997) and his supposedly immoral and, in the words of Adam Smith, 'pernicious' doctrines will haunt us throughout the whole section and beyond. The question of private vices and public virtues, which has exercised a lot of brilliant minds besides Adam Smith, is not, however, fundamental for us here. If the issue of liberty as chance is central – the validity of which we will endeavour to illustrate in what follows – and if the discourses and words of economic theories refuse to acknowledge it, then there are grounds to hypothesize a completely different, society-based theory of evil. The result of this is that ethics and morality are irrelevant to our theoretical purposes here.

Hume (2009) presents a number of themes helpful for kicking off our discussion. In the first place, as announced above, this text throws some doubts on what we will say when studying his other works. It is, in fact, the least intellectually subversive among them, at least for our purposes here. Its Epicurean scepticism is much less pronounced, and hypocrisy à la Mandeville and self-love are given a chance to be useful alongside convention. However, references to the intrinsic goodness of humankind and hints at the uselessness of languages, besides a final sceptical statement and an Epicurean *excusatio non petita* are found everywhere. Rounding it off, the dialogue at the end is a masterpiece of literary subversion of morals.

As with Adam Smith's *Theory of Moral Sentiments* (2009), here too the main issue is the difference between natural and social qualities: society selects some of the former and enforces them by means of thinking in language form and by the sentiments of approbation and the lure of wealth, with the calm and dignity it bestows on individuals. Thus, although passions and morals are related, it is the selective intellectual reduction of them to what is useful in society that counts. It may seem that Smith and Mandeville are both vindicated here, but Hume always has some surprises ready. He knows very well that things could be very different.

'Justice is useful to society' (Hume, 2009, p. 26) because there is scarcity. But if nature were so benevolent as to require 'no laborious occupation' (ibid.), and 'music, poetry and contemplation form [man's] sole business Conversation, mirth, and friendship his sole amusement' (ibid.), 'justice would never have been dreamed of' (ibid.). Goods would need no partition, there would be no property, and justice would not be 'in the catalogue of virtues' (ibid.). But this is not all. In Part II of the same chapter ('Of justice'), he refers to initiatives such as those of the Levellers, who use religious principles to imagine and practise a society based on equality. Although this is laudable, it would require some sort of a censor to be continually checking out inequalities. He goes on to conclude that the present arrangement based upon private property is better, but does not say why it requires no, or little, or feasible, censorship.

On the contrary:

It must, indeed, be confessed, that nature is so liberal to mankind, that, were all her presents equally divided among the species, and improved by art and industry, every individual would enjoy all the necessaries. [. . .] It must also be confessed, that, wherever we depart from this equality, we rob the poor of more satisfaction than we add to the rich, and that the slightest gratification of a frivolous vanity, in one individual, frequently costs more than bread to many families, and even provinces. It may appear withal, that the rule of equality, as it would be highly *useful*, is not altogether *impracticable*; but has taken place, at least in an imperfect degree, in some republics; particularly that of Sparta [. . .] with the most beneficial consequences.

(p. 44; emphasis in the original, here and in all Hume quotations to come)

However, he hastens to tell us, historians insist that equality is impracticable, for it 'would be extremely *pernicious* to human society' (p. 44), for it would 'destroy all subordination' (p. 46), thereby destroying power and property. In fact, calling objects mine or yours is weak, because it means that they 'receive those appellations' being 'foreign to us [. . .] totally disjoined and separated from us; and nothing but the general interests of society can form the connexion' (p. 48). Thus, the laws of justice can find themselves in 'total uncertainty' (ibid.), and, thus, 'statutes, customs, precedents, analogies, and a hundred other circumstances' (p. 50) are used to justify property.

But the ultimate point, in which they all professedly terminate, is, the interest and happiness of human society. Where this enters not into consideration, nothing can appear more whimsical, unnatural, and even superstitious, than all or most of the laws of justice and property.

(p. 50)

This should be borne in mind when we are considering his other works further on, because they make society into a place where only lesser individuals can live contented and thrive. In the second part of Section VI ('Of qualities useful to ourselves'), he comes back to the issue from a different perspective:

> A man, who has cured himself of all ridiculous prepossessions, and is [. . .] convinced, from experience as well as philosophy, that the difference of fortune makes less difference in happiness than is vulgarly imagined [. . .] may, indeed, externally pay a superior deference to the great lord above the vassal; because riches are the most convenient, being the most fixed and determined, source of distinction. But his internal sentiments are more regulated by the personal characters of men.
>
> (p. 126)

Hume[2] is clearly distinguishing between an unprejudiced, natural kind of thought that makes us see the theoretical practicability of anarchist communism, and a lesser, social kind of thought that, for unexplained reasons, prefers to keep power, hierarchies and injustice alive. It also seems to that reasoning that the keeping of injustice (i.e. the perennial need for justice) is much easier than the keeping of equality. This is because conventions, hierarchies and, indeed, inequalities are the only way to manage society by using the chimera of justice and the deception of private initiative (notice the similarity with Adam Smith's invisible hand), for riches are the most convenient source of reciprocal distinction among social men. All this might seem secondary in *Principles of Morals* (2009), but becomes important in the light of Hume's Epicurean scepticism of his other works that we are going to consider here.

The central point seems to be the choice between society, with its evils, and communist anarchism. This latter is open, as hinted so far and as argued by Hume in the other works we will examine, only to the philosopher, the man who, as we will see, thinks by first looking at material reality. We need morals in practice because (as said) we are prepared, in order to have society, to bear a degree of immorality and injustice, without which society would not exist. This is just like in Smith and in Mandeville, as we will see next. Society is based upon evil.

One cannot help relating all the above to the final, highly sceptical, 'A dialogue' (Hume, 2009, pp. 248–78), which, after a bewildering list of moral perversities, reveals itself to be a simple comparison of ancient Greek and modern customs. At the end of it, the notions of *natural* and *artificial* in life and thinking are considered, and no solution is offered. 'An experiment [. . .] which succeeds in the air, will not always succeed in a vacuum' (p. 278). When taken by artificial things, 'the natural principles of their mind play not with the same regularity, as if left to themselves, free from the illusions of religious superstition or philosophical enthusiasm' (ibid.).

The question of whether impressions are the main source of social conventions and morality, or rather ideas, is, in *Principles of Morals* (2009), less relevant than in the other works we are about to consider. Hume is just explaining, seeking to give a realistic appraisal of reality. This reality is that of societies and economic intercourse – hence the choice to let the *historians* have it their way. But the sceptical impossibility of reaching a conclusion is there, and with it are the impossibility and uselessness, outside society, of having a morality. Out there, only nature rules, and the natural principles of the mind function regularly. Power, private property and injustice are solid, but need morality. However, in *Principles of Morals* (2009), man is good by nature and sympathetic: the horns of the dilemma could not be clearer or more radical.

We can conclude the study of this text by considering that, 'industry, frugality, temperance, secrecy, perseverance, and many other laudable powers or habits, generally styled virtues, are exerted without any immediate sentiment in the person possessed by them; and are only known to him by their effects' (p. 234). Languages cannot even help individuals communicate among themselves about it (ibid.). But, there 'is no wonder, that languages should not be very precise in marking the boundaries between virtues and talents, vices and defects; since there is so little distinction made in our internal estimation of them' (p. 236). 'A sentiment of conscious worth', however common it may be, has no proper name in languages. We display with ostentation our worthiness, and keep our failures to ourselves. That is what society is about; let us place all this in context, in Hume and in general.

A Treatise of Human Nature (Hume, 2011) and *An Enquiry Concerning Human Understanding* (2008) are, as is well known, very closely linked. Whatever is said with radical verve in the latter is confirmed in more generic terms in the former. Unlike *The Principles of Morals* (2009), in these works, there is a paramount role for passions,[3] which are at the origin of reason, and for impressions. Empiricism is the right path to knowledge, but we do not know whether we have grasped reality and whether a cause–effect relationship can ever be ascertained. Epicurean unpredictability rules nature, only slightly hidden by an intellectual scepticism that is strong in *Concerning Human Understanding* (2008) and less pronounced, but still fundamental, in *A Treatise of Human Nature* (2011). Morality is, therefore, 'more properly felt than judged' (2011, p. 302). Passions à la Epicurus rule man's rational conduct. Society powerfully limits all this, imposing an artificial regularity. Let us see in more detail.

Impressions are: 'Those perceptions, which enter with most force and violence [. . .] I comprehend all our sensations, passions and emotions, as they make their first appearance in the soul' (2011, p. 7). Ideas are, instead, 'the faint images' of the impressions 'in thinking and reasoning' (ibid.). All our ideas are 'copy'd from our impressions' (p. 52). It follows that ideas must be very clear and simple; when they are not, it is our fault, for we have neglected precision (ibid.). Thus, to him, philosophy (including science) 'pretends only to explain the nature and causes of our perceptions, or impressions and ideas' (p. 46).

'There remain, therefore, algebra and arithmetic as the only sciences in which we can carry on a chain of reasoning to any degree of intricacy, and yet preserve a perfect exactness and certainty' (p. 51). We should be careful not to fall prey to the notion that there are 'spiritual and refin'd perceptions' (p. 52); this only serves to cover many of the 'absurdities' philosophers contrive. It follows that reason is, or at least proceeds from, instinct: 'reason is nothing but a wonderful and unintelligible instinct in our souls, which carries us along a certain train of ideas' (p. 120). The reason why humans are puzzled by the instinct of animals is that they do not acknowledge that their own reason, just like animal reason, is equally instinct (ibid.). Finally, that is why we rely on past experience and observation: 'Nay, habit is nothing but one of the principles of nature, and derives all its force from that origin' (p. 120). We saw, in Chapter 3, the case of agriculture.

Education, and all social things, can as a consequence be misleading. Yet, 'it prevails nonetheless in the world, and is the cause why all systems, upon whatever convincing argument they may be founded, are apt to be repeated at first as new and unusual' (p. 81). 'Reason is, and ought only to be the slave of the passions, and can never pretend to any other office than to serve and obey them' (p. 266). In fact, passions 'can be contrary to reason only so far as they are accompany'd with some judgement or opinion' (p. 267).

To clarify:[4]

> Since a passion can never, in any sense, be called unreasonable, but when founded on a false supposition, or when it chooses means insufficient for the design'd end, 'tis impossible, that reason and passion can ever oppose each other [. . .] The moment we perceive the falsehood of any supposition, or the insufficiency of any means our passions yield to our reason without any opposition.
>
> (p. 267)

It is easy to infer that philosophical work is individual and must be independent from any socially contrived, limited logic. Society is a hindrance to proper philosophical work. Accepting its presence (which, as we will see, Hume nonetheless does) sets powerful limits on the possibility of knowledge and – this is most important – of freedom. Let us deepen this line of thought by looking first of all at the limits of knowledge, and then at what is not to do with it, in particular justice and morality.

The most important ideas, from which everything follows, are that 'an object may exist, and yet be nowhere' (p. 154). 'Now this is evidently the case with all our perceptions and objects, except those of the sight and feeling' (p. 155). The point is that 'whatever we conceive is possible' (ibid.). The mind can just conceive of things in peace, without fear of producing non-practical (for this is the word the metaphysics of capitalism prefers, with a typical metonymy, to 'things that exist nowhere') items.

If whatever we conceive is possible, then demonstration becomes tricky, and highly theoretical, and, as a consequence, confined to 'algebra and arithmetic' (which excludes geometry). To make this point as succinctly and faithfully to Hume as possible, we can quote from the 'Abstract' by Hume himself:

It is not any thing that reason sees in the cause, which makes us *infer* the effect. Such an inference, were it possible, would amount to a demonstration [...] But no inference from cause to effect amounts to a demonstration'.

(2011, p. 410)

In other words, 'whatever we conceive is possible' (ibid.) We can think out whatever we want, but attributing a regularity of behaviour to reality is not possible.

In fact, if a demonstration is achieved, the contrary becomes impossible, and that is a contradiction. All knowledge, therefore, comes down to mere probability (p. 122). 'All our reasonings concerning causes and effects are deriv'd from nothing but customs' (p. 123). 'To every probability there is an opposite possibility' (p. 93).

He goes on (in Section 12) to assert that there is 'nothing in any object' that can afford our drawing a conclusion about it (p. 95); no inference can be drawn, therefore. Inference is only a transference of the past to the future (ibid.). 'Any thing may produce any thing' (p. 116).

We can now introduce the following essential point, and then consider justice, government and morality. In Part 3, Section 1, Hume says that cause and effect are 'as distinct and separate from each other, as any two things in nature' (p. 261), and nobody can distinguish one from the other. Experience, i.e. the observation of their constant union, forms the inference. This last is 'nothing but the effects of customs on the imagination' (ibid.). The 'necessary connection' of cause and effect is not 'a conclusion of the understanding, but is merely a perception of our mind' (ibid.). We 'feel the necessity', but cannot penetrate any further into the connection.

Necessity makes an essential part of causation; and consequently liberty, by removing necessity, removes also causes, and is the very same thing with chance. As chance is commonly thought to imply a contradiction, and is at least directly contrary to experience, there are always the same arguments against liberty or free-will.

(p. 262)

In other words, 'liberty and chance are synonymous'. The consequences of this discovery for economics and politics are, as we will see when we discuss *The Principles of Morals* (2009), momentous. Government is a human convention, although 'it be possible for men to maintain a small uncultivated society without government' (pp. 346–7). However, it is impossible to 'maintain a society of any kind without justice' (ibid.). We turn to this vicious circle.

In Part 2 of Book 3, Hume states, 'that our sense of every kind of virtue is not natural; but that there are some virtues, that produce pleasure and approbation by means of an artifice or contrivance, which arises from the circumstances and necessities of mankind'. This statement takes us back all the way to Adam Smith's *Theory of Moral Sentiments*. Abstinence from possessing the property of others is one such artifice (p. 315), hence the 'origin of justice explains that of property' (ibid.). But, those impressions 'which give rise to this sense of justice, are not natural to the mind of man, but arise from artifice and human conventions' (p. 319). All this is tempered by the assertion (p. 311) that there is reason to argue that the rules of justice are artificial, and in that sense they are not natural. But they are not 'arbitrary' because justice (in general) is a natural virtue.

In other words, morality and the actual artificial parts of justice are not natural and are not from reason (we should never forget that reason is instinctual and comes from impressions). In fact, again in Book 3, Hume openly states that 'The rules of morality, therefore, are not conclusions of our reason' (p. 294). He repeats the concept on p. 295, when he says that moral distinctions are not 'the offspring of reason', for (p. 301) 'morality is not an object of reason'. Decisions about moral rectitude 'are evidently perceptions [impressions or ideas]' (p. 302). That is why morality 'is more properly felt than judged'. Social approbation intervenes on top of all this.

The only way to hold all this together, as in all the other authors we have been considering so far, including Smith and Marx, is to suppose that there is a natural feeling of sympathy in men. This is clear in the 'Conclusions of this book': 'We are certain, that sympathy is a very powerful principle in human nature, and it influences our judgement on morality' (pp. 393–4). It seems evident that, if so, and if society is meant (in Hume, but also in all economic and political theories) to protect property, hierarchies and the sanctity of contracts, there is a clash between the natural man (whose existence as such Hume denies often), or at least the philosophizing man, and society.

Furthermore, it is evident that there is a communicative dimension in society that is completely different from a potential communication among philosophizing men, who waste no words in making ungranted inferences. Societal communication is artificial and perfunctory. Cause and effect, and experience itself, become the object of a peculiar type of rendering in language, for they depend on a logical flaw. Yet, nature presents itself to us with instances of regularity. We must be careful not to derive a more general regularity from that. The big, subversive issue is the question of liberty as chance. To be free, we must free chance. To do so, we must free ourselves from the intellectual limits imposed on us by society, with its silly defence of unprovable goods. The question at stake is, as usual, communist anarchism: freedom versus restricted life, communicated with the wrong, unnatural maieutics.

We are left, therefore, with the task of exploring the main features of human understanding, in a world where we can potentially free chance. The consequences for language, words and the dominant maieutics are, by now, easy to infer and less important, at this preliminary stage, than the exciting possibility that the human mind could free itself from limiting slavery to customs, i.e. for us here, the metaphysics of capitalism.

Before delving into the specific arguments of Hume (2008), it is worth our while reconsidering and summarizing the question of the relationship between knowledge, rationality and society in our modern terms. Although rationality works smoothly, demonstrably and naturally only in algebra and arithmetic, its theoretical productions, however impractical ('nowhere'), do exist and do have a human relevance. The presence of external, material objects, related to each other (nature), makes for the presence of artificial objects and concepts: to all of these only a partial rationality can be applied, for the cause–effect demonstration is impossible. Liberty is chance, and chance cannot be reduced to any set of rules. Thus, society differs from nature only in that society's artificial concepts, objects and connections require irrational (or flawed) thinking to be held together: justice and morality. Let us see in more depth.

Hume's *Enquiry Concerning Human Understanding* (2008) was meant to amend the faults of *A Treatise of Human Nature* (2011); in so doing, nonetheless, it expresses the points concerning human understanding in a much more radical – hence, useful to us here – way. Human reason (p. 18) enquires in two forms: relations of ideas and matters of fact. The former is what can be demonstrated with certainty, i.e. the mathematical disciplines. The latter are hard to grasp and even describe, for, in reality, the opposite of what one sees is always possible: the sun may not rise tomorrow.

Again, the mathematical sciences have a 'great advantage' over the moral ones (Section VII, p. 44), for no ambiguity is possible in them. If we venture to say that, where there is no property, there is no injustice,[5] we need to define both terms (p. 119), and any such proposition is imperfect. All our ideas are copies of our impressions (p. 45), and we cannot think of anything we have not felt before. Ideas are thus not as clear as facts; a degree of obscurity and ambiguity is always present. Section VIII (p. 58) goes as far as proposing that it is precisely such ambiguity that keeps disputes open.

The cause–effect point we have already dealt with is clearly and radically expressed in *An Enquiry Concerning Human Understanding* (2008):

> Suppose a person, though endowed with the strongest faculties of reason and reflection, to be brought on a sudden into this world: he would, indeed, immediately observe a continuous succession of objects, and one event following another; but he would not discover anything further.

The powers of nature that produce facts 'never appear to the senses'; only experience suggests connections: 'This principle is CUSTOM or HABIT' (p. 32). Custom, then, is the great guide of human life (ibid.). Without it, we would be 'ignorant of every matter of fact' (ibid.) and would be impotent vis-à-vis nature.

In fact, and this is very important, 'The only immediate utility of all sciences, is to teach us, how to control and regulate future events by their causes' (Section VII, p. 56). Hence, a cause is 'an object, followed by another, and where all the objects, similar to the first, are followed by objects, similar to this second' (ibid.). But it is very clear that, in the first place, custom and experience count to produce this kind of conclusion (see, for instance, pp. 33, 34, 55, 56, 59–60), and therefore it all comes down to memory, i.e. to confused and ambiguous ideas. This is not human understanding, but rather a type of applied science; let us call it engineering.

In the second place, this type of knowledge is indissolubly tied to society and its survival: we need it to cope with the overwhelming power of nature, but, if so, it is connected to everything else society entails in intellectual terms: ambiguity of expression and such unnatural reasoning as morality and justice. The most obvious problem deriving from this is that, in society, à la Keynes,[6] the future is conformable to the past in the minds of the citizens. This is precisely what Hume notices:

> For all inferences from experience suppose, as their foundation, that the future will resemble the past, and that similar powers will be conjoined with similar sensible qualities. If there be any suspicion, that the course of nature may change, and that the past may be no rule for the future, all experience becomes useless, and can give rise to no inference or conclusion.
>
> (Section IV, p. 27)

If that were not clear enough, here is a reiterated, and even more radical, statement from the Abstract (p. 138):

> Adam with all his science, would never have been able to *demonstrate*, that the course of nature must continue uniformly the same, and that the future must be conformable to the past. [. . .] I will go further, and assert, that he could not so much as prove by any *probable* arguments, that the future must be conformable to the past. [. . .] But our experience in the past can be a proof of nothing for the future, but upon a supposition, that there is a resemblance betwixt them. This therefore is a point, which can admit of no proof at all, and which we can take for granted without any proof.

In order to come to what is relevant for political economy, we can notice once again, with him, that:

> Nothing is more free than the imagination of man; and though it cannot exceed that original stock of ideas, furnished by the internal and external senses, it has unlimited power of mixing, compounding, separating, and dividing these ideas, in all the varieties of fiction and vision.
>
> (Section V, Part II, p. 34)

Placed in the framework thus far described, the above statement simply means that man's faculties are unpredictably great in number, and that it is not easy to extricate what one sees and experiences from what is made up, by mistake or by the mere desire to imagine freely. The limit to all this is constituted by society, which funnels man's faculties towards a limited set of artificial thoughts.

In discussing mathematics, Hume notices the importance of knowing exactly what you must pronounce yourself upon: 'any difficulty in these decisions, it proceeds entirely from the undeterminate meaning of words, which is corrected by juster definitions' (Section XII, p. 119). But, outside mathematics, all propositions are imperfect. For instance:

To convince us of this proposition, that where there is no property there is no injustice, it is only necessary to define the terms, and explain injustice to be a violation of property. This proposition is, indeed, nothing but a more imperfect definition.

(ibid.)

He naturally concludes that this problem presents itself in all branches of knowledge except mathematics.

Thus, it is not only society that reduces man's life to artificial and limited sets of thoughts; furthermore, it is perfectly indeterminate in whatever it does and proposes. Nor could it be otherwise, in a world in which Epicurean chance makes it impossible to connect cause and effect. Just like in Berkeley, the human brain holds the key to both knowledge and ignorance, and, like in Berkeley, Smith and all those thinkers we examined in Chapters 2 and 3, it is deaf to the language of nature and approximate in its own language, despite the continuous striving for precision. What is the solution to this apparently pessimistic puzzle?

To Hume, there is in reality a minority of people, those to whom he is talking, whom he calls the philosophers, who can only share his Epicurean scepticism,[7] helped by their Stoic morality and strength. The others content themselves with inference from experience, i.e. with pretending to a knowledge they do not hold. They could not do so if social language were not simultaneously enormously approximate (to cover up the evident lack of logic in relying on experience only) and apparently, and in intent, looking for closer and closer precision.

In works of *human* art and contrivance, it is allowable to advance from the effect to the cause, and returning back from the cause, to form new inferences concerning the effects, and examine the alterations [. . .] [for] man is a being, whom we know by experience, whose motives and designs we are acquainted with, and whose projects and inclinations have a certain connexion and coherence.

(Section XI, pp. 104–5)

This is an appropriate, but sad, conclusion. Although the potentialities of the human mind are infinite, just like the possible occurrences in material reality, we can know, and operate, and even predict the actions and thoughts of the social and institutionalized individual. In it, in fact, nature has been tamed to a set of 'coherent' projects and inclinations. However similar men are to the other animals, who also 'learn many things from experience' (Section IX, p. 76), they neglect instinct (ibid., p. 77; also, philosophers do, he adds) when they think scientifically (ibid., p. 78). But there is hope, for not all instincts are lost (ibid.): some are still there, and from there we can start.

The presence of society, generated by the 'mutual dependence of men' (Section VIII, p. 64) makes it so 'that scarcely any human action is entirely compleat in itself'. The more complicated social life becomes, the more institutions, rules and individuals are tangled together; the more so, the more 'necessity' rules the presence of society's strictures.

> How could *politics* be a science, if laws and forms of government had not a
> uniform influence upon society? Where would be the foundations of *morals*,
> if particular characters had no certain or determinate power to produce
> particular sentiments, and if these sentiments had no constant operation on
> actions?
>
> (ibid., p. 65)

Let us draw some conclusions for our materialistic political economy purposes
from the many important things Hume adds to the themes of Chapter 3.[8] In the
first place, reality, the material, is made and unmade by chance, in an undeniable,
Epicurean fashion. Yet chance is tied, and limited, by the fact that men think by
analogy and by experience (e.g. statistics). Thus, they refuse to entertain those
thoughts that push them away from the realm of necessity and from what we
decided to call in this book engineering, i.e. science that denies, or at least
neglects, the unpredictability of nature and the impossibility of producing
cause–effect scientific laws.

Inevitably, in the second place, society becomes tied to morality. That is
possible because, despite morality being impossible to determine and clarify, the
social man is perfectly knowable and repetitious in his actions, which are
reciprocally bound to those of everybody else and limited by rules and institutions.
The consequence is that society is the only realm of reality where what we have
called engineering thinking applies and yields relevant results, despite its
philosophical, logical faults. Human societies are precisely those 'enclosures' that,
erroneously (as also observed by Katzner, 2015), Lawson (1997, 2003) deems to
be the source of all the problems with mainstream economic theory. On the
contrary, it is the very presence of such enclosures and their iterative behaviour,
with the general flawed logic entailed, that proves mainstream theory much more
realistic than any heterodox attempt at an amendment (see Micocci, 2002, 2013,
2014a, 2014b).

In the third place, and inevitably, chance is liberty. Outside society and the
economy there is unfettered thought and direct contact with nature in the sense
of the chance to get rid of what we can call, connecting back to Chapters 2 and
3, the triple Marxian alienation of man. Materialism, i.e. the empirical knowledge
that Hume and all the other thinkers we have discussed, including Marx,[9] advocate,
is possible only outside society. If we want to pursue it, therefore, we must
understand it as a tool to help us leave society. In Humean terms, and in practice,
this is easy, for materialism (liberty as chance) can – indeed, it must, both in society
and outside it – simply be pursued by the side of engineering disciplines and actions.
The local regularities of nature seem to allow precisely for this possibility: again,
take the agriculture example.

In the fourth place, political economy, then, is not a tool to help regulate society
or to plan new and alternative societies and economies. It is only a history-based
practice to emancipate us from capitalist society and its intellectuality, helping
return our thought to nature and instinct. We can reinterpret Marx's expression
'critique of political economy' precisely in this sense. This is possible because

Marx can be read as an anarchist thinker of the anti- or non-Hegelian type. This is what we shall keep exploring. But, let us go step by step.

Before moving on to some fresh observations on Adam Smith's invisible hand, we can observe that all the above needs a language that expresses everything in an indeterminate way. Any statement of fact that is rigorous is maths-like, and either cannot apply to practical human life or is a subversion of it, or both. This means that a language suited to the economy and society must be evocative rather than capable of stating things clearly. We will come back to that through our reasoning on materialism.[10] At this stage, we can refer the reader to Micocci (2008/2010, 2012a) and Cassirer (1961).

This is not the place to speculate on the similarities, friendship and overall relationship between Hume and Adam Smith. These are not relevant to our purpose. What matters is to notice that, in Smith (1980, 1999, 2001, 2009), we find the same view on the relationship between necessity and society as in Hume, and the same conservative acceptance of class-based institutional organization. Also, the presence of a wide degree of deception, and indeed its usefulness and necessity, is clear in both thinkers. Routines inspired by experience and by reliance on the knowledge fed by experience is also there. It would appear that Mandeville (1997) is an important, looming presence, for the conceptions of morality and conformism are similar in these three authors (hence, probably, the need for Smith to declare Mandeville's doctrine 'pernicious', to distance himself from him).

There is, however, an important difference between Hume and Smith, and Mandeville. Whereas the last of the three has nothing to say on whether an alternative world, based on totally different conceptions, is possible, in Smith, and much more so in Hume, the choice to side with present-day society is political and dictated by practical concerns. Alternative societies are indeed possible, and some, like Sparta, have even existed, but, if the role of society is that of providing for necessities and building securities and, in Smith, also of increasing the wealth of the nation, then deception, lack of logic, indifference to nature and to the prerogatives of the individual, and a language that evokes rather than refers and explains are admissible. That is the kind of reality political economy starts from, for its goal is not to help change society but to help preserve it such as it is. We must wait for Marx to have a critique of political economy.

The fact that things in life are expressed in simultaneously approximate and precise words means 'The poor man's son, whom heaven in its anger has visited with ambition [. . .] admires the condition of the rich' (Smith, 2009, p. 211), even though 'He does not even imagine that they are really happier than other people: but he imagines that they possess more means of happiness' (ibid., p. 213). What happens is that the person who dreams of a better life cannot connect this feeling with a natural condition, for all his language-based maieutics supplies him with is not happiness, but the means of procuring the vague idea of happiness. He applies himself to this, in the deluded hope that happiness is what society says it is, i.e. a rich man's life.

It is this deception that rouses and keeps in continual motion the industry of mankind [. . .] which first prompted to cultivate the ground, to build houses, to found cities and commonwealths, and to invent and to improve all the sciences and arts [. . .] which have entirely changed the face of the globe.

(ibid., p. 214)

Without this deception, societies would not progress; they would not even resist external and internal pressures. In an astonishing vicious circle, well illustrated by Hume, intellectual limitations cause the capacity of societies and economies to progress, and tie individuals to themselves. The prize is the hope – not the certainty – that your ambition will lead you to socially imagined higher happiness, made of material (but we know this means metaphysical, which matters decisively in capitalism's confusing of the material and the abstract) items you can buy.

The price is Marx's triple alienation. You must give yourself up to yet another set of activities that are presumed to be satisfactory (this even applies to the Marxists: take the notion of general intellect we discussed in Section 3.3): labour. This is, as is well known, the 'commercial man' of Smith's *Wealth of Nations*, the entrepreneur himself. For reasons similar to the deception Smith describes in *The Theory of Moral Sentiments* (2009), the commercial man is supposed to take pride in his work. Why not, after all? He has nothing else, for nature (even his own nature) is out of reach, and he can only understand and express 'artificial' things that, by analogy, look natural. In the end, wealth means the possibility of feeding and sheltering yourself, quenching your thirst and having some amusement; this last point is obtained, in Smith and in capitalism in general, by the addition of luxury to the normal things we do.

Importantly, the invisible hand needs a class society and inequality, and, hence, even more security than that dictated by the man–nature relationship.

When providence divided the earth among a few lordly masters, it neither forgot nor abandoned those who seemed to have been left out of the partition. [. . .] In what constitutes the real happiness of human life, they are in no respect inferior to those who would seem so much above them.

(ibid., p. 215)

He is right, although not for the reasons he thinks: in fact, all men are equal in their triple Marxian alienation and in the absurd language they speak.

As in Hume, stability is easy to get: 'The same principle, the same love of system, the same regard to the beauty of order, of art and contrivance, frequently serves to recommend those institutions which tend to promote the public welfare' (ibid.).

We do not need Hume's philosophers with their Epicurean scepticism, for:

political disquisitions, if just, and reasonable, and practicable, are of all the works of speculation the most useful [. . .] They serve to animate the public passions of men, and rouse them to seek out the means of promoting the happiness of the society.

(ibid.)[11]

Like in Polybius (Polibio, 1979) or Aristotle's *Politics* (1981; especially Book VI), humans have to be conditioned to social life and social theory with education and emotional arousal. We will have to come back to that again and again.

We can conclude this section by observing that we have now discovered that the material of Classical political economy is not the concrete, but society and its maieutics. If this is the case, it is well worth wondering whether, in the analysis of politics and the economy, economists can dispense altogether with confusing reality in general with social and economic reality. This would grant brevity and clarity, a fair correspondence to the object of our research, and an internal rigour. In fact, this is exactly what the Neoclassical economists did.

4.3 Economic arguments as justification

In order to preserve society and hierarchy, the authors we have been considering in this and in the preceding chapter have to separate theoretical discourse of a logical philosophical kind from 'practical' analyses of the economic base with its superstructure. The Neoclassical economists in the last decades of the nineteenth century went further by simply doing without logic and philosophy, thereby determining, in the forms of the mathematical models they borrowed from physics, the transformation of political economy into a metaphysics in our sense here. At that point, material reality no longer mattered and was dutifully discarded. This epistemological absurdity (see, for instance, Micocci, 2002, 2008/2010) is the reason why mainstream economics actually works in practice, by mirroring capitalist social and economic arrangements and interacting with them. The overall logical problem of the abstract–concrete–metaphysical separation naturally remains.

Merker (2009) – repeating an argument that is clear and evident in Marx (Micocci, 2002, 2008/2010) – correctly notices that the turning point in Western philosophy and politics is the system of Hegel and its general consonance with European history and culture. Hegel-like thought has influenced even those people who are not necessarily interested in philosophy, and it has played a subtle yet paramount role in twentieth-century fascism and in the populisms of the twenty-first century. For our purposes, we can summarize this difficult phase of Western intellectual development by seeing it as the irresistible comeback of metaphysics that has inevitably informed of itself capitalism, taking advantage of the dialectical features this last system has. Philosophy and economic and political life came simultaneously to gain similar, dialectical features. The consequences are momentous.[12]

The question has been well known since the days of Parmenides. Metaphysics is always bound to fail, at least as long as we find ourselves having trouble distinguishing between the abstract and the concrete. Considering that, to human understanding, the abstract is forever rendered vain by the need to be expressed in words, the only way to take it seriously is that we think, in the typically fascist mythical fashion, that Being is something we can relate to dialectically, but this is obviously yet another metaphysics, and an ugly and flawed one. Hence, abstract philosophy, though it is the only thing philosophy can do for us, is useless per se; its only utility comes from its supplying us with logical tools. But these only can prove the limits of philosophy itself and, hence, of all natural and social sciences. This implies that 'applied philosophy' is an empty term, periodically filled by occasional fashions: political and economic philosophy, for two instances that interest us here, can only be techniques to manipulate and use in practice the culture and language of the dominant metaphysics. The same applies to the natural sciences; this is a further reason to justify our decision to group these last under the general heading of 'engineering' studies.

We can only struggle continuously to emancipate ourselves from every metaphysics we are presented with. Our tools to do so can be found starting with the authors and arguments considered in the present book and the understanding of real opposition in the sense used by the pre-*Critiques* Kant (see Micocci, 2002, 2008/2010). Hence, also, we can use the anti-Hegelian Marx,[13] who bases himself upon this 'radical' Kant, as Della Volpe and Colletti had well understood (see Della Volpe, 1949, 1963, 1967, 1978, 1980; Colletti, 1969a, 1969b, 1972, 1973, 1974, 1975, 1979; Micocci, 2002). Instead of a political economy, therefore, we can only propose a critique of political economy without any pretension to any practical or applied philosophy. This is a fundamental result.

What has just been said implies that we must reconsider, and explain, the issue of human creativity. Hume's definitions, with their supreme optimism, are a useful starting point. To Hume, 'whatever we conceive is possible', because 'nothing is more free than the imagination of man'. This gives much hope, but is not very compatible with the ideas just illustrated, which are instead similar to Hume's Epicurean scepticism and to its Stoic everyday practicability within the status quo of any historical era. The only way to interpret Hume's conception and hope in a useful way is to rid it of its 'practical' optimism.

If all of the above holds, in fact, the human mind is most certainly, in a potential, theoretical way, capable of 'conceiving whatever' and having a free imagination, but such potential freedom is a rare situation to find in practice, for capitalist reality is powerfully and thoroughly enslaved to the consequences of Marx's triple alienation. The mind cannot 'conceive whatever', nor can imagination roam free, for two binding reasons: first, and most forbidding, simply because Marx's triple alienation blocks and renders bare mind and imagination alike. Second, because, even if a degree of roaming were allowed, or conquered, by the individual, its practical results only would be expressed with the intellectual means of the dominant metaphysics and its language and maieutics, or be lost, even to their creator.[14]

As a consequence, in capitalism, only the 'bizarre' is ever allowed, and rarely so. 'Bizarre' non-artistic works, however, are almost impossible to come by and are obstinately denied when present. Think of the case of the anarchist Marx we are considering in the present book. The malicious reciprocal influence of the limits imposed by the dominant intellectuality and of those imposed by the language and speech render vain any creative breakthrough, big or small. Thus, Adam Smith's invisible hand can simply be disregarded and reimagined by each, autonomously, and not surprisingly unanimously, only to be vaguely confused with microeconomics' perfect competition. The two things become a single concept everybody pretends to understand, and everybody conceives and uses with a different degree of precision, and communicates and discusses without anybody noticing, let alone minding, the Babel Tower effect.

Hume is also right when he says that 'nowhere' things can and do exist, ontologically speaking. The process described above greatly helps their survival. But they are perfectly useless. They wander among us, but their only role is that of showing to the capitalist mind actual instances of such 'non-practical' impurities. Non-practical and nowhere in fact coincide in the metaphysics of capitalism: their only property is that of being objects of refusal and/or scarecrows to the sloppy – those people who have a tendency to dream, i.e. to be creative, to want to see material reality.

The only way partly to preserve Hume's optimism despite such sad considerations lies in working on the detachment of capitalist human understanding from nature, i.e. the distance of its metaphysics from natural reality, including instinct, and from the abstract (from the natural human mind, that is). Philosophy can do it for us: it can help us destroy our illusions about the abstract, uncover the faults of the metaphysics and turn to material reality with an open mind and open senses. What has just been said is nothing to do with yoga, Zen, philosophical mysticism, Russian Nihilism or apophanic religions. It is materialistic emancipation in the tradition of Marx, if one reads him for what he writes, rather than for what 'practical' things he is supposed to say, by Marxists and anti-Marxists alike. Only thus can one practise Marx's Thesis XI on Feuerbach (in Marx and Engels, 1985, p. 121–3) in the light of Theses VIII, IX, X, indeed of all of them.

A 'practical, sensuous' activity (at least at this stage of our analysis) must replace metaphysics and metaphysics' entanglement with language and speech, with their evocative, rather than analytical, structure and content. This we can call silence, which is not different from Hume's faith in the unlimited theoretical freedom of the human mind, especially when conceived in contrast to the limitations imposed on it by the capitalist base and superstructure we have discussed in Section 4.2. However, we need to go beyond the given set of forms our mind is endowed with by our intellectuality and, instead of lucubrating and imagining (i.e. combining and compounding, in Hume's terminology), bring scepticism to its limits and:

- fight against the dominant metaphysics; and
- see what is behind it.

Most likely, at least in our time, we will find another metaphysics, but this should not discourage us.

At stake is not logic, imagination or bare observation. It is the reconnection of human understanding to the material. This might even mean that we discover that no such possibility exists. In fact, the point is precisely not to stop at the imaginable, and even less at the unimaginable. Rather, we must go beyond that difference by stripping human understanding of all we can critically observe and dispense with. There is no denying that this is, at least in part, a metaphysical process, if the senses are what they appear to be to the metaphysics of capitalism. But that might not be, and a realm of freedom, that is liberty as chance, is entailed by this possibility. This is what we must pursue; silence is this effort of optimism.

Chapter 5 will give a more diffused explanation of silence and of its method. Before getting there, we need to complete our description of the economic aspects of capitalism, its economic theorization, their reciprocal correspondence and their effects on the individual. Only then can we carefully consider the weight of language and speech, and their indispensable, simultaneous approximation, precision and striving for precision while only seeking to be evocative. Let us start with the Neoclassical subversion of political economy of the last decades of the nineteenth century, to then go back to Smith and Marx; Hume will help us see things and consider the basic features, and goals, of a materialistic political economy.

It appears very clear that we are discussing a great divide that, however suppressed, keeps resurfacing, especially when we think in radical terms. On the one hand are the (false) securities of organized society and the economy, and on the other the unknown, i.e. what we cannot – and we must not, we have been arguing here – imagine. This unsettling situation cannot be tolerated, lest society and the economy be threatened. Repressing it is no use: no civil or religious regime has ever been able to eliminate all opposition by repression. The smartest move is to pretend that the unknown does not exist, for it is simply a matter of conquering the little that is left of it, and build an intellectual apparatus perfectly detached from material reality and faulty enough in its internal mechanisms to allow for patches of doubt, continuous criticism and even derision. This is what the Neoclassical thinkers did for economics.

In one of those surprising – but still terribly logical in their banality – occurrences, in the few decades starting from the 1870s, several thinkers independently reached similar or complementary conclusions. To Jevons, Edgeworth, Walras, Marshall, and, in part, to Menger, Wicksell and Pareto (to name but the best known), economics was a metaphysical object. Present-day economists, with the ignorance and approximation typical of their profession, call this metaphysics 'abstract' thinking; this is another instance of the evocative power of the precise approximation of capitalist language and speech. To be above criticism, Neoclassical metaphysics had to be 'scientific'. To best avoid the attacks of the materialists, it also had to be perfectly detached from any connection with material reality. This they achieved, with a move this author does not hesitate to call an act of genius.

Inspired, one should presume, by the 'commercial man' of Adam Smith's *Wealth of Nations*, the Neoclassical authors devised the *Homo Oeconomicus*, a mathematical calculator of pains and pleasures endowed with endless desires. These last could have been the object of moralistic attacks and have, therefore, been identified, in another brilliant move, with 'needs'. The endless desires of consumers can thus match the endless creativity of the producer. This last is not

Hume's creativity, but rather the intense desire always to apply engineering to conjure up new products and/or processes of production, in order to meet, and even enhance, the people's infinite capacity to consume.

Production, which had given the Classical political economists so much trouble by being based on natural laws, is shaded and apparently superseded by the fact that, to the Neoclassical and present-day mainstream, the economic process is an endless sequence of exchanges between demanders and suppliers. With this move, we need only appreciate, in nature, the regularity that allows technology and, hence, as shown in Chapter 3, agriculture and, inevitably, industry and eventually services. Thus conceived, human relations need no ethics, and of course we need not bother with politics and sociology, and even less with history. Ahistorical theories, despite Marx's criticism of the Classical political economists, have come back to stay, for they have purged themselves of all their other connections with the rest of social, economic and material reality. Chance has been conquered and thoroughly chained.

All the basic mechanisms of these interactions are described, as already signalled, by the mathematics of calculus. At a more detailed level, chaos theories have recently been added, but their effect is simply that of proposing a similar, more complex, regular irregularity. Some, like Lawson (1997, 2003) and Velupillai (2005, 2014), object to such use of mathematics and the statistical methods it entails. Their reasoning appears solid, but their criticisms are perfectly impotent, as Katzner (2015) also points out. These and all the other critical authors miss the fact that the method of mainstream economics perfectly mirrors the dominant, dialectical intellectuality of the capitalist base and superstructure (Micocci, 2002, 2008/2010). Why should anyone want to change something that works in practice?

Others, such as Barzilai (2013, 2014; see also Katzner's reply, 2014), resort to higher kinds of mathematics to prove a different point: that mathematical tools are used improperly by economists. The result is exactly the same: Friedman (1966) put paid to such types of criticism long ago by saying that things matter when they work (when they are useful and 'practical'). Objecting to the lack of history in economic theory is also no objection, as we saw, for it equates to objecting to mainstream economics itself as a whole. The question, then, revolves, like everything else in the mental poverty of capitalism, around the issue of practicality. Here, mathematics matters in an evil way.

Sylos Labini (1992, 1993, 2004) develops a very tight argument, repeated with the very same wording in his main works. According to him, history must be brought back to economics (he echoes Schumpeter here), and mathematics is not incompatible with such purpose; only, the mathematics of the mainstream is faulty and must be amended. He is very clear:

La questione del realismo dei modelli teorici coincide con la questione riguardante l'oggetto dell'analisi economica. Ora, questo oggetto ha carattere storico [. . .] non esiste nessuna incompatibilità tra matematica e storia: basta riflettere sul significato dei modelli econometrici e sulle equazioni che vengono stimate utilizzando serie temporali di dati. Sono da criticare gli sviluppi puramente formali [. . .] [che] coprono la crassa ignoranza della storia o, più semplicemente, dei fatti da spiegare.

(1992, p. 8)

Translation:

The question of the realism of theoretical models coincides with the question of the object of economic analysis. Such subject has a historical character [. . .] there is no incompatibility whatsoever in between mathematics and history: all it takes is to reflect upon the meaning of econometric models and on the equations that are estimated using time series. What must be criticized are the purely formal developments [. . .] that conceal the crass ignorance of history, or, more simply, of the facts you want to explain.

(trans. A. Micocci)

A second problem is the micro–macro aggregation, which implies a 'psycho-logical–individualistic' purview that leads to society as a sum of supposed individuals rather than as an 'aggregate' (1992, p. 81). It follows, as a powerful instance, that in demand theory the collective demands of the various goods are the sum of individual demands, which are independent from each other. Pertinently (p. 83), Sylos Labini notices that, in Adam Smith, there is, simply, roughly and effectively, an 'effectual demand' to which a 'natural price' corresponds. In fact, in his *Wealth of Nations*, Smith 'harmoniously combines theoretical analysis with empirical and historical analyses' (p. 393). Sylos Labini does not seem to notice that historical and empirical observations are not absent from mainstream economics: they simply are surreptitiously inserted as illustrations, examples and appeals to common sense when the theory is short of explanatory power. The very core of the mainstream is based upon a hypostatization of history (Micocci, 2002).

A third, obvious source of problems for Sylos Labini is the application of the mathematical tools that have been chosen for their discipline by the Neoclassical authors and that still rule the dominant understanding of mainstream economics. The telling instance of marginal productivity '*concepita come una derivata parziale appare dunque come una nozione priva di corrispondenza con la realtà economica. [. . .] una derivata parziale è una derivata parziale e basta*' (Sylos Labini, 1992, pp. 109–10; 'conceived as a partial derivative therefore appears as a notion without correspondence to economic reality. A partial derivative is but a partial derivative', trans. A. Micocci). Nonetheless, '*la teoria tradizionale è criticabile, ma nel suo interno è certamente coerente, ciò che può contribuire a spiegare perché sia così longeva*' (ibid.; 'traditional theory can be criticized, but it certainly is internally coherent, which goes towards explaining why it has lasted so long' (trans. A. Micocci). The use of marginalism is even more devastating in a general equilibrium framework (ibid., p. 116), but it does not matter, given the internal coherence of the theory.

The presence of oligopoly, i.e. of powerful firms market-wise, poses entry barriers and, above all, challenges the marginalist Neoclassical approach to profit (ibid., p. 205). In any case, the entrepreneur (of any type of firm) does not make his/her decisions using mathematical derivatives (ibid., p. 260). If demand at a given price grows, he/she may want to use idle, inefficient machinery or pay higher wages. '*Ma in tali decisioni egli compie calcoli in termini di medie e non di variazioni marginali nel senso proprio*' (ibid.; 'But in such decisions he makes calculations in terms of averages and not of marginal variations in their proper sense', trans. A. Micocci).

The more general problem, hidden by Sylos Labini's use (1992, 1993) of the word history – which he does, polemically, to invite the reader to go back to the Classical political economists (see his 2004) – is that of static versus dynamic. Neoclassical and mainstream models of equilibrium are hopelessly static and do not capture the historical short- and long-term movements of society. Here, Sylos Labini reveals his belonging to the dominant mentality, for he mixes up two logically distinct things: an unpredictable sequence of events (what he calls history, or economic dynamism) and a mathematical scheme that describes one variable at a time to give a theoretical idea of its functioning. The latter is correct, *pace* Sylos Labini, because the error in the former observation is to hypothesize a variety of possibilities for the actual behaviour of societies, economies and individuals. These are instead, because of the metaphysics of capitalism, the realm of iteration and inertia, or, to put it with Hume, of predictability.

As a consequence, although Sylos Labini is right (1993) in criticizing the oversimplifications imposed by the mainstream models (e.g. price determination), he also says that:

> *diviene rilevante il cosiddetto principio del costo pieno, secondo il quale le imprese maggiori pervengono al prezzo aggiungendo al costo diretto un margine proporzionale* (mark-up). *In un contesto statico tale margine non ha significato; l'acquista solo in un contesto dinamico ed ammesso che vi siano imprese che in qualche modo guidano i prezzi.*
>
> (1993, p. 168; emphasis in the original)

Translation:

> The so-called principle of full cost becomes relevant; in it the biggest firms decide the price adding to the cost a proportional margin, the mark-up. In a static context such margin has no meaning; it acquires meaning only in a dynamic context, on condition that there are firms that somehow drive prices.
>
> (trans. A. Micocci)

In other words, his reasoning induces us to infer that the theory and the practice are too far from each other to influence each other. But, one cannot help notice, the latter is clearly the former, because a method can be replaced by another, plus some complications that empirical analysis helps explain. So, what is wrong?

In fact:

Un modello statico è un modello che incorpora una serie di possibilità logiche, indipendenti dal tempo. [. . .] Un modello dinamico è un modello in cui le quantità e le decisioni debbono essere datate [. . .] è inconcepibile fuori dal tempo. Occorre tuttavia aggiungere che un processo stazionario è pur sempre un processo dinamico che si ripete sempre allo stesso modo.

(ibid., pp. 11–12)

Translation:

A static model is a model that incorporates a number of logical possibilities independent from time [. . .] A dynamic model is a model in which quantities and decisions must be dated [. . .] it is inconceivable out of time. It must, however, be added that a stationary process is also a dynamic process, that repeats itself in the same way.

(trans. A. Micocci)

We are talking about the same iterative, rather than repetitive, phenomena to which experience, and statistical observation, can be applied. This is what is being done; the internal logic of such experience and statistics simply does not matter, which Hume and the other eighteenth-century philosophers, including Smith, abundantly warned us about.

Sylos Labini has to conclude, summarizing his critique of marginalism, that '*se sono logicamente coerenti e non si fondano su elementi in evidente contrasto con la realtà da spiegare, quei modelli hanno piena cittadinanza nella teoria economica*' (1993, p. 57; 'if they are logically coherent and are not based on elements in evident contrast with the reality that is to be explained, such models have full citizenship in economic theory', trans. A. Micocci), but he adds (p. 58) that we must '*uscire dall'ambiguità*' (abandon such ambiguity). The only possible way to interpret this statement in the light of the reasoning that precedes it is that the metaphysics of economic theory must be most coherent within itself (as proposed long ago by Cuoco, 1991, discussed in Chapter 2). In other words, once again, material reality does not matter, or at least it matters only when it can be surreptitiously used to point out the faults in the coherence of the theory. That can be done because reality in the perception of economists is in any case consonant to the theory, and repetitious (iterative, in our language here). You can use it a lot, a little, or not at all, just as we have been arguing throughout.

It would, therefore, seem that Samuelson was right when he solved economic problems by appealing to a parable (Samuelson, 1962), with some internal coherence and no requirement for direct correspondence to reality. Although his argument concerns the famous Cambridge controversy about capital, it can be easily extended to the whole of economic thought (see Micocci, 2014b). Additionally, Samuelson also appears to be right when he says (1987) that we can define, and use, economic theory by building a 'Whig history'. In practice, the theories that are actually used are the valid ones, for Samuelson and indeed for us here too, if all we have discussed so far is correct. Finally, if these two arguments hold, then there would be reason to think that mainstream economics is natural, if not to humans, at least to capitalist societies.

How can we, therefore, characterize mainstream economics? It builds a psychology, the *Homo Oeconomicus*, which, though unreal and unrelated to 'reality', fits perfectly well with capitalism as we know it, that is, if we do not notice the dreadful ambiguity in identifying the object of its theorization. The concept of reality is the most macroscopic instance. No one bothers to say what is meant, if they can avoid it. If pressed by need, the average economist refers to the 'empirical' material of his/her research, i.e. to those numbers that are gathered in tables and graphics and refer to theoretical curves and that lack any clear ontological status. They were cherries, washing machines, desires and mark-ups. Now they are a piece in a metaphysical puzzle that is meant to identify them precisely as that piece of that puzzle. Marxian alienation at its most evident is at work here: objects, creatures, accountings, even thoughts and emotions are alienated from themselves in order to become operational. They are just imprecise, precise words.

Their original ontological nature is perfectly useless. What we peddle in capitalism is the alienated item. The role of this alienation is that of making things amenable to language and speech and the general intellectual maieutics. In it, you can safely and smoothly pass from a mathematical derivative (a cost, or profit consideration, for instance) to an average (the same thing for actual entrepreneurs), from technical efficiency of the engineering type à la Marshall to the actual use of inefficient machinery or costly labour. You can even, as Malm (2013) shows, have a whole industry (cotton) in a country (Britain) shift from water to steam, against the advice of technical experts and against all evidence on economic efficiency and product quality, and, by this crazy move, give a powerful boost to your country's economic primacy and indeed to the industrial revolution itself. Nothing of the sort can be done if your logic is sound and your language unequivocal.

If words and concepts had a univocal meaning and referred to a precise object instead of presenting a wide degree of understanding, and if they were put together in a manner respecting such precise meaning, people would not be fooled into mistaking most of their actual life for labour time, let alone giving a monetary value to such an evident conceptual mistake. Centuries of struggle have been waged over these pieces of foolishness.

The most characteristic feature of economics, one that perfectly mirrors the same flaw in the actual goings on of capitalism as we know it, is the perfect lack of analytical content. Individuals maximize and minimize their functions, without bothering with what they are. An entrepreneur can, in fact, be made of an endless array of completely different professional behaviours, institutional situations and commercial management styles, like anybody or anything else. What matters is that we can associate a word/concept with an act/concept, regardless of their actual nature and/or existence. This, in capitalism as we know it, we can certainly do.

A market can be transmogrified in passing from one person to the next: for instance, from the perfect competition of the theory to an actual oligopoly, to the actual market in the main square of your city. Every day, each of us transforms ourself from human to labourer and back to human, without actually ever being either of them, just as none of the markets is a market. The metaphysics of capitalism works because it can do precisely this: it can play with alienated items that have no natural role and no material existence as such. They are always something else. The game would be uncovered only if language and speech were capable of finally identifying their objects and their relationships, which of course they are not, and indeed they must not do so. Like chickens in a cage, we keep behaving as if we were natural chickens in freedom: we scratch the soil looking for food. In fact, with our beaks, which are not made to feed from a manger, we dig in what food is given us as we would in open soil, thus throwing some of it on the ground.

Unlike chickens, however, we talk about what we do. We call the process of forced and artificial nutrition and malnutrition eating. We call the artificial feed we are given food, for it comes in various kinds and compositions worth noticing and lucubrating about all the time. Furthermore, unlike chickens, we attach ethical meanings to any objects around us. Mainstream economics can formally do without mentioning its own ethics, because it takes for granted that the dominant and vague ethics of capitalism as we know it, whether liberal, neo-liberal or fascist, is the right one. In this type of environment, criticisms such as McCloskey's (1985) have no incisiveness. Although there exists a rhetoric of economics, the problem is much wider.

What has been described here has the obvious role of justifying and disciplining capitalism as we know it. Whatever you do, however far from or close to the theory (or, by the same token, the practice), is easy to brand as part of it. If your last act can be assimilated to that of an entrepreneur, then entrepreneur you are, and what we mean by entrepreneur or what it means in general simply does not matter (also because there is no chance of ever having a market of perfect competition). The basic theory can be, and is, complicated at will. The overall feeling is, therefore, that of being channelled and moulded into capitalism as we know it, whatever you do, and yet never fully partaking of it. An act of terrorism and subversion is also part of the game. Whatever we do, whether in favour or against, provided it can be related in words, is part of capitalism as we know it. No subversion is actually possible, therefore, although subversion is actively practised all the time.

In this framework, eminent writers on economics such as Akerlof and Shiller can present books such as their *Animal Spirits* (2009), with self-congratulating language and the illusion of proposing, not only an original argument, but also a proper 'theory'. In it, argument is replaced by episodes, or data. Part 1 enumerates and discusses actual 'animal spirits': confidence, fairness, corruption/bad faith, money illusion, stories. To Akerlof and Shiller, the above concepts are not only incontrovertible in meaning and actually present in economic reality, they also, as a consequence, can help resolve actual economic problems, the most noteworthy being the volatility of financial markets.

If one were not astonished enough at their simplistic reductionism, the rest of the book completes the work by letting the reader know that this is what they gathered from Keynes. Here, Keynes seems to share in the same destiny as the anarchist Marx. His psychological observations and insights, which so much enrich his work and especially his *General Theory* (1983), are transformed into methodological variables upon which the 'theory' is supposedly based.

Akerlof and Shiller have good reason not to feel guilty about the superficiality of their approach. Even psychologists, in fact, simply mistake the *Homo Oeconomicus* of the theory for the normal man of capitalism as we know it. Although this is not completely unjustified, for the metaphysics of capitalism homogenizes and limits all human behaviours and feelings, one could object that, from a mainstream point of view, you cannot do it. Actual persons are supposed to be richer than the theory, at least because they have capitalist creativity: the capacity to invent new needs and to conjure up a new piece of technology at will (under the given theoretical conditions).

Kahneman (2011) is another case of self-congratulating reductionism. He even engages Hume in several places,[15] constantly misunderstanding the radical power of his work and emasculating his sceptical attitude. To Kahneman, Hume's causality comes down to experience. For every problem Kahneman poses to himself, he devises ingenious experiments, which have the common characteristic of mistaking the capitalist man and his sentiments for men and sentiments in general. Every word of his book is embedded in the socialized thinking of capitalism as we know it. The ideas and feelings of the humans he so thoroughly studies are the fully artificial thoughts and feelings of the intellectuality of capitalism. Instead of looking at the basic functions of the human mind, as Berkeley and Hume do, Kahneman studies the effects of the social brain, which he confuses with the human brain.

As in mainstream economics, his individuals are all the same, a homogeneous mass of which each individual is a fraction. Even trivial objects (e.g., a car), in Kahneman's book, look eternal, for they are the objects of the capitalist man's thinking and feeling. They are very much unlike the carriages of Hume and Smith, which were ephemeral epitomizations of the socialized man's need to show off. This is because, for Kahneman, human ideas, feelings and understanding have (inexplicably) changed from those days. In his view, we see more 'complexity' in our times, which means more simultaneous work going on. He simply echoes, obviously and easily, what complexity theory in mainstream economics is about.

It comes as no surprise, therefore, that Kahneman (2011, ch. 23) has a very thorough and realistic understanding of finance and its workings. Additionally, he is well aware that – in open contradiction of what is done in finance all the time – people cannot predict and only pretend to know. This is a very interesting problem: the more capitalistically intellectual and artificial you are, the more finance and its workings (and money in general) are easy to understand for you. The more you reduce human understanding to the trivial things that capitalist intellectuality comes down to, the more you are able to understand finance, in theory and in practice.

After all this complex, erudite discussion, we are left with an unresolved apparent contradiction. On the one hand, the capitalist man may be eminently suited to deal with the most dynamic development of capitalist intercourse, finance and its recently won preponderance vis-à-vis material production (Micocci, 2011a, 2011b). On the other hand, Smith's invisible hand continues to be a problem for those who see capitalism as the unfolding of a subversive modernity. In fact, for Smith, the deception of the invisible hand needs a number of atavistic features in order to create the commercial man and, hence, the *Homo Oeconomicus* of the theory: first of all, a state and a cluster of non-capitalist, non-entrepreneurial dominant classes (Di Mario and Micocci, 2015).

It is evident that capitalist intellectuality does not simply reduce human understanding to manageable variables by pretending that capitalist reality is all there is. It must also tame and reduce the extant parts of the preceding mode of production, which are those, as we have endeavoured to show here, that have produced the radical and subversive philosophies we have been considering in this book, to its own maieutical capacity. This helps explain why the radical power in the works of these philosophers has been defused by being forgotten, and also helps explain the often-found derogatory remark that Marx is a sort of Enlightenment philosopher.

Setting the official record straight is not within the scope and aim of the present book. It suffices to notice the problem and to keep it in mind while we go on with the actual task we have set ourselves: to sketch the importance of the flawed human understanding of the capitalist era in order to contribute to a logically sound, materialistic political economy oriented towards emancipation. We have at last understood, with this last section, that the solution can only be a critique of political economy, as Marx correctly named it. Otherwise, what you produce is economics as justification, an apology for capitalism and for its metaphysics, whatever your intentions are.

4.4 Present-day trends

In studying capitalism, if you do not conceive of materialism as a critique of political economy, you must inevitably conceive of it as a political economy. In that case, you have to accept the whole erroneous apparatus of the metaphysics of capitalism, together with its language and speech. In fact, economic categories (and everything else, obviously) are the outcome of the flawed processes of capitalist human understanding. If you want to intervene in them without challenging the metaphysics as a whole, you can only contribute to their historical resistance. As a result, there has never been a true challenge to capitalism in history.

The cunning that the political and economic system deploys to preserve itself has obviously taken many historical forms. Xenophon (Senofonte, 1997), in his *Cyropaedia*, offers a discussion of the basic mechanisms that underlie them all: hypocrisy as precise and imprecise approximation. After an admiring description of the Persian education system and its ideals (courage, justice, sincerity, fairness, lack of cunning and calculation, simplicity in deeds and in speech), he unfolds the tale of the very young Cyrus, about to go to war to help Astyarte of Media. Cyrus's father, Cambyses, is inevitably worried for his safety and accompanies him as far as the border, taking advantage of the trip to administer the truly important teaching a king is to give his successor. In war, he tells Cyrus, fairness, courage and personal value are not the only thing you need to practise. You also have to trick and con.

Strategy and the fight itself, like the management of a kingdom, are in fact a clash of reciprocal cunning and deception. An ambush is a typical case, battle tactics another. You must outsmart your enemy. Cyrus's vehement reaction is expected: why then has he been taught to be always straightforward, just, honest and brave? Cambyses's answer is logically perfect. He reminds his son that hunting has also been a fundamental part of his education, killing animals both with weapons and by laying traps. Is this fair and honest and brave? Of course not. A rabbit in a trap and a lion killed by sword and spear have been deceived into accepting an uneven struggle they have no chance of ever winning. The moral value of bravery and straightforwardness miserably evaporates before the injustice that is built into reality. From whichever end you look at it, this is a statement on the inevitability of hypocrisy and an acknowledgement of the artificial nature of ethics.

There is no way to reconcile nature and society in human understanding in Xenophon, just as there is not in our modern times. Society can only work if it imagines itself isolated – and protected – from nature. This does not prevent its individuals' forays into the exploitation of nature by hunting or agriculture, nor does it prevent nature being named among the things you can explain and interact with, as if they were society. The words and speech around that have only one purpose: as they cannot grasp and describe the actual categories of the object of study, they approximate them grossly enough to allow discussion, while simultaneously striving for precision in identifying the item. What is hunting? Deception, unfairness, injustice and hypocrisy, if inserted in an upbringing aimed at justice and honesty, or just a case of the inevitability of organized society's strength?

Like Cyrus, when you accept the categories society creates, you must accept their inbuilt ambiguity. Whereas Xenophon's Cyrus makes the most of his father's teaching by looking Persian in simplicity of life and straightforwardness, while deceiving friends and foes, Marxist political economists have kept the illusion, indeed the deception, of their revolutionary goal, while contributing to capitalist discourse. This is the framework in which we must read the unreasonable past polemics on the anti-Hegelian Marx already referred to repeatedly. Despite the simple truth that, if capitalism is dialectical, class struggle must not be dialectical if it is not to preserve capitalism (Micocci, 2002, 2008/2010, 2012a), for it would not be a tool for revolution, Marxists have kept denying the so-called anti-Hegelian Marx.

The latest twist of this constant attempt to deny radical thought and revolution and keep the Engels–Lenin Hegelian apparatus is the attempt to deny the division between a young, directly anti-Hegelian Marx and a late Marx who is simply not Hegelian. We have sought here to go beyond this whole debate by referring throughout to just the anarchist (sometimes anti-Hegelian, sometimes non-Hegelian) Marx. The old debate limited Marx's anti-Hegelianism to his youthful period (as proposed in Della Volpe, 1945, 1949, 1963, 1967, 1978, 1980; Colletti, 1969a, 1969b, 1972, 1973, 1974, 1975, 1979; Rosenthal, 1998; for the background to the present discussion, see Micocci, 2002, 2008/2010, 2012a). But, all of a sudden, to present-day Marxists, the young Marx appears as a Hegelian thinker, whereas the late Marx appears to be a writer far away from Hegel (Balakrishnan, 2014, 2015, is the typical *New Left Review* endorsement of a newly established fashion).

The aim of such a move is clear. It is to rescue the Marxist Leninist apparatus by inverting the debate. The late Marx, with his Engels-corrected technicalities, is branded as non-Hegelian, whereas the fact of the anti-Hegelian young Marx is denied, against all evidence, in order to connect it to Engels's corrected technicalities. The result is the same as always: the categories of bourgeois economics are rescued and left within the intellectual framework whence they come. In this situation, they can be operated on by those like Cyrus, pretending to be Persian-educated while, in fact, employing the strategies of those they are engaged with, with their corrupted customs in war, politics and at home. The important thing is to keep chance in chains.

It follows that markets, entrepreneurs, rates of exchange and any other economic category that mainstream economics takes as beneficial to the economy, provided you do not bother about the definition and the theory–reality correspondence, are now malevolent. The market is the cause of all evils, and you can call it what you want (the invisible hand, capitalism, capitalist competition, the law of value, the struggle for profit, and so on). You can add tables and graphs, but nobody is bound to bother if you use (as we have argued everybody does) a vague definition, for technical readers concentrate on your tables, as do politically engaged readers, as they only want to know the quantity of injustice meted out. All of them want to know, in fact, which little cause they can fight for or against without rocking the boat, or, in the best of cases, whether they can save a soul instead of destroying the system that damns them all.

To the rescue of both the Marxists and the mainstream comes the question – which, like all questions in economic thinking, is typically ambiguous (is it empirical or theoretical?) – of whether capitalism can ever complete its development. If it could, then a type of Marxist socialist revolution might even come about. But, to everybody's relief, this appears to the capitalist mind well beyond 'practical' lengths of time. Capitalism, in fact, would seem at the end of its development to be the equalization of profit rates in all sectors, for capital will have exploited all avenues for its profitable reproduction. Another way to put it is that, if perfect competition were ever achieved, the result would be that there would be no way to keep those high profits that keep firms operating.[16] At this point, at the equilibrium, there would be a static situation that is impossible to solve if all rates of profit are equal. Finally, there is the problem of the exhaustion of natural resources, which is not new, for it was proposed by John Stuart Mill (1998). See also Micocci (2015).

The only way for capitalism to avoid the inevitable 'stationary state' is to keep developing asymptotically, approaching its completion but forever lacking that final piece; once more, the language of calculus is perfect for the task of describing capitalism. This keeps both the supporters and the opponents happy in the comforting certainty that their work will never see a radical end. Additionally, this certainty gives powerful help to the effort to isolate capitalism from nature, the material in general. In fact, it has a distinctive dialectical flavour of the Hegelian kind, which theory-wise pleases the Marxists as well as the mainstream (see e.g. Barkley Rosser, 1999, 2000), and in practice pleases everybody else, who can go on as if economic and political life were iterative (with conflicts looking catastrophic but always ending in a vulgar Hegelian compromise; see Micocci, 2012a). Even Mill's moderate dream (1998) that the stationary state could end the reciprocal market violence of capitalism is a pious illusion.

Globalization is to no avail, for even international trade seems to point to an inglorious end in a stationary state: 'countries have become less specialized in the export of particular products, and therefore more similar in terms of their export competition. Comparative advantage, or international differences in relative efficiencies among products, has become weaker over time in many countries' (World Trade Report, 2013).[17] This is perfectly suited to the tragicomic language of capitalism as we know it, which sees catastrophe looming behind every corner while heading towards the next lack of events. Thus, everybody is frantically working at reversing this international trend, on the small scale with the 'glocal' fashion, or on a large scale with new wars and conflicts and economic impositions that destroy some productive areas, putting the problem of the stationary state off to the next day.

But is what we have been describing a theoretical or empirical point? Each of the arguments concerning the stationary state is theoretical when we display it at first, but cannot remain standing as such, and must be supported by empirical reference, direct or indirect. The terms that are used tend to be those that make this problem less intelligible. Capital running to its most profitable uses, for instance, is a powerfully evocative image for everybody, but what does it mean in practice? Which capital, which capitalist? Do we ever check whether this is so? No need to do it, of course, because reality is far too complex (in its iterative working) to allow for unanimity in the judgement of results when the object is so vague, and yet tables and figures can be produced. When things, on rare occasions, look straightforward, problems with mathematics and statistics are invoked to keep the final judgement 'controversial'. Economists are proud of this last feature, which to their distorted mind signifies 'pluralism'.

In other words, to economists, a market is a market is a market. However long the merry-go-round of the various meanings attached to it has been going on, at the end, you are back with the same vagueness as at the starting point, for precise meanings are confined to erudite academic literature, and precise practical actions and uses are too hard to pin down. A cost can be a mathematical derivative, an average or, more likely, an accounting item, and yet, at the next spin of the merry-go-round, everything goes on again, iteratively, yielding another combination of the same items. You do not need a precise language to operate in such environment, on the contrary, but there is plenty of room for ethics.

This last factor in fact is, as pointed out by Hume, artificial in the same way as economics is and, as a consequence, is both compatible with and complementary to it (or Marxism). Its definitions and uses are as unreachable as those of economic ideas, and are implicit in them, as in the mainstream, or explicit, as in justice-seeking Marxism. A third option, the fascist one, sees justice as juxtaposed with economics and politics (Micocci, 2012a). The overall ambiguity allows for a wide variety of usages of ethics, which in times of crisis is brandished like a sword to threaten this or that economic idea. The whole exercise is useless for the many reasons we have been reviewing thus far, but it nonetheless takes place, owing to the evocative power of capitalist language and speech. It serves as a safety valve for sublimating (metaphysically shared) emotions.

The only way to define all this is by the concept introduced in the earlier chapters of a social inertia that holds capitalism together, the modern with the ancient, the theoretical with the 'practical'/empirical, the just with the unjust, catastrophe with positive work at stability, just to mention the common questions we are presented with in capitalism as we know it. The social inertia, or, in other words, the asymptotic tendency of capitalism towards its own realization, is a rational thing, a part and a consequence of its general metaphysics. It is but a vulgar version of the Hegelism that imbibes of itself capitalism as we know it, but it is fundamental because it performs that work of triple Marxian alienation to which we have been referring throughout.

Repressing and perverting human natural emotions in fact helps preserve the need for (capitalist) talk. Anything that cannot be expressed in speech is 'imprac-tical', and whatever sentiment and emotion or impression we get is transcended in speech through the logic and maieutics of capitalism as we know it. Lovers describe their love (which means that it lacks that pure bliss of madness that erotic passion provokes, as Smith mentions in *The Theory of Moral Sentiments*, 2009), and sick people their sufferings with the same tools as they describe their worsening/recovery (in the words and the deeds and the proofs of the medical tests, which are very much like the data of economics). Open passions are relegated to the realm of the impossible and go unrecognized when they take place. The worker and their family always complain, the rich person and their family vent their artificial feelings to the benefit of the lower classes, as Smith notices in his description of the invisible hand. The media multiply it all, although it would spread even without their help.

This last aspect has been well understood, and used in practice, by the fascist and Christian movements. To them, there are local homogeneities that give rise to a shared cultural bedrock that constitutes a communitarian link. This supposed unanimity makes the enforcement of what already exists (capitalist intellectual and emotional homogeneity) both easy in practice at the beginning and an exciting col-lective task all the way through. There is no conceptual difference from capitalism in general, except for a totalitarianism that is well known in mainstream economic theory: Arrow's impossibility theorem (Arrow, 1951). Predictably enough, fascism is not incompatible even with mainstream economics (Micocci, 2012a).

The fact that capitalism harbours its fascist continuation should come as no surprise. First, fascism is a possible solution to the need never to fully develop in a market direction. Second, fascism is built into the intimacy between capitalist ideas (in favour and against) and (social) ethics. Third, it is the only existing argument available to justify the idea of community. True liberals and Marxists should have fought this as hard as possible, whereas, instead, they have gone along with it. Fourth, it helps tame and channel the distorted and perverted emotions that are produced by capitalist triple alienation in the right social, political and economic direction. Fifth, it supplies a language that is logically similar to capitalist language, but even more evocative (Cassirer, 1961), making a continuous, bland Aristotelian catharsis possible and thus helping stability and governance.

A world marred by an ongoing social inertia that blocks its historical evolution cannot, however, remain blocked for long. Before nature, with its non-predictability, makes itself felt in a catastrophic way with a rupture with oblivion, the inner forces of the system tend to exceed the boundaries imposed on them. Capitalist metaphysics bases itself on money, without which no transaction would take place. Money has the most perfect metaphysical features, for it is independent from both the intricacies of the theories about it and the material world. As well argued by Rosenthal (1998; see also Micocci, 2011a, 2011b, 2014b; Di Mario and Micocci, 2015), its Hegelian features make it the most central of capitalist items: both an economic object and a political and social glue. By recognizing money, you acknowledge your belonging to the system (your triple Marxian alienation, we have said over and over again in this book). But money, in the form of finance, has exceeded all boundaries of capitalism as we know it.

If we think of money as capital, we cannot help noticing its independence from the will of men, states and theories. Also, to the chagrin of justice-seeking Marxists, money is independent from anything material, including the extraction of surplus value from labour (see also Mann, 2011). As long as this last is forthcoming at a good rate, capitalism can use it, such as during the Industrial Revolution or in the age of mass consumption. But the multiplication of capital[18] is much more rewarding when left to itself, i.e. to what Marx would call the M–M' (with M' > M) circuit. Here lies the next, and only, dynamic frontier of capitalism as we know it. Shut in the darkness of your office or home, sitting at a computer, you complete your alienation from yourself, your fellow humans and nature by making millions you will never be able to spend.

We can explain this starting from Marx's *Capital*, which also allows us to keep defending our anarchist Marx. As is well known, there are terrible differences between the three volumes of *Capital*. The first was directly published by Marx, whereas the second and the third were revised, and published, by that Hegelian character Engels. In his Preface to *Capital*, Volume 3 (1978), Engels confesses his difficulties in accomplishing his task. In fact, the volume is uneven, unlike Volume 2, but is also much more original. Let us see.

Volume 1 (1978) shows that Marx has a clear project: explaining capitalism as an enormous circulation of money, in which capital and greed are the historical servants of the concept of value. That cannot be argued without the strong presence of the triple Marxian alienation. The extraction of surplus value from labour is much more important here than in Volume 3, despite Engels's hands on the latter. In Volume 1, Marx's limit is that he sees finance (M–M') as a sort of Mercantilist operation, despite being very clear about value, greed and circulation.

Volume 2 is the least interesting for our purposes, although it does contain some important definitions. The volume tends to concentrate on accumulation by exploitation, with numerical examples. Yet, capital is described in it as being periodically hoarded in the form of money to feed the process of production. It is finance as imagined by the bourgeois writers, ancillary to material production, but Volume 3 changes this.

In Volume 3, in fact, we find the main characters we need to explain the present-day preponderance and independence of finance: independent, interest-bearing capital, the banker, the swindler. The first has not always existed, but has taken its modern role with capitalism. Capital leaves the hands of private individuals to become a social thing; a sort of *ante litteram* socialism is formed, with injustice at its base and managers in charge of true dictatorships over capital. Money comes from commercial capital, which is in fact credit capital, for commercial trips historically produced this expedient. The common aspect of its variety is its international nature. The whole argument, however, is necessarily inconclusive and unresolved. We will, therefore, depart from it to finish our story.

Let us start from an observation in Volume 2 that brings us close to the argument developed here:

> [We need to go on] a different method of investigation. Hitherto one has been satisfied with uttering phrases which upon close analysis are found to contain nothing but indefinite ideas borrowed from the intertwining of metamorphoses common to all commodity circulation.
>
> (Marx, 1978, Vol. 2, p. 118)

In this spirit we go on.

In a recent book, Lotz (2014) has the intuition of something similar to what we have been developing here. Money is a true Universal in the Hegelian sense. It unifies people and annihilates time, transforming capitalism into an endless present, and the monetization of life becomes the true centre of capitalist human understanding. Unfortunately, like most Marxists, he does not see the thoroughly anti-Hegelian nature of his own correct and very Marxian reasoning. Feuerbach's hypostatization critique that is at the origin of Marx's historical (materialistic) method (Micocci, 2002) is perfectly – and surprisingly, given the brilliant intuition Lotz has – absent. Thus, he has to resort to Adorno (whom he corrects in important points) and to Heidegger's explanation of Kant's schemes of the mind and time. The metaphysics of capitalism has been rescued again.

Lotz, as a consequence, mistakes metaphysics for abstraction. His Heideggerian Kantian man has a mind schema (very much similar, despite its hopeless limitation, to what we have called here and in Micocci, 2008/2010, prolepsis) and can only see the social importance of money. As a consequence, for lack of a solid theoretical argument, Lotz has to resort to quotations from Marx isolated from their non- or anti-Hegelian context, and to touching examples from reality, i.e. that conventional reality he cannot justify, which coincides with what is reported by capitalist intellectuality with capitalist words and maieutics. Inevitably, the moral tone is there, as if we needed moral arguments to feel pity for our fellow human beings; we do, in his book as we do in capitalism, because we are triply alienated.

The result is, despite the brilliant intuition at its base, yet another cosy fiction of reality. Such is the price, which is strongly reiterated in the conclusions, of his non-abandonment of the dialectics. Lotz's capitalism can only be criticized for its defects, not for what it is. In his capitalism, which is but a wider version of Adorno's 'culture industry', even affects are – not surprisingly – monetized, and inevitably language too. To Lotz, 'social theory as philosophical theory can only be preserved in dialectics, since otherwise the categorical structure of what we call "society" gets reduced either to social anthropology or mental constructivism' (Lotz, 2014, p. 156). Hopefully, our reasoning so far should have proved the very opposite.

We can now turn to see Marx's conception of finance capital in more detail. That will help us further our general reasoning and introduce, in the conclusions, a society-based hypothesis of evil, or at least of social evils.

4.5 Materialistic political economy

We cannot draw the contours of a materialistic political economy in the sense we have been seeking to pursue here if we do not properly understand the essence of money. Lotz (2014) mentions several times the expression that money 'is nothing'. This, of course, seems to point to a clear meaning in the mentality of capitalism. In another typically capitalist lack of logical rigour, the expression in fact indicates a paradox: money is nothing because it is everything. This paradox identifies value, empirically determining prices,[19] which include wages.

We, in turn, do not understand finance and its present-day preponderance if we do not understand this typical character of money and of capitalism itself, which has acquired its maturity with the coming of present-day capitalism. Here, Marx can be a useful initial guide. Commercial money, credit capital and the absurdity of the interest rate have transformed the 'commercial man' into Marx's own 'capitalist', and eventually into the present possessor of financial rent.

We can proceed, as banally as possible, moving from *Capital*, Volume 1, to Volumes 2 and 3. Marx starts by asserting, in Chapter III, Section I, that, 'it is not money that renders commodities commensurable' (1978, p. 97), but, on the contrary, it is the fact that all commodities are realized human labour (ibid.). This might appear like a powerful limitation: only commodities produce value by their 'immanent' (ibid.) labour time. But circulation, in Marx and in capitalism, is a much more complex thing. Capitalism does not contain commodities only; it is worth reminding the reader here that the mistaken view that commodities are the basis of capitalist economies is shared implicitly by the mainstream and explicitly by the Marxists. It is not necessarily in Marx, as we shall endeavour to show in what follows.

In the same chapter, Marx crucially notices that commodities are not sold:

> for the purposes of buying others, but in order to replace their commodity form by their money form. [. . .] This change of form becomes the end and aim. [. . .] Money becomes petrified into a hoard, and the seller becomes a hoarder of money.
>
> (p. 131)

Circulation (p. 132) is the name of the game that transforms everything into money/gold, for 'the desire of hoarding is in its very nature insatiable' (p. 133). The hoarder is a Sysiphus-like labourer (ibid.). But, 'While hoarding, as a distinct mode of acquiring riches, vanishes with the progress of civil society, the formation of reserves of the means of payments grows with that progress' (p. 141).

'The functions of hoards, therefore, arise in part out of the function of money [. . .] [home circulation and home payments], and in part out of its function of money of the world' (p. 143). In fact, Chapter IV (Part II) starts by unequivocally saying, 'The circulation of commodities is the starting point of capital' (p. 145). Marx goes on by saying that, 'The circulation of money as capital is [. . .] an end in itself, for the expansion of value takes place only within this constantly renewed movement. The circulation of capital has therefore no limits' (p. 150). The capitalist, the 'possessor of money', aims at 'profit-making alone' (p. 151), which is a 'never-ending process'. This is decisive.

In fact, 'value is the active factor in a process', and commodities are its 'disguised mode' (p. 152). 'The capitalist knows that all commodities [. . .] [are] a wonderful means whereby out of money to make more money' (ibid.). Hence, the circulation of capital 'suddenly presents itself as an independent substance', independent from money and commodities alike (pp. 159–63); value becomes 'capital', value in process, money in process. The circulation can, as described by the Mercantilists, reduce itself to 'money that begets money'.

> In the case of interest-bearing capital, the circulation M–C–M' appears abridged. We have its results without the intermediate stage, in the form M–M', *'en style lapidaire'* so to say, money that is worth more money, value that is greater than itself.
>
> (p. 153)

It follows that M–C–M' is 'the general formula of capital as it appears prima facie within the sphere of circulation'.

There is, of course, no need to emphasize the importance of that 'prima facie'. Chapter V concludes by admitting that merchants' capital and interest-bearing capital were well known since Aristotle and beyond. But they were not modern enough. The point in capitalism, in its industrial phase (p. 163), is that value mainly originates from the labour immanent in the commodities. But capital as such is there, waiting for its chance to free itself from this cumbersome connection with material reality. Let capitalism run its course.

We witness in this first volume an ambivalent situation for capital. It oscillates between a producer of surplus value through the labour embodied (immanent) in manufactured goods and a creator of a multiplication of itself. This last requires, in order to display its full potential, an advanced capitalism. It requires an interest rate, i.e. a usury price that is not usury. To get that, it must evoke the idea of a productive use, of a role related to manufacture. This engenders the well-known mistakes of the mainstream, and mainstream Marxist, economists. Let us go on with Marx.

As mentioned several times, Volume 2 is the place where Engels's Hegelian vocation can be witnessed at its most thorough. Nonetheless, the merely technical subjects of the volume leave a couple of important points for us to progress. Let us start from Part I, Chapter IV. Here, Marx is unequivocal. After explaining 'the movements of capital' (p. 108) as the interaction of the various actors including the 'owner of productive capital' (a different person from the one who buys labour and commodities), he discusses the 'circuit', which produces sudden 'revolutions in value' (p. 109):

> The more does the automatic movement of the now independent value operate with the elemental force of a natural process, against the foresight and calculations of the individual capitalist, the more does the course of normal production become subservient to abnormal speculation. [. . .] These periodical revolutions in value therefore corroborate what they are supposed to refute, namely, that value as capital acquires independent existence, which it maintains and accentuates through its movement.
>
> (p. 109)

He continues, in contradiction to Samuel Bailey, saying that value functions as capital-value or capital, determining value, only insofar as these remain 'identical' to themselves. Marx's reasoning coherently develops towards the inevitable, i.e. the necessity of 'monopoly or big-money capitalists, who may operate singly or in association' (p. 110). Capital is starting to acquire its preponderant, present-day form, independent from the exploitation of the working class[20] because it is independent from material production. In fact, on pages 119–20, Marx warns us that seeing capitalism as a 'social character of production' rather than a 'mode of exchange' is a mistake quite in keeping with the bourgeois horizon.

Part III, Chapter XVIII, as a consequence, points out that, 'productive capital, money-capital, and commodity capital [. . .] [as different portions of the total capital value] are constantly side by side and function in these different states' (p. 357). The metamorphoses of capital become more and more complicated. The time needs of material production depend mainly upon their material nature rather than the working period; thus, the 'magnitude of money-capital' at the disposal of the individual capitalist matters. 'This barrier is broken down by the credit system and the associations connected with it, e.g., the stock companies' (p. 361). Disturbances in the money market, therefore, matter very much (p. 362).

We have, by now, all the elements we need. Let us see some more particulars in order to appreciate Marx the anarchist's foresight and the time that has been wasted denying it[21] in its straightforward simplicity. Part IV of Volume 3, which Engels (p. 4) himself admitted to have taken trouble to amend to a complete, fully developed form (especially Part V), starts by discussing commercial capital, which 'is now the exclusive operation of a special kind of capitalist, the merchant' (p. 270), 'capital functioning in the sphere of circulation' (p. 278), surplus value realized in the sale of commodities. Chapter XVII continues this discussion, which is interesting because one cannot understand the metamorphoses of capital without accepting its metaphysical nature.[22]

Chapter XVIII tells us (p. 311) that, with the growth of the capitalist mode of production, merchants' capital has the ease of 'entering retail trade, speculation, and the redundance of released capital'. Chapter XIX delivers us, finally, to finance. Here money-dealing capital, which is a portion of industrial capital in money form operating specific technical functions (p. 315), is introduced. Its movements can be resolved in C–M and M–C, but is 'carried out by a special section of agents, or capitalists, for the rest of the capitalist class' (p. 316). Some capital must in other words be kept on board all the time, entrusted to a special type of capitalist, and this becomes an 'international commerce' (p. 316). Marx separates it from credit capital, but points out that even here the M–M' movement occurs.

The discussion spills over to Part V, in which the 'money begets money' concept is furthered (p. 345), for the money advanced comes back with a surplus-value. At this point, we need the presence of an interest rate, i.e. of a purely metaphysical item that does not exist as a 'natural' object. What is meant by 'natural rate of interest' is, Marx tells us (p. 356), 'the rate fixed by free competition', but there are no 'natural' limits to the rate of interest (ibid.). It can become 'arbitrary and lawless'. Interest (ch. XXIII) flows to the money-capitalist. Interest and profit of enterprise are 'determined by separate laws' (p. 375), but, in the preceding chapter, Marx had warned us that, 'the development of large-scale industry money-capital [. . .] is not represented by some individual capitalist [. . .] but assumes the nature of a concentrated, organized mass [. . .] subject to the control of the bankers, i.e., the representatives of social capital'.

An interest is an independent form of surplus-value (p. 377) yielded by capital as such, out of the production process. 'If all capital were in the hands of the industrial capitalists there would be no such thing as interest and rate of interest' (ibid.). So, a capitalist can expand the value of its capital by 'lending it out as interest-bearing capital' or by using it as 'productive capital' (ibid.). Of course, to think that all capitals can be converted in the first form is 'preposterous'. But 'productive capital' is the antagonist of such capital, just as wage labour is the antagonist of productive capital (p. 379). Interest-bearing capital is 'capital as property' (p. 379) rather than capital 'as function'. It therefore, we add, generates rent.

Chapter XXIV reminds us that all this means the straight M–M' movement. But Marx is explicit: money becomes capital, and this last appears as a mere thing (p. 392). 'The social relation is consummated in the relation of a thing, of money, to itself' (ibid.). We only see 'form without content' (ibid.). 'The actually functioning capital [. . .] presents itself in such a light, that it seems to yield interest not as a functioning capital, but as capital in itself, as money-capital' (ibid.). This worsens to fetish capital. 'As the growing process is to trees, so generating money (τόκος) appears innate in capital in its form of money-capital'.

In capitalism as we know it, with its metaphysics, this is all we need to understand the coming preponderance of finance as the most natural form (in the sense of being the most metaphysical form) of increasing the value of capital, especially when compared with material production. This last is tainted and marred by its relationship with nature and its, at least potential, relative unpredictability. Not so with money, the metaphysical features of which can be used by the triply alienated capitalist man, and understood after they have been gained. The game, to use Hume's words, becomes entirely predictable. We have overcome the natural limits of nature and chained chance. We remain with the need to shelter, feed and cloth ourselves, but what could come more à propos than that? Precisely this need feeds the illusion of the finance–material production relationship, at least in the evocative language of capitalism as we know it.

The idea of capital as fetish, reiterated by Marx, for instance on page 399, in a polemic with the Economist, is only a simple rhetorical polemical tool. Remaining in Part V, to the chagrin of Engels and of many Marxists, we come, with Chapter XXVII, to the importance of stock companies, which to Marx transform property from private to 'social' (p. 437): 'the property of associated producers', who socialize the capitalist function. In other words, capitalism spreads to a socialized set of functions anybody can get in touch with and even belong to, and above all which everybody must end up understanding in their complication simply to survive in capitalism as we know it.

> This is the abolition of the capitalist mode of production within the capitalist mode of production itself. [. . .] It establishes a monopoly in certain spheres and thereby requires state interference. It reproduces a new financial aristocracy, a new variety of parasites in the shape of promoters, speculators and simply nominal directors; a whole system of swindling and cheating by means of corporation promotion, stock issuance, and stock speculation. It is private production without the control of private property.
>
> (p. 438)[23]

Capital creates the superstructure of credit, and social property is risked by the speculator, as we all know since 2008. 'Success and failure both lead here to a centralization of capital, and thus to expropriation on the most enormous scale. [. . .] Its accomplishment is the goal of this production' (p. 439).

Marx goes on with the role of 'gambling on the stock exchange' (p. 440). It is interesting to point out (Part V again!) that (Chapter XXXII), 'the banker

[. . .] [by receiving and lending the money] appears in the role of a supreme benefactor' (p. 506).

> With the growth of material wealth the class of money-capitalists grows; on the one hand, the number and wealth of retiring capitalists, rentiers, increases; and on the other hand, the development of the credit system is promoted, thereby increasing the number of bankers, money-lenders, financiers.
>
> (p. 510)

Our discussion of Part V runs towards the end with the warning (Chapter XXXIII) that bankers, financers and stock-jobbers are 'bandits', exploiting national and world production (p. 545). This is reiterated on page 571, for instance.

> The monetary system is essentially a Catholic institution, the credit system essentially Protestant. [. . .] It is *faith* that brings salvation. [. . .] But the credit system does not emancipate itself from the basis of the monetary system anymore than Protestantism has emancipated itself from the foundations of Catholicism.
>
> (p. 592; emphasis in the original)

Modern crises make the money-capitalist and the usurer emerge (p. 599). Indeed (p. 600), the credit system is a development of usury, adapted to the capitalist system. 'The banking system is the most artificial and the most developed product turned out by the capitalist mode of production' (p. 606). If everything so far said holds, it is clear that here Marx means something very close to what we have been arguing so far. It is akin, for the meaning of 'artificial' in the quotation above, to Hume's sense when he discusses morality/ethics. Also, it is appropriate to conclude, to show the persistence of the anti-Hegelian Marx despite Engels (ah, how Part V must have troubled him!), that Marx goes back to his old critique of Saint Simon and Proudhon and the 'socialist' credit system (pp. 607–8): Hegelian (more precisely, bad Hegelian) absurdities. In fact, 'it is in the nature of things that interest-bearing capital assumes in popular conception the form of capital *par excellence*' (p. 609; emphasis in the original).

This whole discussion of Marx, however, cannot be taken as a conclusive proof. Volume 3 of *Capital* is particularly uneven, and Part V is simply inconclusive. It is not clear how far Marx understands the difference between ancient and modern credit systems, nor where, for him, this whole development will lead capitalism. In fact, he lacks knowledge of the modern base for the preponderance of finance: communication by computers. We can only say that in it we find more proof of the need for a materialistic political economy that studies the metaphysics of capitalism, i.e. not its material nature, but its immaterial, intellectual confusion with its language and maieutics. History is fundamental to this purpose, as we will see in the next chapter.

However, if this is so, then we can use political economy only as a tool for emancipation, from capitalism in particular. The problem of how we know that we have at last gained a firm grasp of the material in fact remains. But this is not a political economy problem. If everything that has been developed so far in the book holds, political economy is a tool for emancipation. It cannot be a positive tool for managing life, social or asocial. It is the abolition of political economy of all kinds, mainstream as well as materialist, that is the object of materialistic political economy itself (Micocci, 2014a). A materialistic political economy is about metaphysics and is merely a destructive tool.

The present-day preponderance of finance is the most evident terrain on which the Hegelian efforts of the economic mainstream and of mainstream Marxism founder. The illusion that capitalism is about commodities, enhanced in Marxists by the theme of Chapter I of Volume I of *Capital*, is dispelled. We need to understand the metaphysics of capitalism as we know it. The production of commodities is only another historically transient form of the irrational way humankind operates for its material survival in a societal context. In a vicious circle, it needs political economy. This is an evident case of a sublimated, artificial ethics à la Hume.

Let us summarize: if money as capital (i.e. value), as Lotz (2014) also agrees, is the centre and indeed the essence of capitalist activity, then Adam Smith's invisible hand is safe. The 'commercial man' can entrust his wish for happiness to money, and his pretence and representation of the sentiments entailed to words and language. He will be triply alienated all the time, but he will pile up money as capital, or wish he did and, hence, keep working in, and buying into, the metaphysics of capitalism, lest his dreams be shattered. It is true enough that, in this framework, those who have 'nothing to lose but their chains' could be the subversive (but not the revolutionary) subject. It is as true as the fact that such paupers exist.

In other words, capitalism's invisible hand is founded on injustice, even more so the more finance gains independence and preponderance. Even if that were not true, as Smith hopes to be the case, there remains the need to accept the triple Marxian alienation in order to understand and participate in the system, as this is based on the flawed metaphysics that requires such triple alienation to exist and to act. Whether man is naturally good, as Hume and Rousseau propose, or is not, the fact is that there are two orders of evils in capitalism: practical injustice, which engenders the need for further violence and injustice to be corrected, and alienation, which keeps the horrific game of violence and injustice alive.

4.6 Conclusions

Economic discourse in the form of an 'artificial' ethics (meant as a set of human behaviours that are needed for social life and civilization) disciplines capitalism. As a consequence, in a world in which profit (in the form of M–M', whatever is between the two in practice) is the cause of wealth, finance only can grant the fast-track means to happiness. Happiness itself is completely artificial and, in a circular way, it originates in those concepts, words, speech and maieutics of which mainstream economics – and, unfortunately, most mainstream Marxism and heterodox economics – are the best and most sublime interpreters. This grants the survival of the invisible hand of Adam Smith, a world of injustice, illusions, deceptions and rent-based upper classes that is coming to its glorious explosion with neo-liberal ideas and the present crisis.

In capitalism as we know it, human beings (and all other natural objects) do the things that come naturally to them without the need to do so. The alienated capitalist individual bases him/herself on the metaphysics, the general intellectual discourse, but this last is fiction. It is the outcome of the long-lasting effect of the mediating, dialectical mind that fears ruptures-with-oblivion, well interpreted by Hegel (and, on the left, by Lenin, Gramsci and Che Guevara). The capitalist individual is exactly like de Cervantes's Don Quixote (de Cervantes, 2013): an alienated fool who believes and has made his own his age's fiction, and goes on to enact it.

As in Don Quixote, even madness needs to be faked, intellectually built out of a model. In Chapter XXV (vol. 1), when Don Quixote decides it is time to go mad about love like every '*caballero andante*', he sends Sancho Panza to communicate his madness to Dulcinea. After making sure that Sancho can find him when he comes back, he is asked by Sancho to do what he had proposed himself earlier on: to give proof of his crazy deeds.

> *Y desmudàndose con toda priesa los calzones, quedò en carnes y en pañales, y luego, sin mas ni mas, dio dos zapotetos en el aire y dos tumbas la cabeza abajo y los pies en alto, descubriendo cosas que, por no verlas otra vez, volviò Sancho la rienda a Rocinante, y se diò por contento y satisfecho de que podrìa jurar que su amo quedaba loco.*
>
> (2013, p. 360)

Everything in capitalism, as for Don Quixote, is perfunctory and alienated: not even madness needs to be natural, nor belief in it. Davis (2006) should not marvel at what urban copy show is set up in Dubai.

It is reasonable to suppose then that, although we shall likely never know whether human nature is evil or good, the source of evil lies in social behaviour: the very intellectual alienation of all deeds and feelings we perform makes injustice, maiming, killing and prepotence artificial, easy-to-tell deeds. They can be explained, and thereby justified. For instance, left-wingers can thus demonstrate for peace while displaying images of the militaristic Che Guevara, or condemn the international oppression of Cuba while backing its domestic oppression by the Castro family. As with de Cervantes's book, a second volume (and then, in practice, another, and another) must be written, because fake second volumes are coming out, just like in the fiction itself, in which Don Quixote discovers his deeds are fairly famous and is not amazed by it.

The core of the question is that, if the categories of the metaphysics of capitalism are accepted, then the mainstream economists are right,[24] as argued in the present chapter. We have to emancipate ourselves from economic categories by emancipating ourselves from the flawed metaphysics of capitalism. This is an intellectual task that requires no organization and no violence. It only takes the courage of accepting the liberation of chance.

Some might want to remark that these are eighteenth-century issues. Sadly, no twentieth-century author has produced such clear and radical thinking, which is the reason we had to resort to older works. This goes towards proving that the present argument about the intellectual poverty of capitalism is correct. If capitalism is the way we have described, it prevents radical novelties, or hides them when and if they appear. Only 'practical' things are allowed. In the next chapter, we will discuss a historical materialistic political economy – silence – from a non-practical (in the capitalist sense) point of view.

Notes

1 Some of the arguments in this section have been previously discussed in Micocci (2014a, 2014b). This is a fresh re-elaboration, enlargement and evolution of those arguments.
2 We should not forget, in considering these problems, the undeniable influence of Epictetus, who is cited and discussed in Hume (2009). But we had announced this.
3 Kayatekin (2014) uses the role of passions in Hume to explain his difference from Hobbes, natural law, rationalism. Such discussion does not matter much to our discourse here, as we will soon see.
4 Guyer (2011) makes much of passions in Hume, and also infers a similarity with Kant. But, as we will see next, his reasoning is geared to morality, which makes it inappropriate for Hume.
5 This is a salutary warning when connecting evil with society, which we will soon do.
6 See, for instance, apart from his Treatise on Probability, Chapter 12 of his *General Theory* (Keynes, 1983). This is not meant to endorse in any way the argument for a Humean Keynes. Carabelli (1988), Chick and Dow (2001) and Dow and Hillard (1995) misunderstand common-sense philosophy (in Hume's time, common-sense philosophers were very much against him).
7 Meeker (2013) also notices the radical scepticism of Hume.
8 Some might object that this section omits the discussion of the so-called New Hume Interpretation (see e.g. Wright, 1983; Strawson, 1989; Read and Richman, 2000). The reasons will be obvious from the following argument. What we do here is too peculiar to be referred to that kind of literature.
9 Who, however, is guilty of saying precious few things on this fundamental issue.
10 In the light of what has been said above, we can confine the consideration of Hume (2006) to this footnote. This work discusses natural religion in order to attack pragmatism and all approaches that over-rely on words. In Part 1, the sceptical arguments are shown to be defeated by the need to conform, and, in Part 2, the difference between a single case and a general homogeneity is stated. Parts 3 and 4 are on the senses and have a critique of religion similar to Feuerbach's hypostatization critique. Parts 5 and 6 discuss the role of the mind and of ruptures, without deepening such issues. Part 9 insists on the absurdity of a priori metaphysics and mathematics, repeating what has already been covered in the present section. Part 11 shows the weakness of the Christian God, and Part 12 comes back to analogy. Being a dialogue, quotations from this work are difficult to obtain.
11 Please note the 'useful'.
12 I gained more confidence in the present argument after hearing Gennaro Sasso at a seminar in Rome in January 2015. Of course, he is not responsible for anything I say here. Thanks are due to the Scuola Romana of the Istituto Italiano di Studi Filosofici, with the usual, emphatic, disclaimers.

13　Suddenly, as we are about to see, at least in the Anglo-Saxon literature, a new majority reading of Marx has been invented, erasing the past. The Young and Late Marx have been inverted into a youthful Hegelian and a mature non-Hegelian. Here, we stick to the reading in Micocci (2002, 2008/2010).

14　Or, alternatively, engender in the creator such a powerful pressure and solitude as to make him/her sick in the body and in the mind. Some of us even might have lived through such stories. The outcome is always the same: the result of the creative mind for the dominant metaphysics is equally un-understandable, or frustratingly not accepted (and completely erased), even in the rare cases when it is considered. As a compensation, its author, in case he/she can make him/herself conspicuous to the collective memory, is admired for his/her useless self-sacrifice.

15　See especially his pp. 51–2.

16　In fact, in practice (Micocci, 2008/2010), firms avoid competition, seeking a market niche or market predominance. Stiglitz (2013, p. 44) also comes to similar conclusions.

17　Online. Available at: www.wto.org/english/res_e/publications_e/wtr13_e.htm (accessed 25 February 2016).

18　This term is preferable to that of valorization, which is dependent on labour exploitation and cannot ever reach the rates of multiplication yielded by financial speculation.

19　And solving the absurd 'transformation problem', which is a mathematical conundrum that exists only in theory, whereas it is solved in practice all the time in reality (see Micocci, 2012b, for a more diffused explanation).

20　This, of course, remains, and is even enhanced, or the manufacturer will want to become a financial capitalist. That is why all types of government in the world gave in to the neo-liberal rolling back of the welfare state: they wanted to preserve their material production base, that is to say their GDP, growing. See Mann (2011).

21　See Micocci (2011a, 2011b, 2014b) and Di Mario and Micocci (2015). The Marxist literature is so vast and homogeneous that there is no point discussing it here.

22　Well explained in Rosenthal (1998).

23　We have left out of the quotation the parts concerning transition and contradiction, for they simply prove what is taken for granted here: capitalism is dialectical, and this is its problem, for Marx and for us.

24　Katzner (2015) is slowly coming to see the point, from a mainstream perspective.

References

Akerlof, G. A., and Shiller, R. J. (2009) *Animal Spirits*, Princeton University Press, Princeton, NJ.

Aristotle (1981) *The Politics*, Penguin, London.

Arrow, K. J. (1951) *Social Choice and Individual Values*, Yale University Press, New Haven, CT.

Balakrishnan, G. (2014) 'The Abolitionist – I', *New Left Review*, 90, 101–36.

Balakrishnan, G. (2015) 'The Abolitionist – II', *New Left Review*, 91, 69–100.

Barkley Rosser, J. (1999) 'On the complexities of complex economic dynamics', *Journal of Economic Perspectives*, 13, 4, 169–92.

Barkley Rosser, J. (2000) 'Aspects of dialectics and non-linear dynamics', *Cambridge Journal of Economics*, 24, 311–24.

Barzilai, J. (2013) 'Inapplicable operations on ordinal, cardinal and expected utility', *Real-World Economics Review*, 63, 98–117. Online. Available at: www.paecon.net/PAE Review/issue63/Barzilai63.pdf (accessed 25 February 2016).

Barzilai, J. (2014) 'Demand theory is founded on errors', *Real-World Economics Review*, 68, 62–5. Online. Available at: www.PAECON.NET/PAEReview/issue68/Barzilai68.pdf (accessed 25 February 2016).

Carabelli, A. (1988) *On Keynes's Method*, MacMillan, London.

Cassirer, E. (1961) *The Myth of the State*, Yale University Press, New Haven, CT.

Chick, V., and Dow, S. C. (2001) 'Formalism, logic and reality: A Keynesian analysis', *Cambridge Journal of Economics*, 25, 6, 705–21.

Colletti, L. (1969a) *Ideologia e Società [Ideology and Society]*, Laterza, Bari, Italy.

Colletti, L. (1969b) *Il Marxismo e Hegel [Marxism and Hegel]*, Laterza, Bari, Italy.

Colletti, L. (1972) *From Rousseau to Lenin*, NLB, London.

Colletti, L. (1973) *Marxism and Hegel*, NLB, London.

Colletti, L. (1974) 'A political and philosophical interview', *New Left Review*, 86, 34–52.

Colletti, L. (1975) 'Marxism and the dialectics', *New Left Review*, 93, 3–30.

Colletti, L. (1979) *Tra Marxismo e No [In between Marxism and Not]*, Laterza, Bari, Italy.

Cuoco, V. (1991) *Statistica della Repubblica Italiana [Statistics of the Italian Republic]*, Archivio Guido Izzi, Rome.

Davis, M. (2006) 'Fear and money in Dubai', *New Left Review*, 41, 47–68.

de Cervantes Saavedra, M. (2013) *El Ingenioso Hidalgo Don Quijote de la Mancha [The Ingenious Gentleman Don Quixote of la Mancha]*, Catedra, Madrid.

Della Volpe, G. (1945) *La Teoria Marxista dell'Emancipazione Umana, Saggio sulla Trasmutazione Marxista dei Valori [The Marxist Theory of Human Emancipation, Essay on the Marxist Transformation of Values]*, Ferrara, Messina, Italy.

Della Volpe, G. (1949) *Per la Teoria di un Umanesimo Positivo. Studi e Documenti sulla Dialettica Materialistica [For a Theory of a Positive Humanism. Studies and documents on materialistic dialectics]*, C.Zuffi Editore, Bologna, Italy.

Della Volpe, G. (1963) *La Libertà Comunista. Sulla Dialettica [Communist Liberty on Dialectics]*, Edizioni Avanti! Milan, Italy.

Della Volpe, G. (1967) *Critica dell'Ideologia Contemporanea [Critique of Contemporary Ideology]*, Editori Riuniti, Rome.

Della Volpe, G. (1978) *Rousseau and Marx*, Lawrence & Wishart, London.

Della Volpe, G. (1980) *Logic as a Positive Science*, NLB, London.

Di Mario, F., and Micocci, A. (2015) 'Smith's invisible hand. Controversy is needed', *ESHET Conference*, Rome, 15–18 May.

Dow, S. C., and Hillard, J. (eds) (1995) *Keynes, Knowledge and Uncertainty*, Elgar, Aldershot, UK.

Friedman, M. (1966) 'The methodology of positive economics', in *Essays in Positive Economics*, pp. 3–16, 30–43, University of Chicago Press, Chicago, IL.

Guyer, P. (2011) 'Passion for reason: Hume, Kant and the motivation for morality', Presidential Address, 108th Eastern Division Meeting, APA, in *Proceeding and Addresses*, 86, 2, 4–21.

Hume, D. (2006) *Dialogue Concerning Natural Religion*, Mineola, Dover Philosophical Classics, New York.

Hume, D. (2008) *An Enquiry Concerning Human Understanding*, Oxford University Press, Oxford, UK.

Hume, D. (2009) *An Enquiry Concerning the Principles of Morals/Ricerca sui Principi della Morale*, Laterza, Bari, Italy.

Hume, D. (2011) *A Treatise of Human Nature*, Clarendon Press, Oxford, UK.

Kahneman, D. (2011) *Thinking Fast and Slow*, Penguin, London.

Katzner, D. W. (2014) 'Ordinal utility and the traditional theory of consumer demand', *Real-World Economics Review*, 67, 130–6. Online. Available at: www.PAECON.NET/ PAEReview/issue67/Katzner67.pdf (accessed 25 February 2016).

Katzner, D. W. (2015) 'A neoclassical curmudgeon looks at heterodox criticisms of microeconomics', *World Economic Review*, 4, 63–75.

Kayatekin, A. (2014) 'The relationship of morality to political economy in Hume', *Cambridge Journal of Economics*, 38, 3, 605–22.

Keynes, J. M. (1983) *The General Theory of Employment, Interest and Money*, MacMillan, London.

Lawson, T. (1997) *Economics and Reality*, Routledge, London.

Lawson, T. (2003) *Re-Orienting Economics*, Routledge, London.

Lotz, C. (2014) *The Capitalist Schema: Time, money and the culture of abstraction*, Lexington, Lanham, MD.

McCloskey, D. (1985) *The Rhetoric of Economics*, University of Wisconsin Press, Madison, WI.

Malm, A. (2013) 'The origin of fossil capital: From water to steam in the British cotton industry', *Historical Materialism*, 21, 1, 15–68.

Mandeville, B. (1997) *The Fable of the Bees and Other Writings*, ed. E. J. Undert, Hackett, Indianapolis, IN.

Mann, G. (2011) 'Value after Lehmann', *Historical Materialism*, 18, 4, 172–88.

Marx, K. (1978) *Capital*, Vols I–III, Progress Publishers, Moscow.

Marx, K., and Engels, F. (1985) *The German Ideology*, Lawrence & Wishart, London.

Meeker, K. (2013) *Hume's Radical Scepticism and the Fate of Naturalized Epistemology*, Palgrave MacMillan, London.

Merker, N. (2009) *Filosofie del Populismo* [*Philosophies of Populism*], Laterza, Bari, Italy.

Micocci, A. (2002) *Anti-Hegelian Reading of Economic Theory*, Mellen Press, Lampeter, UK.

Micocci, A. (2008/2010) *The Metaphysics of Capitalism*, Lexington, Lanham, MD.

Micocci, A. (2011a) 'The preponderance of finance and the present crisis', *Studies in Political Economy*, 87, 49–64.

Micocci, A. (2011b) 'Marx and the crisis: A necessary theoretical premise', *International Journal of Political Economy*, special issue on Marx and the crisis, 40, 3, 72–87.

Micocci, A. (2012a) *Moderation and Revolution*, Lexington, Lanham, MD.

Micocci, A. (2012b) 'Economics students – Encouraging critical thinking', *WEA Newsletter*, 2, 1, 6.

Micocci, A. (2013) 'Pensare da soli [Thinking on your own]', *Il Cannocchiale Rivista di Studi Filosofici*, 2, 145–60.

Micocci, A. (2014a) 'Unusual Humean issues in materialistic political economy', *Journal of Philosophical Economics*, 7, 2, 22–6.

Micocci, A. (2014b) 'Smith's invisible hands in neoliberal times', paper presented at IIPPE Conference, Naples, Italy.

Micocci, A. (2015) 'Traditional issues need novel thinking', pp, 131–54, in Figus, A., *Land and Water Will Save Us from the Crisis: The Role of universities*, Eurilink, Rome.

Mill, J. S. (1998) *Principles of Political Economy*, Oxford University Press, Oxford, UK.

Polibio (1979) *Storie* [*Histories*], Mondadori, Milan, Italy.

Read, R., and Richman, K. (2000) *The New Hume Debate*, Routledge, London.

Rosenthal, J. (1998) *The Myth of Dialectics*, MacMillan, London.

Samuelson, P. A. (1962) 'Parable and realism in capital theory: The surrogate production function', *Review of Economic Studies*, 29, 3, 193–206.

Samuelson, P. A. (1987) 'Out of the closet: A program for the Whig history of economic science', *History of Economics Society Bulletin*, 9, 2, 51–60.

Senofonte (1997) *Ciropedia* [*Cyruspaedia*], Newton, Milan, Italy.

Smith, A. (1980) *Essays on Philosophical Subjects*, Bryce, J. C., Wightman, W. P. D. (eds), Clarendon Press, Oxford, UK.

Smith, A. (1999) *The Wealth of Nations*, 2 vols, Penguin Classics, London.

Smith, A. (2001) *Lectures on Rhetoric and Belles Lettres*, Bryce, J. C. (ed.), Clarendon Press, Oxford, UK.

Smith, A. (2009) *The Theory of Moral Sentiments*, Penguin Classics, London.

Stiglitz, J. E. (2013) *The Price of Inequality*, W. W.Norton, New York.

Strawson, G. (1989) *The Secret Connexion: Causation, realism, and David Hume*, Oxford University Press, Oxford, UK.

Sylos Labini, P. (1992) *Elementi di Dinamica Economica* [*Elements of Economic Dynamics*], Laterza, Bari, Italy.

Sylos Labini, P. (1993) *Progresso Tecnico e Sviluppo Ciclico* [*Technical Progress and Cyclical Development*], Laterza, Bari, Italy.

Sylos Labini, P. (2004) *Torniamo ai Classici* [*Let Us Go Back to the Classics*], Laterza, Bari, Italy.

Velupillai, V. K. (2005) 'The unreasonable ineffectiveness of mathematics in economics', *Cambridge Journal of Economics*, 29, 6, 849–72.

Velupillai, V. K. (2014) 'Towards a political economy of the theory of economic policy', *Cambridge Journal of Economics*, 38, 6, 1329–38.

Wright, J. (1983) *The Sceptical Realism of David Hume*, Manchester University Press, Manchester, UK.

5 Silence

5.1 Introduction

After defining the metaphysics of capitalism in Chapter 1 as an intellectual construction aimed at providing an ultimate system of meaning to reality, we have been studying its overwhelming dialectical structural features. These serve to pacify the collective mind by pretending, among other things, that its laws are similar to those of nature. From that point, we have been able (starting in Chapter 2) to explore the technicalities of the discussion by using those modern authors (particularly, but not exclusively, eighteenth-century thinkers) who could help us operate outside the all-pervasive dialectical, moderate mind of capitalism as we know it.

We have, in other words, taken ourselves out of the socialized, anti-individual capitalist world whose main intellectual interpreters are Kant and Hegel, with their philosophical mind that can philosophize for everybody precisely because, in a world where all individuals are homogenized, communication is granted. This is not a new story, nor is it strictly capitalist. We can trace it back, for the most obvious instance, to the Christian roots of European culture.

Tacitus (Tacito, 2000, 2007), to consider the earliest solid, explicit example, warned us against monotheism (Tacito, 2000), as it is conceived only in the mind, by which he meant a collective mind. Before monotheism, as every Roman pagan could explain (see, for instance, Cicero, Cicerone, 2006),[1] religion was about nature and the material and their devastating force – what in Chapter 4 we have called, with Hume, chance. The Jews and the Christians were, as a consequence, inhuman (Tacito, 2007), and only the criminal stupidity of Nero could transform them into innocent victims, symbols of a human love and a sheepish meekness that other witnesses of the time (e.g. Ammiano Marcellino, 2001, among many) tell us they never had nor ever desired to have, let alone practise.

Having clarified that, Tacitus can also enlighten us (Tacito, 2000, 2007) about the political importance of psychology and mass psychology. These matters are so well deployed in his works that it is hard to disentangle them, for instance in the form of quotations, from the stories he tells. For Tacitus, as for us, in the presence of collectivization, politics becomes the realm of banality, of a boring application of the same mechanisms in an iterative fashion, just as we propose capitalism would do much later on, in a much more powerful and pervasive way.

Tacitus could look at a polity that had not yet been fully conquered by the mental barrenness of Christian – and later capitalist – homogenization. In a pagan, non-capitalist setting, individuals could strive to improve themselves by using both mind and body to transcend the banality and heaviness of everyday practical cares. This is well rendered by Sallust, in a historical conjuncture (Catilina's plot) that is earlier than Tacitus but similar in cultural terms: the stern and austere customs of the ancients, which had made Rome great, were hard pressed and challenged by base and inhuman socialized desires, well epitomized in a comparison to herbivorous animals, compelled by the poverty of their diet to be slaves of their bellies and unable to aspire to high, individual goals: '*Omnes hominess qui sese student praestare ceteris animalibus summa ope niti decet ne vitam silentio transeant veluti pecora, quae natura prona atque ventri oboedentia finxit. Sed nostra omnis vis in animo et corpore sita est*' (Sallustio, 1994, I, p. 76).

Sallust's words and his reference to the limitations of sheep are an appropriate bridge to Giacomo Leopardi, a Classical scholar, poet and philosopher who, with his typically eighteenth-century cultural background[2] (see Biscuso and Gallo, 1999; Micocci, 2000), has been a looming presence throughout this book. In his 1829–30 '*Canto notturno di un pastore errante dell'Asia*' ('Night song of a nomadic Asian shepherd'), he has his imaginary Asian shepherd ask the Moon:

> *Ancor non se' tu paga*
> *Di riandare i sempiterni calli?*
> *Ancor non prendi a schivo, ancor se vaga*
> *Di rimirar queste valli?*
>
> (Leopardi, 1998, ll. 5–8)

'Why is the Moon not yet tired of studying from above the world such as it is?'

After wondering what could be the use of the material world (p. 373, ll. 97–9), the shepherd turns to ask why he is made so unhappy, and is even bored by it, while his flock not only forgets all pains soon, it also:

> *giammai tedio non provi*
> *Quando tu siedi all'ombra, sovra l'erbe*
> *Tu sei queta e contenta; e gran parte dell'anno*
> *Senza noia consumi in quello stato*
>
> (1998, p. 374, ll. 111–16)

> *Ma, s'io giaccio in riposo, il tedio assale*
>
> (1998, p. 75, l. 132)

Animals are not bothered by the pain of reality, and are not bored by lack of events and emotions. They are equally serene under all circumstances, and seem impermeable to ennui, let alone bitterness or spleen. When they do not eat they ruminate.

The word '*tedio*' in Leopardi's *oeuvre* signifies, at least to the present author, that condition that assails the social man when he is faced by the painful and unsettling incoherence and incommunicability between his bodily sentiments and the social thoughts expressed in words and speech that he is continuously bombarded with, whether he likes it or not. Socialized thoughts are so pervasive as to obfuscate and render it difficult to make sense of bodily sentiments. Such an alienated condition, as discussed earlier, is well represented and criticized in Rousseau. Take, for an apt instance, his *Emile* (1975). In XCI, he notices, and chastises, the absurd fixation of modern men that life is short. What they mean is the contrary, i.e. that they do not know how to employ their time. They are bored.

Men either endeavour or pretend to be running somewhere all the time, and seek to avoid, by erasing it, the time that separates them from the goal they have set for themselves at any given time. In so doing, they mistreat and insult nature; in the instance of travel Rousseau discusses in XCI, they sit in their means of transportation with the full intention of getting bored by the trip. To achieve that, they concentrate on their departure and arrival points, completely disregarding whatever is between: travelling itself. They miss what is most interesting, and useful, and natural: the discovery of what lies between the two ends of the trip. They miss reality, and above all they miss mystery (Rousseau would concede the first, but he has no room for, nor does he give any helpful hint about, this second, which is instead paramount for us here). The trip might make you meet the imaginable, the unimaginable and, very importantly, the unconceived: that which is without us. This is liberty as chance.

Like Leopardi's shepherd, Rousseau's alienated contemporaries do not exert body and mind simultaneously. They only use one at a time, and sometimes neither, as in when they sit in the darkness of their carriages longing to get where they are going. Their lack of physical and mental exertion is the result of the boring iterations of social life, which requires neither bodily nor mental qualities apart from bovine endurance of the same facts and reasonings presenting themselves to you all the time. All minds are homogeneous, and philosophical problems are trusted, as stated above, to a theoretical philosophical mind that one day, in the person of the next Kant or Hegel, will inform them of where the world is heading, and perhaps even of the meaning and use of life.

Deprived of Tacitus's inhuman enemy, for Christianity was unavoidable by their time, and of a revolutionary anarchist hope, for Marx was yet to come, Rousseau and Leopardi can only draw pessimistic conclusions. The boy Emile will marry his childhood sweetheart; the Asian shepherd will identify his '*tedio*' with the cruelty of his mortal condition. They help pose the problem of human understanding, while despairing of a solution. That is for us to devise, which we will do in the present chapter in an open-ended way. We will seek to unchain chance, in order for it to take the place of pessimism.

However, so far in the book, we have also sought to dispel the illusion, held by Leopardi, Rousseau and the other thinkers we have been considering, that nature's existence needs no proof, and that we can just devote ourselves to the study of its hidden and non-hidden objects and structures. We have, if everything so far argued is correct, lost capitalist hope. All we know is that we can, if we so wish, leave the limiting intellectual world of capitalism as we know it by operating upon the imagined and the unimaginable, while waiting for nature, or, as we will develop later, the unconceived, to unfold or not to unfold on its own, without necessarily sending us a signal. Such a signal might well be catastrophic in the dominant intellectual sense of our days. Indeed, only if that is so might what is argued here prove worthwhile.

In order to prepare for the final, emancipative argument, it might prove useful to anticipate here a few considerations that follow from what has been argued in the preceding chapters. It is of paramount importance to remind the reader that, in capitalism as we know it, facts do not count as such. However much they affect the lives of the individuals involved, they count only as pieces of that continuous, harmonious flow of the metaphysics that throws them up, only to quickly replace them with others that are very similar but proposed as something different. The same applies to the actual, individual human beings. This poses obvious problems with the ontological status of what is being dealt with, which is most evident, as proposed earlier, in economics and political economy. We will keep working on this problem, here and in the conclusions.

Second, even if we do not claim to have a chance to actually know, or even touch, nature (the concrete, the material as such, as if capitalism did not exist), we have science as engineering. The tendency of natural environments to individually and provisionally adapt to whatever devastation human beings inflict upon them in fact poses a false logical problem. Adepts of the metaphysics of capitalism might argue that this demonstrates our ability to go on indefinitely, for capitalism as we know it and nature have always adapted to each other and are likely to keep doing so. Anti-capitalist ecological activists also belong to this group, as previously observed, but, as we have said, the logic of the anti-capitalist argument presented here abandons any such hope. Science as engineering is challenged.

What we have called the adaptability of nature to human endeavours is in fact only so apparently, and from the point of view of the dominant metaphysics. It is simply the human submission to the needs of engineering activities to win its daily bread. From this point of view, nothing has changed from past historical records. Humans will always submit to their need for food and shelter. Although the possibility of disasters remains as high as ever, jeopardizing human survival as ever, the whole exercise reveals itself as empty rhetoric. This will come in very useful in what follows.

Section 5.2 will sort out some remaining basic philosophical questions. They are, needless to say, to do with the thinkers we have considered thus far, and in particular Marx the anarchist. Inevitably, the section will discuss the important questions posed by Marx's Theses on Feuerbach, especially Thesis XI.

Section 5.3 will expand the discussion of words and language. It will do so by framing them in the wider question of revolution, which has been prepared in Section 5.2. The section will also consider the issue of boredom and the psychological reactions engendered by politics, in the spirit of Tacitus, as mentioned above.

Section 5.4 discusses and describes our historical political economy of a materialistic kind. It starts from a problem posed in Section 5.3, which follows from some of the arguments presented on evil and its social and intellectual features in Chapter 4. Economic value will be regarded as being central to capitalism, but not to a post-revolutionary setting.

Section 5.5 will describe emancipation from capitalism as a process that leads to destroy (any) metaphysics in order to open up to the unconceived (which is wider than liberty as chance).

The conclusions of the chapter will summarize everything, delivering the reader to Chapter 6, for the overall conclusions.

5.2 Questions of philosophy

Let us start by summarizing a topic we have been analysing in progressive detail throughout the preceding chapters, that is, the forced socialization determined by capitalism. In the first place, we have seen that there is a main, typically capitalist, mechanism that we have expressed as something similar to Marx's triple alienation from the self, the others and nature. This is almost completely determined (with which even mainstream Marxists would agree) by the way the relations of production are thought about and practised, although, we have been showing, the phenomenon is much wider and deeper.

There is, in fact, a metaphysics – a dominant, all-encompassing web – that comprises all the rest and interferes with everything, be it public or strictly private, that is performed under the aegis of the capitalist relations of production. It reduces everything, all the time, to a few dominant maieutical devices that are iteratively repeated, in an apparently different form or concerning apparently different facts, and it makes anything that is not structured along those lines not only unthinkable but also impossible to understand. Its words and speech, as anticipated in the preceding chapters and as we will see in more detail next section, are both a powerful limiting tool and a versatile emotional controller. As in Adam Smith (2009), it is words that evoke emotions, and not the other way around, although the fiction that this latter procedure still functions is left in place. Capitalism is ruled by its intellectuality.

Marx's alienation is thus easily widened and generalized. Although the ensuing homogenization of human bodies, minds and emotions ensures the smooth functioning of the political and economic system, as testified by the practical utility of mainstream economics, which does without reality, there remains the worrying question of the separation from nature. In fact, the intellectuality of capitalism as we know it, although producing an intellectual bubble that is isolated from nature, cannot completely erase nature itself. The concrete is out there, but appears as an object of scientific conquest (for capitalist metaphysics has, inevitably, an unlimited faith in its own science) and of actual, economically productive conquest, sustainable or not. The economic exploitation of nature nonetheless worries capitalism, for Kantian real oppositions are impossible in capitalism, whereas in nature they are possible.

The idea of nature's threats, however unlikely from the statistical point of view (statistics itself being yet another mixture of intellectual maieutics and repressed emotions), is nonetheless useful. They are transcended to produce social cohesion (aimed at the protection of society from nature) and a fiction of subversion, such as the green and ecological movements that sublimate capitalist dialectics into an even more intellectual paroxysm. As a result, capitalism can keep (not) understanding nature its own way: according to the poor maieutical devices of its dominant metaphysics. The language of nature, as argued by our eighteenth-century philosophers, is forever severed from us. Capitalism's words and speech are all we are left with. More human homogenization and alienation ensues, and no escape appears possible.

All the efforts made by the thinkers we have been reviewing in the preceding chapters can thus, in and by capitalism as we know it, be set aside and forgotten. Their attempts to conceive of knowledge and reasoning as 'human understanding', i.e. as individual processes placed in a social setting, becomes useless, and pointless or non-practical, in capitalist parlance. There is in fact only one, eternal and iterative, social setting, the different possible historical forms of which can be exaggerated at will by the use of words, and adjectives in particular. Any brief look at the pro- and anti-capitalist literature of all kinds provides a list of such noun-cum-adjective characterizations of capitalism (late capitalism, long century, and the like). The capitalist person can move overnight from being modern to postmodern, whether they are a model petty bourgeois individual, a third-world peasant struggling for life, a woman or a homosexual, all fictional categories singled out at need to signify non-subversive differences: see, for instance, Benn Michaels (2008).

Humans are transformed, like in Thucydides's Histories (Thucydides, 2005),[3] into knowable and known beings, whose speeches can be reported even when they have not been heard directly: as any reasoning can be made out by means of another reasoning, no surprise is possible. Not only do institutions funnel thought, but human nature itself is limited and easily described. No wonder then that a theoretical philosophical Mind is all we need to do philosophy, as in Kant and Hegel. The capitalist individual projects itself into a theory, hypostatizing. Everything the manager of that 'Mind' makes it do and say as a consequence applies to everybody else. If everything so far argued is correct, who can deny that this procedure is correct? Like mainstream economics, but in a wider sense, Idealist philosophy does without reality, and in so doing it also does without human beings, apart from the puppeteer who manages the Mind itself.

The imagined can be easily managed, and so can the unimaginable. The two resemble each other, for they are opposite in a poorly dialectical sense. The most evident and unnoticed instance of this trick, not dissimilar in method from that of a street conjuror, is Hegel's *Phenomenology of Spirit* (2008). In it, in far too many places, some of which have been pointed out earlier on, the meanings of other and different are eliminated, with the latter continuously replacing the former, while the various words that signify them are kept. Different men are bestowed with an otherness, which thus pretends that men are indeed, in general, other from each other, while meaning, instead, simply different. Men who are truly other are, as a result, erased from the picture. They are inconceivable. One consequence we have examined throughout the present book is that, by such tricks, Marx has been reduced to the role of a socialist agitator.

It goes without saying that Hegel's approach, for us, is just a historical turning point, i.e. an arbitrary historical occurrence that summarizes a pattern that is amenable to generalization. Such a pattern is precisely the progressive preponderance of the imagined, which intellectually rules the unimaginable, constraining it within its limited and limiting borders, but this is what happens inside that insignificant historical thing called capitalism. Outside might lie the unconceived. Whether this is nature (the material, the concrete) or not, does not and cannot matter here. In fact, all we can do at this stage is:

- lose hope in the maieutical devices of capitalism;
- destroy them;
- recover mystery by exploring the possibility of the unconceived.

Seen from this perspective, capitalism as we know it comes to amount to a mechanical device that periodically turns its wheels to determine another configuration, with its winners and losers (which are analysed by the theorization of microeconomics). The game, as everybody can tell, is rigged in favour of the privileged classes. Here, the mainstream Marxists are right, but, as we have seen in the preceding chapter, they are right because they repeat what Adam Smith had described as the invisible hand and the combination of masters and workers against one another in a struggle over the level of wages.

The mechanics of capitalism as we know it looks very much like a lottery machine,[4] both from an economic and a political point of view. All that is required of the players is that they have faith in the system. If you trust that the wheels deliver statistically analysable results, you deem it worthwhile to place your stakes. Never mind that some, through being on the side of the possessors of wealth, are bound to reap more benefits than you, or are cushioned in their fall. The punter tries his/her hand precisely because he/she trusts statistical chance, and because he/she thinks to have at least a partial and limited advantage, similar to (but likely smaller than) that of the lucky, privileged minority: say, a degree from a good university, a peculiar work experience, an understanding of the game itself. The setting is Adam Smith's deception (Di Mario and Micocci, 2015) of the invisible hand.

The statistical inference that the punters trust, the tricks and advantages that they believe they hold, and the faith in the substantial neutrality of the system (corruption and dishonesty are accepted as inevitable, because they are only incidents, and anyway they are just another instance of the often-referred-to simultaneous precision and approximation of all capitalist things and concepts that can be rendered in words), as well as the supine acceptance of the intrinsic class inequality with its unjust consequences, are all instances of the same thing: the metaphysics of capitalism. They all proceed from the flawed capitalist reasoning that is unable to identify abstract categories (e.g. numbers are foregone and replaced by statistical inference) and refuses to see what they themselves call material reality (e.g. the class inequality that rigs the game). As Hume would put it, in the minds of the common people, for the working of the system, tomorrow must resemble today.

All this is intellectually transcended, and summarized in a word that is evocative and vague enough to perform its role of precise agglomeration of imprecision: hope. Capitalist hope, that is a socialized hope, is this: the symbol of the undeniable incoherences of the system (a lottery that is simultaneously mechanical and rigged, fair and unfair), which only the metaphysical precision of approximation can render logical and usable to the dominant maieutics. Lovers of capitalism can use it to produce their praises of the system, and those who oppose it (e.g. the mainstream Marxists) can use it to prove its unfairness. Neither of them can use it as a starting point for an alternative.

In fact, in capitalism, the alternative is the unimaginable, i.e. the dialectical 'opposite' (in the sense of a contradiction) of the imaginable: to a system, another system is opposed. Anarchism is a priori ruled out, for its consideration, going beyond the imaginable and the unimaginable, is not possible to the maieutical means of the metaphysics of capitalism. Capitalism thus produces socialism, unsustainable processes of production produce sustainable processes of production, in theory and – this is the most powerful aspect of the metaphysics of capitalism – in practice. One could hypothesize that this was clear to Adam Smith, who in fact could think of nothing challenging capitalism except the wild liberty and unprejudiced brains of the barbarian nations and the pernicious logical rigour of Dr Mandeville. We could also hypothesize (see the preceding chapters and Micocci, 2002, 2008/2010, 2012) that we are facing the reason why Marx felt that he had to challenge Hegel first and abandon, or simply forget him, later.

The power of the metaphysics of capitalism is so overwhelming that a present-day Marxist journal can even approvingly publish a 1931 radio broadcast by Carl Schmitt (Schmitt, 2014) that asserts that Marx was a Hegelian thinker: 'it was precisely the Hegelian method and dialectic that Marx employed' (2014, p. 389). The Hegelian importance of the 'economic determinations' in society, which 'nowadays is easily understood' (p. 389), was 'quickly and confidently' (ibid.) grasped by the young Marx, led by 'philosophy, or rather Hegelian philosophy' (ibid.). In fact:

> Hegel's dialectical philosophy of history, if properly employed, provides a powerful means to free the concrete here and now, the *hic et nunc*, from the sphere of irrational intuitions or emotionally guided impressionism, and install man as the master over the irrationality of a fate ordained by God, nature, or providence.
>
> (p. 391; emphasis in the original)

Not only are we inside the main preconceptions behind Nazi theories. We also are fully within the metaphysics of capitalism, with its foolish pretension to rationally rule the world, excluding what does not fit. Needless to say, none of that is in Marx. Obviously enough, like Heidegger, Schmitt was terrified by the similarity between men and animals that animates our eighteenth-century thinkers, including Adam Smith, and makes their philosophy so conducive to libertarian outcomes.

> The scientific certainty [. . .] of the correctness of this Marxist claim [that the industrial class will bring about a classless society, a view 'uncorrupted by the status quo', AM] is, in structure, thoroughly Hegelian, and can only be understood in Hegelian terms.
>
> (p. 392)

What count are society and its activity as a harmonious, choral set of operations:

> Whoever is not positioned actively and vitally within this process [the Spirit actualizing itself, AM], whoever is not involved, is incapable of knowing, and sees and hears nothing, despite being constantly thrust this way and that by events. The bearers of the world-historical struggle, by contrast, located in the right moment of this process, know this process.
>
> (p. 393)

As Merker (2009) also points out (as earlier discussed), this is a clear statement of what we have been arguing throughout. It is the homogenizing power of the metaphysics of capitalism.[5]

Schmitt being a Nazi, and the Marxists being his enemies, graphically renders one of the main points argued in this section and in the whole volume. Not only do facts and ideas not count in themselves, because they are promptly and iteratively replaced by others, which are similar and yet claim to be different, even other, they also lend themselves to different interpretations that appear to clash precisely because they do not clash. Conflict is dialectical; the solution is moderate and comprises both determinations in a variable combination. Smith's invisible hand can be both ugly and beautiful, communism dictatorial and democratic, the market mono- or oligopolistic. The same logical tools make you a Nazi or an anti-Nazi. In all this, it is not material reality that is being talked about; therefore, the doubt about the existence of the material itself need not be addressed. The process, the actualization of the Spirit, cannot waste any time. It is the only knowledge available.

We must necessarily wonder again, at this point of the discussion, what revolution is. To do so, we cannot avoid starting from the most pertinent thinker: Marx. In what follows, we will examine a text of his that we have not yet discussed in our attempt to sketch the anarchist Marx: his much quoted Theses on Feuerbach, probably written in the 1846–7 period and published by Engels in 1888.

In order to better understand the Theses, we can start by bridging Marx with this book's argument that language contributes to the confusion about reality we have been describing. The Marx–Engels couple that worked on *The German Ideology* (Marx and Engels, 1985) did not posit a language of nature, which appears implicitly in other examples of Marx's writings, but a language of life, which can be misunderstood in the Hegelian sense. In Marx and Engels (1985), very much in tune with the Theses on Feuerbach, we read that:

> For philosophers, one of the most difficult tasks is to descend from the world of thought to the actual world. *Language* is the immediate actuality of thought. Just as philosophers have given thought an independent existence, so they had to make language into an independent realm. This is the secret of philosophical language. [. . .] The problem of descending from the world of thoughts to the actual world is turned into the problem of descending from language to life.
>
> (p. 118; emphasis in the original)

Going further does not clarify the issue of the language of life:

> The philosophers would only have to dissolve this language into the ordinary language, from which it is abstracted, to recognize it as the distorted language of the actual world, and to realize that neither thoughts nor language in themselves form a realm of their own, that they are only *manifestations* of actual life.
>
> (ibid.; emphasis in the original)

There is, nonetheless, enough for us to be content with for the time being. Kant's and Hegel's philosophical Mind is evidently criticized as not materially relevant.

The Theses on Feuerbach are our starting point for the discussion of revolution (which will continue in the rest of the chapter) because they are about emancipation. Their subject matter is materialism: the abolition of rational mysticism (for the general importance rational mysticism has in Marx's thought, see Micocci, 2002) and the search for sensuousness, i.e. for a relationship with nature. Circumstances must change (Marx does not specify – and this is very important – whether on their own, by man's action, or both) as well as human conscience. The point is to change the world. This, we have seen, is simply impossible to any form of Idealism, which instead presumes to know reality by immersing itself in the metaphysics it itself produces, as well explained by Schmitt (2014), who praises Lenin for fully understanding such absurdity.

The main difference between the argument of the present book and Marx lies in the role of sensuousness. If everything so far argued in fact holds, we cannot, at least at the present stage, even know whether we grasp or ever will grasp the material, for we simply cannot even say that the material exists, but on our side we have instinct and that peculiar and mysterious thing we have called prolepsis (see Micocci, 2008/2010, about the philosophical origin of this term in Epicurus). We cannot know whether or not they are the right things, but we can follow their impulses and see where they lead. We can hypothesize, as a consequence, that instinct and prolepsis are a helpful connection to what Marx calls, with a vague and abused word, sensuousness.

Thesis I (Marx and Engels, 1985, p. 121) informs us that all preceding materialisms, including Feuerbach's (Marx actually mentions no other names), were conceived as 'objects of contemplation' instead of 'sensuous human activity'. This is obviously fundamental, for Marx and for us too. Human individuals must themselves take over the task of understanding material reality. Marx does not explain why this is so, although it is clear to us: it serves to escape capitalist homogenization and alienation. Marx also attacks Idealism. Crucially, he ends Thesis I by saying that what he has called human sensuous practice has the significance of 'revolutionary'. That means a 'practical–critical activity'. This is a good way to approach what we shall define later on as revolution and emancipation.

Thesis II poses the problem put forward by Berkeley (2004) in a most interesting way. It proposes that thinking 'isolated from practice' is a purely 'scholastic question' when it is conceived as the dispute between the reality and the non-reality of thinking. This is most interesting for our purposes here. It contains an intuition of what the present volume proposes as a tool for emancipation from the metaphysics of capitalism as we know it: individual, practical thought dictated by an open logic, non-dialectical in the sense that, besides dialectical relationships, it accepts ruptures with oblivion, real opposition. Only in this way, which Marx did not propose explicitly, can emancipation make room for the unconceived. This last point is the true object of investigation, because the practical–critical part only serves to emancipate us from the metaphysics, but leads us nowhere in discovering whether reality exists and has a logic, and, if it does, what it is.

The consequences of all the above are beautifully summarized in Thesis III. Man is able to challenge circumstances by 'dividing society into two parts', one of which is above society itself; this latter is the practical–critical activity. By change of circumstances, Marx continues, what is meant is the circumstances of human activity. It amounts to a 'self-changing' that can only be rationally understood as 'revolutionary practice'. There is no danger of overemphasizing the anti-Hegelian and anti-Idealistic force of this Thesis. Anticipating what is being proposed from a rather different perspective in this volume, Marx is saying that we need to see the separation between society and nature in general. We can only operate in the former, hoping to get out of it. The implication is, as has been argued here in many other ways, that you must leave nature free to go on. No *Geist* is at work, for there is no common man–nature purpose.

Marx's contention that revolution is a practical–critical activity is a way of saying that it is an intellectual operation. It needs sensuousness, or, as we propose here, openness to the unconceived and attention to instinct and prolepsis. It is an individual task, but it is everybody's task: it is a collective endeavour, requiring no organization and no internal differentiation of roles (e.g. party and cannon fodder, as pretended to by many misguided practitioners of 'Marxist' class struggle, above all Lenin). Additionally, it erases the typically capitalist petty bourgeois distinction between practical and non-practical (the capitalist useful) we have already criticized several times in the preceding chapters.

Marx continues his criticism of Feuerbach's rational mysticism in Thesis IV, thus furthering the critique of the Idealist Mind. This last question is in fact taken up in Thesis V, where he points out that Feuerbach does not want 'abstract thinking' but 'contemplation'. Contemplation itself does without all sensuous–practical features. It is a sort of Idealistic philosophizing Mind.

Thesis VI concludes that, 'the human essence is no abstraction inherent in each single individual'. It is 'the ensemble of the social relations'. This requires careful scrutiny. Marx is saying that Feuerbach 'abstracts from the historical process', thus presupposing an 'abstract', i.e. 'isolated', individual (this explanation is crucial), which leads to a 'dumb generality' that appears to 'naturally unite' the many individuals. Marx, in other words, is saying that:

- there is no such thing as human essence, i.e. human nature;
- this is so because social relations determine the individual.

This, we have endeavoured to show, means that, in Marx as well as in our present argument, the social man is not a man but a limited, stunted creature maimed by society. Liberation is necessary.

Thus (Thesis VII), 'religious sentiment' is a social product, and each man is determined by his society (by history). It is easy to infer from this that social life is essentially 'practical' (Thesis VIII). 'All mysteries which lead theory to mysticism find their rational solution in human practice and in the comprehension of this practice.' Theory and practice are one and the same thing, and they are a powerfully limited thing. History explains the social man because it makes it simple, as argued by the eighteenth-century philosophers we have reviewed in the preceding chapters. No essence of man can or must be sought in the social man, who is a lesser creature than man.

In Thesis IX, Marx attacks 'contemplative materialism' and its contemplation of single individuals and of civil society. The point of materialism is another, of course. We must move from civil society as a standpoint (Thesis X) to 'human society', 'social humanity'. The meaning of this last Thesis is unmistakable: civil society is secondary and historical, and studying it does not help unless it is a 'practical–critical' activity: an emancipation from it, to discover, or maybe create, human society (not 'a' human society!). Operating within society and within history is no emancipation (this is straightforwardly anti-Hegelian, there is scarcely the need to point out). We must move above society, outside it, and from there observe. Only thus can we hope to notice the unconceived, we might add. Chance can then be liberated.

In fact, the question is well known, and is explained in the much-abused Thesis XI: the point of philosophy is to change the world, not society. This can only be done by freeing ourselves and by freeing chance. The two things are one and the same.

What Marx says in the Theses must be seen in the larger framework of the argument put forward in this volume. It is very important to dwell a little on the meaning of change and its role in the description of revolution. Changing reality means changing the individual, liberating it from the metaphysics of capitalism by means of a 'practical', logically sound intellectual activity of emancipation. The point is not to operate within or against society, but to seek to do everything humans can do. In all likelihood, this means erasing society. But this does not matter at all, for society is, by definition, something that is bound to come to an end.

We have finally systematized everything we have been arguing so far by liberating it from the erudite debates we have had to face earlier. Now, we know that we have in front of us a practical, individual task that can be defined as sensuous only in that it aims to free itself from the triple alienation and from the metaphysics of capitalism as we know it.

5.3   Individual, society and evil

It is well worth starting this section by going back to the question posed by Leopardi's Asian shepherd: is nature boring? Why is it so to some human beings, and not to itself (to animals, plants, rocks, the Moon)? Why do animals appear to be content with their lot, a lot that looks so miserable to some human beings, and why do they even meekly submit to the butcher's knife, or the predator's fangs, for that matter? We have seen with Marx, in the preceding section, that man can and indeed must pose himself above society, but can he pose himself above nature? Does he need to do that to study it, as for society?

The whole discussion pursued so far has made it clear that capitalism operates as if there could be something alien, and more powerful than nature itself, out there. The *Geist* is the most obvious example; God, or more precisely a conception all in the mind supposedly shared by the vast majority, is another. Even the intrinsic notion of nature itself could be thought of as such power, but, alternatively, with our eighteenth-century thinkers and Marx, we can think of nature as a set of material things freely driven by their physical features. These last they have, or appear to have, in common with us.

The above problem constitutes the core of the ontological impossibility of a capitalist metaphysics we anticipated in Chapter 2. If we stick with the philosophical language of capitalism as we know it, leaving the formulation of an alternative for later on, we notice in fact that the various categories that constitute capitalist reality have a variable ontological status. On the one hand, we get the Spirit, God, or even history and natural evolution. These are posited as if they fully transcended the material. They are considered as other from the concrete, with the proviso that, to the capitalist mind, other simply means different. Thus, although they might actually and truly be other, they are called so while they are thought of as dialectically different and they are thus employed, with a typically capitalist, logically flawed convolution.

On the other hand, as noticed so many times, one has the material items of reality. These are simply ontologically suspended. They include material objects (tractors, strawberries, TV sets), non-material objects (parliaments, prices and quantities, moral values such as private property), as well as feelings (economic needs and desires, national pride, but also supposedly natural and private feelings, for these are only signified when they are socialized in words and speech). In this case, capitalism need not pose any logical problem of otherness and diversity. All of these things are speakable, however ontologically different. They depend on words and speech, i.e. they depend upon the existence of capitalism as we know it. This last, in turn, depends on believing, or even pretending to believe, in words and speech as if they were the result of an impeccable common logic: the metaphysics itself.

We are dealing, as observed so many times, with the confusion, in capitalism as we know it and in its metaphysics, between the material and the abstract. Neither of these two exists. The former is transcended into metaphysics, just as the latter undergoes the same process in the opposite sense, of a declension into metaphysics. Now you can go to a supermarket, for a banal example, without feeling the absurdity of such an operation. Instead of wanting or needing something, you make a choice by surveying the shelves. Instead of picking an egg because an egg is but an embryo with a nutritional value, you marvel at the various boxes and at the types of egg they contain. As the perfect fool you are, you go back home happy because you have bought the cheapest and worst owing to your budgetary constraints. The naturalness of hens and eggs has become the perverted poetry of microeconomics. To use a cruel comparison: instead of falling in love, you have found yourself a lover. The former cannot be explained and spoken of in words, whereas the latter can. This is what counts.

Here is the problem with Marx's sensuousness discussed in Section 5.2. No sensuousness is required; no sensuousness is possible. Capitalism is like art to the Russian Nihilists (see Pardjanadze and Micocci, 2000): a copy of reality you peddle all the time as if it were the embodiment, the essence and the beauty of reality itself. This final point no longer matters, for in it the danger of real opposition, and more generally of a complete lack of determinations, challenges the smooth dialectical functioning of the capitalist mechanism. The one thing that actually counts is the mechanism itself, which is all the metaphysics of capitalism is about. It is not material, and yet it conditions the material. A few words about the material are therefore in order.

From our alternative point of view, we cannot say that the material exists, but, to capitalism as we know it, it appears to exist, in that it is substituted, in everyday usage, by the metaphysics. You come back from the supermarket with an egg *qua* commodity, not with an egg. Its material existence is so unimportant that it does not matter that you needed just one and come back with a dozen, and you needed a good one and came back with a dozen bad ones. Remaining shreds of instinct and prolepsis make you enjoy your egg, or your sex with a lover with whom you are not in love, by sudden and confusing flashes of naturalness that you cannot help, and the origin of which does not matter, for even that can be resolved in thought. To the metaphysics of capitalism, they are instinct (an empty word to indicate everything you cannot explain in animals) or the activity of nervous terminations (another empty but apparently meaningful 'scientific' fact).

So, is nature boring? To a capitalist person, it most certainly is. He/she (provided the material exists) is unable to do anything with it, unless it is transcended in words and speech, the only way for the metaphysics to operate. A valley can then become a breathtaking landscape, the sea immense, children joyous. Nature is replaced by its copy. The funny consequence is that the beautiful valley can now be cut in two by a useless motorway. This would only provoke the rage of those who oppose it, the lovers of nature, who will pour words on the devastation and even quantify it in terms of prices. Worst of all, they even feel able to quantify it in its own terms: biodiversity, natural equilibrium, beauty ravished and the like.

We can lift ourselves above society as Marx prescribed, but we cannot, if everything so far argued in this book stands, lift ourselves above nature, unless we have a firm grasp of what the physical limits to be crossed are, but this is not possible at the present stage. As a consequence, nature is both boring to the capitalist individual and infinitely satisfactory and exciting. It is boring to a capitalist rendering, for it can only take the repetitive forms of normal science and normal, banal speech. It is boring to the capitalist idler, who can only wrack his brain looking for words that signify what he sees and feels, because what he sees and feels must be identical in form and content to what everybody sees and feels, or it would be incommunicable, i.e. non-existent.

The above is precisely the reason why nature is not, nor can it be, boring to the non-capitalist mind and body. First, because it is to do with both mind and body, which the capitalist person does not use simultaneously, as already explained. Second, because a non-capitalist individual observes in the sense of feeling. (Is this perhaps what Marx calls sensuousness? We submit it is, although this is an erudite dispute of little importance.) Perception is thus enhanced. Third, because nature hides, but may reveal its ontological status to observation. We want to know, as repeatedly stated, even whether it exists. Fourth, because nature is not merely dialectical, by experience (the various cataclysms that we know of) and by logical thinking wider than capitalist, which must contain all possibilities. Fifth, because it appears, however poor our ontological profundity is at the present, capitalist stage, as though it is consubstantial to us.

Can we say any more than the above? Of course not. That is why descriptions involving human feelings have always been trusted to special forms of expression that are hard to penetrate, such as poetry and drunken conversation, from which you always emerge as unsatisfied as before, despite the feeling of having enjoyed something daring. Hence, the need to iterate them, and we are back to this most important feature of capitalism and of social intercourse in general. We can now see the role of words and speech in full: they cover the whole degree of human intercourse, from the fully artificial (plenty of useless words, e.g. a one-night stand pick-up at a bar) to the fully human, which, of course, we cannot demonstrate to be fully natural (e.g. a *coup de foudre*, which involves no words).

We can further illustrate the role of words and speech in repressing natural impulses in capitalism (which also applies to so many non-capitalist instances, say, Aristotelian moderation) by discussing Nussbaum (2015) on anger. Although she acknowledges the original nature of anger being that of a sentiment, Nussbaum argues – in a sense correctly, if the metaphysics of capitalism is what we have been studying so far – that it can become an eminently rational thing. As a consequence, obviously enough, it can be conquered and dominated, as previously proposed by many ancient and modern philosophers. There is obviously a simple mistake here: anger can be controlled, as we all know, on many occasions, but there is no need, nor are there any grounds to do so, to connect this common phenomenon to rationality, and to make anger a rational thing.

The problem is that Nussbaum has so deeply internalized the capitalist equation between individual and society that, to her, anger is 'a central threat to decent human interactions', though she acknowledges that some argue that it has some 'usefulness and value' (2015, p. 41). In fact, 'Anger brings some benefits that may have been valuable at one stage in human prehistory. Even today, vestiges of its useful role remain' (ibid., p. 56). The Hegelian actualization of the Spirit has struck again. Capitalism is no longer in need of anger, and humans are no longer primitives.

> As Aeschylus notes, however, forward-looking systems of justice have to a great extent made this emotion unnecessary, whether in personal or in public life. Like Athena's citizens, we are now free to attend to its irrationality and destructiveness, and we should do so, focusing first on intimate personal relations, and then the political realm.
>
> (ibid.)

An emotion can be unnecessary! Only the metaphysics of capitalism can produce such monsters. Everything else descends from this absurdity. Why not attend to the irrationality and destructiveness of envy, or of smelly armpits, or of faith in your rival football team? Anger is irrational to the metaphysics of capitalism, and it is destructive only in the sense that it claims destructiveness among its prerogatives. Thus, its destructiveness can be talked about and be circularly attributed to its cause (anger itself), while the destructiveness deriving from the suppression and sublimation of anger (e.g. football collective frenzy, which has substituted the innocent venting of competitive feelings for the rival team) can be endlessly talked about and attributed to the most preposterous causes (parochialism, unemployment and the like).

Most terrifying of all is the smooth and inevitable Hegelian passage criticized by Marx in 1843–4 (see Marx, 1992) from 'intimate personal relations' to the 'political realm'. The two are so homogeneous that, once you solve your per capita problem, you solve it at the society level. What is frightening is that this conception has moved, in the span of a few decades, from being a horror subject for science fiction to a perfectly normal thing proposed by a respectable philosopher. There is no need to emphasize how useful the comparison of humans and animals has been to Adam Smith and the other eighteenth-century philosophers we have been considering in the present volume. It saved them from giving in to the collective, sterilized mind of capitalism.

One cannot help thinking that there is nature in anger, but there is certainly boredom in lack of anger, and repression, and those finely distilled hatreds and envies that cause the most atrocious collective crimes in society. The same applies to each of the other sentiments, indeed to every sentiment that can be rendered 'rational' by words and speech. This is a most important theme, which can only be introduced here but that requires a much deeper and more careful analysis. We are talking of evil.

What is evil, in fact? A perfectly normal thing (violence, scheming, unjustified hurting) that cannot, however, be justified in non-rational terms, although the non-rational terms are precisely those that are damaged by it. Evil becomes rational when it can be argued by means of the metaphysics of capitalism, and cannot be tolerated by those parts of the capitalist individual that are not completely conquered by the metaphysics itself. Such parts, branded as 'irrational' by the metaphysics, cannot therefore stand a number of rational actions. The suffering entailed is worsened by this very fact: your pain is not compatible with the maieutics of capitalism. It can only be uselessly vented and shown, its loneliness pitted against the collective others, who have no means to partake in it. They can only mince words.

For our purposes here, (capitalist) evil is a calculation (akin to a 'rational' thing), with the means of the metaphysics of capitalism that detach you from the material nature of what you deal with (but not from the capacity to act on that material), based on an incomplete set of information and, inevitably, a flawed reasoning. Considerations concerned with individual suffering are withheld, and this is very easy to do for all the reasons we have been exploring so far. The basic logic is the same as that of the *raison d'état*, or of 'all the worse for him/her', 'serves him/her right', or Hegel's butcher's desk of history. If you feel bad, you are not fit for life, and you deserve to undergo evil, but if you can take it, you contribute to society's progress.[6] The personal and public coincide.

Now we are equipped to analyse a very useful work by Moretti and Pestre (2015) on the language and contents of 'Bankspeak'. These two authors notice a change in the language of the World Bank (WB) and attribute it to a change in morality and politics. We will see that this is not the case. Having done that, we will be able to face a short piece by Noam Chomsky (1970/1980), who erroneously attributes a liberation potential to language.

Moretti and Pestre (2015) count the relevant words in the WB reports. This is very easy to do these days, with the aid of a computer; this is just further proof that technology helps us see in a finer-grained way, but has no power whatso-ever to change things. There must of course be recurring words in the reports (loan, country, prices, and so on). But 'a major metamorphosis has taken place' (2015, p. 75) in language from 1958 to 2008. 'It's almost another language, in both semantics and grammar' (p. 76), with a key discontinuity point at the turn of the 1990s. Since then, 'the style of the Reports becomes much more codified, self-referential and detached from everyday language' (ibid.) The neo-liberal era has struck.

To Moretti and Pestre, the WB moves quite suddenly from its original job of referring to the material items that must be the final objects of its loans and from controls based on missions in the field to 'advise, suggest, assist', to something quite different. 'Empirical' (Moretti and Pestre's chosen word) objects start to disappear. Management of the economy in order to get growth and development through the interaction of states, governments, banks and the WB gives way to less empirical objects. It is clear that Moretti and Pestre labour under the illusion that words can unfailingly represent material objects. So great is their illusion that they mistake the economy, or economic growth, for empirical facts, material objects endowed with a concrete existence, which of course they are not in the first place.

We have seen, in fact, that this is not the case. Even those objects that, unlike the economy, or growth, or development, are material to start with, cannot and do not exist as such. What counts is the general, flawed logic of the metaphysics of capitalism, which operates in its own metaphysical way, but, to continue with the analysis of Moretti and Pestre's paper, we can translate what they say as follows: the WB seems to lose interest in those items of economic theory and of practical economic policy that are usually described as concerned with material production. The implication is, just like in all economic theories, that this is not a good thing. Even Marxists would argue that the growth of material production is a good starting point for anything you might want to do.

However, as anticipated, by the 1990s the WB had moved on to a different style and content, which reveal a different field of operation in practice. The first change, predictably enough, has to do with finance. A whole new vocabulary is introduced that has to do with that. A second set has to do with 'management': goals, agendas, opportunities, challenges, strategies are now everywhere in the reports. This brings in, instead of surveys and missions, reports and programmes, like in the first historical phase, 'focusing, strengthening and implementing, monitor, control, audit, indicators, expertise'. Everything is geared to 'enhance *effectiveness, efficiency, performance, competitiveness* and – it goes without saying – promote *innovation*' (p. 80; emphasis in the original).

Moretti and Pestre show that such terms have replaced those words that refer to 'empirical' material production with the ensuing 'income, poverty reduction' and the like. Unsurprisingly, a third set of terms is present, having to do with 'governance'. This last word is as frequent as 'food' and occurs a hundred times more often than 'politics'. Governance has attracted three main adjectives (global, environmental, civil) and other terms such as dialogue, stakeholders, partnerships, communities, accountability and the like we all hear every day, but they do not wonder why such words are accepted by the people who are at the receiving end, from social scientists to the engaged common people. The idea that capitalism is iterative seems to be the most unknowable one to the metaphysics of capitalism. It could not be otherwise: if people were aware of this main characteristic, they would be in revolution.

Moretti and Pestre's work is very thorough and complete, but, given the different nature of our investigation, we can directly jump to their conclusions: 'Aside from individual words, it's the nature of the Bank's language that is changing: becoming more abstract, detached from concrete social life; a technical code, detached from everyday communication [. . .] Solutions are [. . .] the same for everybody, everywhere' (p. 87). An analysis of the grammatical patterns leads them to further conclude: 'This recurrent transmutation of social forces into abstractions turns the World Bank Reports into strangely metaphysical documents, whose protagonists are often not economic agents but principles [. . .] of so universal a nature, it is impossible to oppose them' (p. 91). The word disagreement is hardly mentioned in the reports. 'An infinitely expanding present emerges, where policies are always in progress, but also *only* in progress' (p. 99; emphasis in the original).

While the preponderance of finance is easy to explain with its purely metaphysical properties (as explained earlier on), what can be clearly seen from Moretti and Pestre's conclusions is that they are fully immersed in the metaphysics of capitalism as we know it. They do not object to the iteration of words and concepts because they do not even see it. They object to their 'metaphysical' content and to the role the Bank plays in spreading neo-liberal thought as the only available economic option. They naturally confuse abstract and metaphysical and seem to think that social forces are material instead of being the *ex post* definitions of a historical conjuncture.[7] What they want is the dominant discourse to take the features they like, because they know that this is possible, as we have endeavoured to show in this book. But, being possible, it is also a form of perfect political, intellectual and cultural impotence.

What is argued above also shows the uselessness of fighting against the cultural models that are imposed from above. The only result is that another model, similar in nature and structure and claiming otherness to mean difference, is produced, which is as amenable as the other to discussion. This is posed as pluralism and democracy, but of course it is not. Hence, the need for an anarchist position to guide emancipation efforts, but it is not so easy to find a radical position among anarchists (that is why we have referred so often to Marx the anarchist). They often accept a dialogue on the metaphysical ground of capitalism.

One relevant instance of this problem can be found in a 1970 paper on language and freedom by Noam Chomsky, published in *Abraxas* (vol.1, no.1; 1970/1980). It goes without saying that it is not our purpose here to criticize Chomsky's theories of language. The point is simply to show how insidious the metaphysics of capitalism can be, and how the precise imprecision of its words and language appears laden with meanings that are only in the head of the user and of his/her reader and/or listener, and how such vague meanings can be easily and immediately lost and regained.

After a brief introductory reasoning on language and freedom spanning from Schelling to Rousseau and Kant, Chomsky (1970/1980) connects (p. 143) language and freedom on the basis of language being a means to ascertain whether other organisms have a human-like mind. This is relevant because, to him, humans are by nature rebellious against oppression. From this, he moves on to infer that, if language is human and rebelliousness too, we can use language to understand the human mind. The point, surprisingly for a self-declared anarchist, is to reach the possibility of outlining the fundamentals of a 'rational social order' (p. 144). In fact (ibid.), it is precisely the limits of the human mind that (he claims to be in the steps of Rousseau here) allow the possibility of continuous improvement.

He thus enrols under his Rousseauian banner Wilhelm von Humboldt, to come to criticize the state that makes the individuals undergo its 'arbitrary' goals. Chomsky is well aware that Humboldt has no conception of the momentum of the commodification of labour, but Humboldt, who is very important to Chomsky, is not a 'primitive' individualist à la Rousseau. No savage rebellion, but a freely associated community (whatever that might mean) is what counts. Chomsky continues, stating (p. 153) that we must give value judgements on future society, for these can, and must, follow from a conception of human nature, which can be studied through its creations and deeds. No doubts à la Berkeley, Hume and Marx bother him.

As a consequence, à la Humboldt again (p. 155), we can study language because this originates from the properties of the mind, producing an infinite use of finite means: an iteration without end! Chomsky is clear that a further reason for taking this approach to the study of human intelligence is that language (p. 156) lends itself well to these purposes. A 'humanistic' social science (ibid.) can be developed, which can be a tool for social action. Action, however, cannot wait for a full development of such a science.

It is evident that Chomsky is labouring under the same illusion as Moretti and Pestre (2015). Nature in general and human nature are there, and we can only perfect our knowledge of them. Language is productive and constructive. As a consequence, the metaphysics of capitalism does not exist. It is part of human nature. It can only be reformed towards 'humanistic' forms whose humanistic features are circularly defined by the metaphysics itself. So, why do some people think otherwise, and love anti-humanistic ideas (e.g. the WB people)? The answer can only be that they are perfidious. Thus, violence against them can be justified by need and by humanitarian concerns, but this is one of the wrong arguments this book argues against. Evil is in social actions, not in individuals. It cannot be counteracted by social action, lest it is simply replicated.

5.4 Materialistic political economy as history

Economics and political economy appear to have cleverly avoided responsibility by their, respectively, perfect and approximate refusal to engage evil (but not ethics, as pointed out several times, for ethics is that sublimation of the presence of evil that lends itself to be talked about). They claim to be techniques even when they pose themselves, like political economy, as multidisciplinary tools. The problem of evil becomes the responsibility of the individual or, in most Marxist orthodoxies, the class.

However, from the point of view of the present argument, precisely the contrary is true. Economics and political economy, by supplying a flawed and partial picture of how to handle the technicalities of social reality, are in themselves evil. It is not the politician or the consultant who applies them who is bad. These last are just puppets programmed to be more or less stubborn or pliable in the use of the chosen economic ideology. The case of the summer 2015 negotiations between Tsipras's Greek government and the EU is very telling. The much-maligned German minister, Schauble, is just the stern defender of an evidently wrong economic ideology he clearly and sincerely believes in. He is exercising a fully democratic right and, in sticking to it, he is defending those European treaties that many European governments have half-heartedly signed, knowing they could not respect them.[8]

Tsipras and his collaborators foolishly opposed the EU arguments Schauble defends by putting forward 'reasonable' corrections that, in their opinion, would slow down the speed with which Greece sinks into the hopeless crisis the treaties have caused. This is but a typical case of the vulgar Hegelian dialectics of capitalism, which always and inevitably – all arguments being reciprocally valid, substitutable and amenable to mediation – favours the strongest, who can negotiate by simply imposing the inevitable. In fact, the capitalist dialectics, despite its inbuilt moderation, appears to operate as if there were always one or a few global catastrophes around the corner. In the Greek case, there were many possible catastrophes, for instance the treaties, the danger to the Euro, the breaking of the EU, the other countries in Greece's condition, the isolation of Greece itself. Such catastrophes, needless to say, are instead – and cannot be otherwise – mere dialectical relationships or sheer hullabaloo.

It follows that, in the capitalist intellectuality, dissenting minorities cannot present themselves at official discussions by appearing reasonable and practical and by forwarding feasible proposals. They must, on the contrary, present themselves as the mindless bearers of catastrophically impossible proposals and/or sheer hullabaloo. That would uncover the capitalist (dialectical) game, compelling the majority (the self-styled carriers of the only reasonable, practicable and feasible proposals) to avert the (perceived, and yet impossible) danger of catastrophic events by dialectically mediating, and thus 'destroying', the outrageous proposals of the minority. In the end, the minority gets the basic 'reasonable' core of its proposals passed, which would have not happened had they presented them directly, as Tsipras did. Such is the sad absurdity of capitalist intellectuality,[9] of which economics and political economy are the most sophisticated interpreters.

Once the negotiations based on economics and political economy (the Greece example is particularly meaningful in this respect, because its delegation included self-defined Marxists) are finished, there remains the problem of what in capitalism is called reality. People will in fact start undergoing the consequences of what has been decided. Although, in our neo-liberal era, the state has been granted much wider scope in terms of its capacities for repression (majoritarian electoral systems, continuous threats from terrorism, the concept of governance, the EU treaties themselves, are all cases of restrictions of democratic rights), they can only help cope with the tip of the iceberg of people's sufferings and complaints. Who takes care of what lies under the surface of the water?

The answer is, of course, economics, political economy and their practitioners, again. Their methodological detachment from reality makes them the best-suited entities to mismanage the beautiful precision of the treaties, the programmes and the plans. Stiglitz (2005) is a spectacular instance of such very common praxis. In his book, he lists a set of possibilities that were suggested by economic ideas, corresponding to some perceived facts, and yet could not be transformed into economic policies. The mesmerizing mixture of theory, empirical evidence and pious illusions he spins throughout his book best renders the intellectual confusion of the metaphysics of capitalism.

Such confusion is much more elementary in structure in the minds of the true neo-liberal economists, because their ideas are silly, and hence all the more appealing, because they fish into whatever is left of the distorted emotions of the capitalist individual. Also, and as importantly, they have absolutely no regard for empirical reality.

Neoliberal economists are, in other words, the only bearers of what they perceive to be a (capitalist, hence logically flawed) utopia. They can do whatever they can, as long as they claim it to be in the name of their lesser utopia. Any action incoherent with it is allowed, for an explanation for it can always be found. Any action coherent with it that hurts common people can be justified on the same ground. In the end, when the crisis deepens (which cannot be otherwise), and despite the reforms towards the market no more market has been introduced, they can always blame the government. Like Stiglitz, they are fighting against an invincible Leviathan of their own making.

Not only is the moderate and dialectical intellectual structure of economics and political economy by definition flawed, because it posits a metaphysics based upon an unjustified and unjustifiable dialectics; it also, in the practice of its adepts, loses, dilutes and distorts its very basic tenets during the reciprocal interaction with the metaphysics of government, politics, society and the rest. The same happens on the side of their victims and opponents, who work in the framework of the same metaphysics to alter what is going on rather than stop it. Violence counters violence. To sufferings, other sufferings are offered. Words hide, make banal and replace whatever pain and loss has been produced. Individuals – those who suffer – are totally disregarded.

Empty terms such as liberation, reform, justice, and even brotherhood and comradeship, transcend into metaphysical items the physical loss of bodies and the feelings entailed. The system is thus granted its institutional regularity, with the advantage that the iteration this whole process comes down to might have delivered a slightly different configuration of the same old world. If such has happened, the metaphysics of capitalism can let loose the cataracts of 'noun-cum-adjectives'. 'Alternative systems', 'socialist', 'non-capitalist', 'non-austerity' outcomes have been obtained. The supporters can (always metaphysically) rejoice, while those who have lost their battle can metaphysically wring their hands and pull their hair out. Whether it is the Bolshevik revolution, World War II or Tsipras's defeat by the EU, the pantomime is always the same.

In fact, although the human losses are pedantically recorded and conveyed to the mass media for the show (a sideshow to this is the 'battle' for full information and the recovery of what governments withhold), the pattern is always the same, perfectly disproportionate to the tragedy enacted. The Greek case becomes more important than the geographically adjacent disaster of the immigrants drowning in the Mediterranean Sea, or the Middle East atrocities. This is precisely the question: evil is not in the actual evil acts that are perpetrated. Evil lies in letting the iterations of the metaphysics of capitalism, produced by its socially enforced, flawed understanding of reality and even of itself, go on undisturbed. Evil is also those who count the casualties to present the bill to the governments, which entails the absurdity of comparing governments by the number of casualties they produce. Who can pay the dead and maimed back, and how? Yet, this is what the whole game is about: a mechanical application of the logic of mainstream economics by everybody, including the Marxists.

The first impression is, however, that evil-doing (violence of all kinds, up to murder) is natural to humanity, from Cain and Abel onwards. The present argument cannot fully confute that impression. Only, it points to the following two facts: first, that violence and murder might not always be qualified as evil. They are so when they are meditated within the socialized intellectual framework (even, therefore, when they are individual). Capitalist violence should not be confused with natural violence. Second, if the definition of evil as an outcome of enforced sociality holds, then the solution lies in trying non-enforced, non-mind- and emotion-numbing types of sociality. The success of such a search would, of course, free us from social evils, not from natural violence.

In any case, if economics and political economy are evil in the sense submitted here, it is evident that they should be discarded, or their role changed. Their purpose should not be the one they have at present of helping organize and keep society, in both a positive (the devising of economic policies) and a negative (the criticism of economic policies and of economic systems) sense. Most important of all, they are no use for progressing towards an alternative, non-capitalist way of life. Their only purpose, in fact, is that of operating within the metaphysics of capitalism, dealing with the imagined and the unimagined by keeping the unconceived away. They are useful in analysing and helping the continuation of capitalism and its metaphysics, but they have no other role.

In order to understand capitalism by means of the economic disciplines, one must thus look at it as a historical subject. Capitalism does have an economic structure (a base) we must make sense of. To do so, we need to frame it historically and study its connections with the superstructure. Marx was right: we need a historical subject that studies the dialectical structure of the metaphysics of capitalism, but, in all the preceding pages, we have challenged the material, concrete ontological status of reality. Capitalist 'reality' is metaphysics, and the material, concrete part can be doubted in its existence simply because the metaphysical part has so alienated us as to make the establishment of truth on this matter impossible, at least for the time being.

Meillassoux (2010), whom we will discuss again in the next section, re-proposes a quasi-Humean and quasi-Berkeleyan 'contingency', but he resolves it in un-demonstrated and un-argued mathematical laws and, most importantly, he keeps all the 'normal' structures of philosophy, thus making his recourse to contingency vain. He never quotes the works of Pierre Raymond (see Sotiris, 2015), whom he should know about, who argued against such mechanistic and teleological mathematics. This also applies to Badiou (see, for instance, 2009), making a discussion of his thought superfluous here. Everything is brought back to the normality of capitalist times.

We can now put the theoretical discussion we have been developing so far to good use. In the world such as we (think we) are presented with, the need for emancipation constitutes the core of materialism. Until we have liberated ourselves from the dominant metaphysics, we cannot trust our senses and our emotions. Whether a concrete, material world exists is a question not worth asking at this stage, but rather the most obvious final goal and mystery of the materialistic thinker.

The dominant metaphysics, as pointed out by everybody since Adam Smith, is determined by its economic base. To this we must turn and from this we must start. By their mirroring the dialectics of capitalism, economics and political economy speak to us, before, and more relevantly than by, their discussion of specific facts, of the metaphysics of capitalism. A telling instance that has been sketched through the preceding pages is the inevitability of the preponderance of finance. If we do not understand the intellectuality and the stunted emotions that are at its base, we cannot explain anything concerning finance, i.e. anything concerning the capitalist economy.

A materialistic historical political economy inevitably relegates economics and the various ideas that go under the umbrella term of political economy to the role of case studies. The economic disciplines must historically interpret capitalist reality. We look at them from outside.

The need to start every attempt to go beyond capitalism from a historical political economy should now be established. The capitalist individual has no need of its natural attributes, and he/she is not interested in understanding them, let alone deploying and developing them, because he/she is a *Homo Oeconomicus*. Such a creature, being endowed with rational speech, has all it takes to survive in the metaphysics of capitalism. He/she can use the market, supply and demand, the interest rate in all their various, variable and uncertain meanings and usages, and makes no effort to perform the declension from any theoretical, univocal meaning to actual, precise and approximate pseudo-meanings. The material appears to be thoroughly and easily studied because it is replaced by the metaphysical. Commodities and material production can give way to finance.

We can call a political economy that studies this stuff materialistic because its purpose is to strive for rather than gain the material, the concrete at the end of the metaphysical tunnel. Even if the concrete does not exist, the point for every materialist is not the local achievement but the exploration of reality in the direction of the unconceived. The tool to do so is the criticism of the imagined and of the unimagined. Like Hume's philosophers, we must direct our efforts towards the liberation of chance, which coincides with our own liberation from the metaphysics of capitalism as we know it. Here we can introduce another connotation of our materialism: we must, and we can only, let the material be free to operate by its own laws or lack of laws.

In other words, a materialistic political economy can only be a backward-looking enterprise. It studies the past in order to free us from it, and in so doing it opens us to the future. It must consider everything it studies as amenable to sudden disappearances, i.e. ruptures with oblivion. This entails accepting, not only real oppositions besides dialectical relationships, but also the possibility of a complete lack of determinations. A materialistic political economy frees the future from the fetters of the past, to the chagrin of those who hold (for some un-understandable reason that no one has ever been able to fully and convincingly explain) that no future can be built without being married to the past. Lenin and Gramsci are two world-renowned examples of this attitude, which we can now call, without hesitation, evil in our present sense.

The Humean features and origin of the present approach, discussed in the preceding chapter, lead to a materialistic political economy (Micocci, 2014) that can be unhesitatingly called a 'critique of political economy'. Whether this actually corresponds to what Marx gave the same name to cannot be decided here, and probably cannot be resolved at all. If Marx is not the Hegelian thinker that the vast majority of Marxists have been interpreting, imitating and worshipping, but the anarchist, anti- and non-Hegelian author we have been liberating in the preceding pages, the Marxian ancestry of the present proposals must be recognized and dutifully acknowledged. But, even if Marx were the Hegelian pedant Marxists love, there would be no denying the Marxian roots of what is being presented in this section. The great authors are here to give us their ideas, but also, and perhaps more importantly, to make us think out new ideas of our own.

Thus, a critique of political economy consists in using political economy, from a materialistic point of view, to destroy political economy. For every concept and historical deed, we must be able to work out a logical critique based on the principles so far explained. Economic concepts and (historical) economic facts are the fetters on the human body and soul we must be able to release by countering them with a sceptical analysis that does without the necessity of metaphysical cause–effect connections. This is particularly difficult in the social sciences, in which many debates are precisely about finding out the cause(s) of a certain effect. This is not to say that we must, for a present-day instance, exonerate the Germans from their responsibilities in the Greek disaster, but, as explained throughout the present book, we need to look at things from outside and look for the possibility of releasing chance from its chains.

The whole Greek episode, like any other, must be framed within the metaphysics of capitalism, with all the occasions on which the capitalist game has been played when there was a chance not to do so being identified. Also, the effort of the student of any historical episode should go towards identification of the poverty of capitalism's language, and the attempt to uncover it. A silence in the sense proposed here consists precisely of an attempt to go beyond the precise approximation and useless abundance of capitalist language, because it is not by participating in capitalism that emancipation can progress. Unfortunately, an emancipative language à la Chomsky (1970) cannot exist.

Should we then drop class struggle and the fight for 'normal', capitalist justice and freedom? The answer is a clear 'no' both if class, and political struggles in general, were Adam Smith's functioning of capitalism we discussed earlier, or Marx's indictment of the futile attempts to mistake political and class struggle for revolution, also analysed earlier. If capitalism, like any other institutionalized society, is based on evil, then injustices are there, and they are often lethal. Fighting them equals fighting for life. Plus, fighting for workers' rights, and especially the reduction of working time and the right to free leisure time, is fundamental to our materialistic purposes. Only by detaching oneself from the furious rhythm of capitalism can we cultivate alternatives.

We can now see in further detail why Lotz's (2014) argument cannot help us. Although he is right in pointing out the fundamental importance of the mental schemas that refer to money and transform it into a true Universal, and the fact that time is thus annihilated into an endless present, Lotz gets lost. Instead of noticing the enormous tragedy he is describing, he goes looking for touching examples. As he is unable to see the radical side of things, he has no use for the radical thinkers we have proposed here. He goes back to dialectics, and to capitalism as we know it; he accepts tragedy because he does not see it fully.

Orlean (2014) is similarly useless for us. He sees clearly that value is a convention and not a substance, but Keynes's influence on him is too strong. Conventions to him are, as to Keynes, something worth having and keeping. As a consequence, he does not connect them with culture and intellectuality. He can thus correctly interpret finance as a rational activity, without seeing its historical role, and accept financial crises as one inevitable aspect of capitalism that can nonetheless be helped. Instead of drawing general conclusions, he turns to explain the present crisis, hoping to shift the balance of suffering from one side to another, but suffering itself appears inevitable.

Instead, sufferings are not inevitable and should not just be shifted from one social sector to another. They can be avoided, just like money, prices and values. Here, the common capitalist thinker might want to notice that, in the recent past, those who study primitive human eras have been re-evaluating the hunter–gatherer civilizations, because they were less cruel and warlike than agricultural civilizations (an easy summary of the studies in this field is Patou-Mathis, 2015). However plausible, attractive and coherent with what is being proposed here, such an argument cannot be sufficient to supply a final proof. In a framework of liberty as chance, no final proof (fortunately) can be offered, and everything is in constant potential movement. That is liberty as chance.

We could, for instance, produce a situation ourselves in which social evils are avoided (which, of course, does not mean abandoning the study of the past). Such a situation can only be based on circumstances, and these are not completely under human control. Thus, even if we could arrive at a situation without social evil, and happily live in it, we must be aware of the peculiarity and changeability of it all. However idyllic, it would suddenly or slowly change. This last, however, is not a fault, nor is it something to be feared. On the contrary, it is a thoroughly enjoyable thing. Here lies the main difference from capitalism and its economics and political economy.

Whereas capitalism, economics and political economy are furiously bent on protecting their circumstances in the foolish way we have seen, i.e. by denying a role to reality in general, a materialistic political economy would not be a tool for planning and construction. Once it has completed its negative role of destroying capitalist economics and political economy, one can hypothesize that its political and social ideas would be perfectly useless in a situation of liberty as chance. Planning, if needed at all (which we cannot say here, before emancipation from the metaphysics of capitalism), can at that point be thought of as engineering: the exploitation of the relative local adaptability of nature to human labour we have been observing in the preceding chapters.

Saying any more on this issue would direct us back to the metaphysics of capitalism and to its need to protect itself by fencing itself in physically and metaphysically. The great difficulty at this stage is not so much the description of the role of a materialistic political economy (see Micocci, 2014), but that of liberty as chance. Resorting, as usual, to Marx's own language, we can describe it as the potential to discuss human emancipation as a 'practical question' (Thesis II, Marx and Engels, 1985, p. 123), achieving a 'sensuous human activity': practice, as in Thesis I (ibid.). We must work towards the 'coincidence of the changing of circumstances and of human activity', a 'revolutionary practice' (Thesis III, ibid.). We propose these brief references in the belief, which has been argued in this whole work, that Marx kept a firm coherence in this anti- and non-Hegelian matter.

By revealing the absurdity and the evil limitations of economics and political economy, a materialistic political economy, or any other general approach of this type,[10] cannot tell us anything about silence and liberty as chance. It can only prepare us, by emancipating us from the metaphysics of capitalism, to go towards starting a comprehension of it. There is nothing disappointing in this; on the contrary. It is precisely the fact that we can rationally predict nothing about them that makes them objects worth exploring and even, at least in the case of the present author, irresistible objects of desire.

Another way to put this matter is by defining it as an attempt to let nature follow its course while going along with it. For those who need examples, the only one the present author can offer is the abandonment to sexual ecstasy, but then, if what argued so far is true, few will know what is meant by that.

5.5 Emancipation

It is time to put everything together. By definition, one is intellectually limited and, if what we have been arguing thus far is correct, excessively bound to what words can convey, but words are all we have here, and this section might prove the toughest part of the book, both for the writer and for the reader. Instead of offering alternative languages and rules, we will seek to solve the problem by sticking to the established philosophical language we have been using so far.

The hope is that, by its having survived across historical ages, philosophy might prove to be relatively independent of the constraints of our era.

Unsurprisingly, to begin with we can state that emancipation coincides with revolution, which changes the understanding (not the meaning) of this latter term. If emancipation is from capitalism and from its intellectual structure and language, then inevitably the basis and the superstructure of capitalism should also end up being swept away by its practice. Here precisely lies the difference between the idea of revolution as emancipation and the current usage of this term. In capitalist revolutions, both actual/historical and theoretical, the base and the superstructure are superseded by alternative (i.e. different) types of organization, which are juxtaposed with them. As a consequence, in order to make themselves operational, revolutions must dialectically interact with the old base and superstructure.

It is precisely this dialectical interaction that grants that:

1   in the first place, there is no complete exit from capitalism; its methods and intellectuality are borrowed and reused;
2   the collective organized violence that we have argued to be a characteristic of the dialectical, moderate dynamics of capitalism is also kept;
3   inevitably, there is no emancipation;
4   the revolution must content itself with its justice, equality and economic growth results, thus entirely surrendering to the logic of economics and political economy.

The historical instances of such a pattern of development are so common and well studied in modern and contemporary history that there is no need to undertake any discussion of this issue here.

It is, instead, relevant to seek to figure out at least something of the evolutionary process that follows from the considerations of emancipation developed so far. As said earlier on, we are in the first place describing an individual process of self-liberation that must necessarily operate in the sense of being the arithmetical sum of independent individuals, but, in capitalism as we know it, if a unanimously collective event does not take place, the dominant metaphysics simply excludes the revolutionary minority from communication, denying its presence by its inability to acknowledge the nature of what those individuals are doing. Silence (the process of emancipation), by its very existence, will indict capitalist language, its metaphysics and its base and superstructure. Thus, our task is at once very simple and very complex. How many people must start the process of recovering their 'otherness' for the system not to be able to survive because a communication problem will set in?

One cannot even try to imagine what may happen at this point, although a warning is in order: if evil is what we have so defined earlier on, the danger of organized collective violence on the part of the challenged institutions is high. Here, the problem is not, as the superficial reader might observe, the usual thing with revolutions. The question is more general, and it is indeed a vicious circle: if evil is in institutionalized societies and it takes the form of organized, justified and motivated violence, the elimination of evil can only coincide with the elimination of institutionalized society. There is no other way to counteract organized violence. As already signalled, fighting back, besides provoking further sufferings, helps preserve, and indeed justify, organized violence itself. The whole thing must be erased by calling oneself out of its collectivized, homogeneous logics.

Of course, the same reasoning applies to the absurd and inhuman single features of capitalism as we know it. This is precisely what makes it look so inevitable and impossible to fight, unless one is a Leninist or something similar, in which case you think you can fight it by adopting its methods, but doing it better. The outcome of this last approach has been amply shown by history to be a non- or even an anti-revolutionary practice, i.e. a perfectly capitalist practice, but reasoning about these items, despite appearing at first sight inevitable, is a big mistake. It should be clear by now that the logics and language of capitalism use and allow confrontation only with what is compatible. The rest is not only not useful (practical): more relevantly for us here, for this is the key to the whole construction and to emancipation itself, it is unpredictable.

Unpredictability in the sense of potential lack of determinations – the unconceived – lies at the very core of our whole argument and constitutes the main incompatibility with the metaphysics of capitalism as we know it. This is liberty as chance, the unspeakability of nature (which does not deny the possibility of describing it and using it). The core difficulty is accepting that unpredictability changes your life and makes it incommunicable with present-day capitalism.

This simple thought could perhaps have been said in many fewer words, and without so much erudition, but it was necessary to show that we are not talking about a new need, or a need determined by the faults of capitalist intellectuality alone. We are not even talking about an anti-capitalist revolution. The question is general and has always been present in recorded history. As we are facing it these days, we are doing so by noticing capitalism's faults in this respect.

We have been denoting the character of revolution by calling it 'the unconceived'. What this term means is the lack of relationship between liberty as chance and the speech and words of capitalism. We have also called it 'silence', especially with reference to its realization in the form of emancipation. From the point of view of the metaphysics of capitalism, in fact, the type of emancipation proposed here is a form of silence. The individual, instead of joining the rest of the others in peddling only what can be said, turns his/her attention to whatever is not that type of activity, to the point of, if need be, apparently doing what capitalism, its religions and even most anti-capitalist activists condemn: nothing at all.

In fact, the whole point of the unconceived is its perfect lack of potential certainty. It may not even exist at all. It is very far, therefore, from what Meillassoux (2010) calls contingency. This last is very much a Humean type of presence and is, therefore, characterized by a wild changeability that cannot afford any standpoint from which to operate in the traditional way, but it is not to do, at least in Meillassoux (2010), with the unconceived. On the contrary, Meillassoux's contingency can be talked about and rendered with one important part of the typically limited language of capitalism: mathematics. After dazzling us with long discussions around uncertainty, Meillassoux returns us to where we were in the first place.

Meillassoux (2010) does not perceive and does not investigate the gap between individual and collective perception and the acceptance and possibility that contingency might do something else, completely outside any logic, however local and contingency-based, we can bestow on its development or lack of development. If there exists a movement of things besides the self-contained bubble of capitalism (which we can fairly hypothesize, but for which no final proof can be given), other logics or lack of logics can exist. Only silence can help towards accepting and perhaps understanding that, and in the end perceiving it, if and when possible. Liberty as chance instead cannot be rendered by ordinary language: it only potentially exists to our perception (individual, not collective or institutionalized) when we can pin it down, which is always too late.

Hume, in other words, dared too little in this direction. We must go back all the way to Epicurus (see also Micocci, 2002, 2008/2010) to find a radical expression of the infinite power of possibility. By going back to Epicurus, we can also finish our discussion of Marx the anarchist. It is worthwhile mentioning as a start that, in the preface to his doctoral dissertation (Marx, 1990), Marx quotes Hume (p. 7), among others, to argue that philosophy (against Hegel) must be pursued to its utmost limits, ending with the assertion that Prometheus, the creature who hated the gods, was the greatest saint and martyr of the philosophical calendar (p. 8).

Let us see how Marx's dissertation on Democritus and Epicurus, despite its missing parts, allows us to complete our attempt to separate Marx from the interpretations of the Marxists. In fact, it contains some very important philosophical considerations that confirm the soundness of what we have called 'Marx the anarchist'. It will also help understand better the issue of silence and emancipation.

In this work, Marx is engaged in separating Democritus from Epicurus and in rebuilding the reputation of the latter, unjustly dismissed by most commentators, ancient and modern. He seeks to return 'Epicureans, Stoics and Skeptics' to the mainstream of philosophy (p. 9) by proving the profundity of their positions. In fact, the 'subjective form' these philosophers represent has been so far 'almost completely forgotten in favour of metaphysical determinations' (p. 12). Epicurus, unlike Democritus (p. 17), seeks to give an objective form to the world that can be grasped by the senses, subtracting it from opinion. This point is important per se and also because it helps to explain the key question of materialism, its difference from the view put forward here, and the interpretations of the Marxists.

Marx, in fact, always kept a schizophrenic attitude in his materialism. On the one hand, as anticipated in his dissertation we are considering here, the material exists objectively and can be the object of scientific analysis. On the other hand, Humean doubts crop up all the time in his work, including the dissertation itself. The dissertation is indeed a good example of this ambivalence. Democritus is a believer in empirical observation (p. 18), a supporter of 'positive science'. He believes he can learn and systematize his erudition. But to Epicurus, positive science does not lead to perfection (p. 27): you need philosophy and logic. Democritus's necessity is only a particular case. Chance and humanity will also count. Chance is by far the most important, as Marx emphasizes (p. 22). That is why Epicurus denies disjunctive judgements. It is to abolish necessity.

Abstract possibility (p. 24) is the opposite of real possibility. The former is limitless, 'like fantasy'; the latter is delimited by intellect. Abstract possibility is an exercise for the subject rather than a thing that matters for the explained object. Here, Marx remains in the field of what can be thought. He does not see the possibility, which we have introduced as fundamental, of the unconceived. Epicurus's goal is of course *ataraxia*, mental tranquillity conditioned by the need not to contradict what is perceived as existing. But, where the empirical and sceptical philosophers see only necessity, Epicurus is giving importance mainly to chance, in what Marx calls a 'dogmatic' way.

Moving on to the question of the atoms (Part 2), Marx notices that, in Epicurus, it is repulsion, the reconquering of otherness, that grants self-consciousness (p. 38). That is why we also find more concrete forms of repulsion in Epicurus, such as the contract in politics, or friendships in the social realm (p. 40). Man is alienated, he is different from his essence (p. 41), and his activity is that of always posing contradictions. 'Every determination takes the form of an isolated reality', in Epicurus's atomistic theory (p. 50). Matter and form, existence and essence, in their opposition produce material reality. These are real oppositions. In fact, 'abstract singularity' is freedom 'for existence', not 'within existence' (p. 52).

The only way to make sense of material reality, for Marx's Epicurus, is to give time a paramount role (p. 54). Time is determined as an 'accidens of the accidens', pure change. Time makes and unmakes, all the time causing death and disappearance, and human perception of material reality. Man's sensitivity is time, the place where natural processes are reflected and acquire a phenomenical feature. Time and appearance consume each other in their appearing as phenomena. Disappearance is always around the corner, and always perfectly unpredictable (although Marx does not elaborate this point this way). The senses in Epicurus are the only criterion in 'the dominion of concrete nature, like abstract reason is the same in the world of atoms' (p. 58).

Meteors (V) afford Marx some more, very relevant and enlightening analyses. Celestial bodies in fact give Epicurus an enormous problem, because they appear eternal and unchanging. The contradiction between essence and existence, form and matter, appears erased. Celestial bodies are universal. But here, Epicurus's preoccupation with fear and superstition can also be put to good use. Any determined and univocal explanation of the celestial bodies is wrong. Here, self-consciousness can go beyond what it has done so far (take the same form as the natural matter) and take an autonomous form. Whatever challenges *ataraxia* is not eternal. There is an absolute freedom of the self-consciousness, which is conceived in the form of singularity. Epicurus is, for this reason, the greatest thinker of the Greek Enlightenment (p. 68).

Human individuals fight fear by being other even from what appears eternal and immutable. There is a perfect opposition between the consciousness of the self and the universal that depends on, and we may say it makes, everything changeable and – Marx does not use this word, at least in the Italian edition we are basing ourselves upon here – unpredictable. The knowledge of nature is a continuous process of producing otherness to what you think you have found. It is a process of individual liberation – an emancipation. It goes without saying that it is nothing to do with Hegel. The individual solves his/her relationship with nature by admitting of many explanations: the principle of what can be thought, represented, of chance, of abstract identity and liberty is a lack of determination (from '*Quaderni sulla Filosofia di Epicuro*', in Marx, 1990, p. 82).

In other words, as promised at the beginning of the present section, the language of philosophy has been used to clarify what the maieutics of capitalism cannot even conceive of. Each of us is alone with our understanding of everything. One can choose to join the institutional metaphysics, or to look for a personal *ataraxia* in the sense of a liberation from the fear that univocal explanations, i.e. metaphysics, instil in us. The only way out of the (any) metaphysics is by simultaneously allowing for the presence of the unconceived (the undetermined, liberty as chance, death and its opposite, as Lucretius would put it), i.e. what is other than us, and by a personal making sense, on a purely singular and individual ground, of the material reality around us. This last requires a few words of explanation.

To Epicurus, Marx and most of the thinkers we have been considering in the present book, the senses are our only way to register the reality around us, which we can use both for our survival and for making philosophical and scientific sense of, but, unlike Epicurus, we have no certainty that atoms, or whatever else we can think about or even experimentally prove, are at the origin of the concrete reality out there. As a consequence, any attempt to relate to it and make final sense of it is forever jeopardized. Both reality and our approach to it might be wrong. This is the main difference between the 'Enlightenment' thinkers (including Marx and his Epicurus) we have been discussing here and the thesis proposed in this book. What we propose here is a use of the complete lack of determinations material things might amount to.

Such a complete lack of determinations might look terrifying to the metaphysics of capitalism, but is instead the most complete form of *ataraxia*. By always expecting the unconceived, we nurture optimism. By giving up on capitalist hope, we build a much wider and more exciting type of hope. In it, the banality of the everyday cares can be kept, because the burden of necessity and of their being means to higher social and individual ends has been lifted. They – take the usual example of agriculture – become comfortable routines we can mindlessly attend to with no effort. It means, for a powerful instance, that we are liberated from the slavery of work, from the empty and evil rhetoric that human labour is a good thing, as exemplified in Section 3.3 by the collective intellect discussion, or by the absurd struggle for a 'just' salary or wage.

All the limited and limiting hopes of a material or ethical improvement that capitalism instils in us can be abandoned without our necessarily abandoning the useful (practical) core that lies at their origin: the need to interact with nature to win our daily bread. Our minds would in fact be with our bodies, or, more precisely given the framework of complete lack of determinations, they would be seeking to work together. Thus, conversely, philosophy would lose its characteristic of complex intellectual labour open only to those who are in the know. It is easy to predict that in this world of silence there would be no way for Adam Smith's 'deception' of the market or for all the other capitalist expedients to lure the individuals. Institutions will naturally disappear (not 'wither away' slowly, as Lenin famously put it) with the disappearance of economic intercourse. That is why, in Section 5.4, we classified the role of materialistic political economy as historical.

The acceptance of perfect unpredictability in the sense of lack of determinations is a relaxing possibility. Reality, however doubtful its presence can be, is there for our perception, and we can fully enjoy it. In fact, every instant we relate to it we do so expecting the possibility of the unconceived. In this framework, common activities take up intensely, indeed fascinating, new potentials. Even a walk down the street to fetch bread becomes a walk into the unknown, instead of a boring duty. Imagine the effect on sex and on sentimental relationships. In short, things would regain their presence for the individual. Words to describe them would most of the time be unnecessary. There would be no way to build a metaphysics.

What is liberty then? The mixture of the imagined, the unimagined and the unconceived, in the sensual immersion in the perception (true or not) of nature. Liberty, at least at this stage, is nature itself, unless, as hypothesized already earlier in the book, man does not belong to nature, but the most important thing that we should notice is that emancipation in such a lack of determinations is a continuous process without end, or with an end that at the moment it is impossible even to conceive. So is liberty, therefore. Nobody, at least until some new element is introduced that changes the general framework presented here, can claim to have reached a result. Everything can be other from itself and from the observer in no time, and understanding coincides with time itself, as expressed by Marx's Epicurus.

Each generation is thus freed from the influence of the former generation, even when history is perfectly recorded. Life coincides with time, which coincides with sensuousness (do not forget prolepsis, however). Everything is valid for the length of time it is valid. Again, the example of agriculture and of its apparent submission to human effort is very telling. It works when it works, but we know it can change any time, even in the direction of a catastrophe. Paradoxically, although this, at least to the present author, means to negate the presence of a god of the Christian, Jewish and Islamic type, it can perfectly contain a god of that type. But such a hypothesis would be an individual accommodation that does not entail that need to impose it on the others that has characterized monotheistic religions.

From the point of view proposed here, we can also reconsider all the works that have pointed out the physical and mental repression required to hold together a modern state in general, and capitalism in particular. From Hobbes onwards, we can easily see that repression comes down to the only means institutions have to prevent emancipation. Capitalist collectivization, with its ethical and communitarian goals, appears as a way to keep people within the boundaries of institutionalized society. Indeed, repression of all kinds appears as the main source of the continuous peddling of words and speech by which the metaphysics of capitalism operates. With its characteristic of not being capable of expressing simple, individual thoughts, it needs subtler and subtler discussions, and more and more simultaneously precise and approximate concepts.

That is why economics of the mainstream kind can do without reality, and Marxist approaches consider economic concepts instead of wondering where material reality is. Nothing is real in any case, and the material is secondary to the general game. That is also why economics and political economy work, for good and bad. Like in Aesop's fable of the wolf meeting the dog and wondering about the latter's visible welfare, the choice is between a fettered luxury and an unpredictable and mysterious life in the wilderness. From this perspective, economics and political economy do the poor thing that the Grand Old Duke of York does in the famous nursery rhyme. They command their troops (their concepts and the corresponding objects), marching them up and down the hill, and noticing with great statistical pomp that, 'When they were up/They were up/And when they were down/They were down/And when they were only half-way up/They were neither up nor down'.

As a final point for this section, we must signal that what has been presented here has nothing to do with an excessive, Enlightenment faith in reason. This is not meant to deny the influence of Enlightenment thinkers on the present reasoning (we have been considering here Marx the anarchist as one of the Enlightenment thinkers). In fact, the negation of the philosophical Mind of Kant and Hegel in the first place and the second, important negation of the body and mind distinction inspired by Epicurus make reason and rationality empty terms for our purposes here. Finally, given the evident role of the lack of all determinations, the very idea of faith is simply out of place.

Rather, one might want to notice the role of the unconceived, but such a role is in itself perfectly unpredictable. It even may not exist, or not reveal itself, at all. All we can safely state is that, in the process of emancipation, the pretended difference between body and mind blurs, but, to come to the only possible conclusion, the whole reasoning of this section means, for us now, that only one thing is possible to us: the elimination of the metaphysics of capitalism. Given all we have been arguing thus far, and despite the few intuitive matters put forward throughout the present section, its debunking is all we are faced with in practice. The most important tool that we hold in our hand to do so is a (historical) materialistic political economy of capitalism, as described in Section 5.4.

It is to that task that we must turn. The 'practical', continuous anxiety typical of the metaphysics of capitalism to always plan, defend and organize the future must not influence us. By building and applying a materialistic political economy as a critique of political economy, we also contribute to a resolution of the issue of the ontological problem of the metaphysics of capitalism that we have introduced since Chapter 2. Whether the solution is the one we propose here that comes from Epicurus and Marx but is neither Epicurean nor Marxist, or it is any other, by criticizing the metaphysics of capitalism, we are working towards the solution of the equivocal ontology of capitalism itself and of its metaphysics.

Although, by now, it should go without saying, it is well worth reminding the reader that there is no guarantee of success. Indeed, this is one more feature that differentiates what we are submitting here from all the other criticisms of capitalism. The theoretical argument proposed here is emphatically not a recipe for conducting one's life or a revolution. It is, obviously, the very opposite: a call for individual responsibility.

5.6 Conclusions

Let us start from the most obvious. What has been argued thus far prevents the possibility of a theory of anarchism, while proving that anarchism is the only possible outcome of the emancipation process presented here. Anarchist theory coincides with the unconceived: it can only be practised. It is the most appropriate application of what Marx recommends in his Thesis XI on Feuerbach. The issues of feasibility and of what anarchism would look like can only be solved by individually progressing towards emancipation, and that can only be done by the arithmetical sum of everybody's efforts. This also answers the erroneous argument proposed by those who oppose anarchism: it works only if everybody does it, believing in it. Indeed, but that is, ontologically speaking, a 'natural' outcome, as we have argued in Section 5.5. It is easy, as long as we start from the critique of political economy. Silence is a materialistic political economy.

Naturally, the outcome of the process might be very different from how we conceive anarchism in our capitalist days, but this is precisely what anarchism is about. That is why words cannot convey anything positively, but can only be used to outline the destructive part of the process. This makes them extremely different in usage from what happens in capitalism as we know it, where they are used to sanction the precise approximation and the absurd ontological status of capitalism itself. They are part of the collective conditioning of human intellects and feelings towards what can be said in the form of noun-cum-adjective. In the process, they help evil act. They are there to cause it, then justify it, and eventually condemn it. Economics and political economy supply the general analytical framework.

We started this chapter by considering, with Leopardi's Asian shepherd, whether or not nature can be boring. The point is not to reply with a 'yes' or 'no'. Rather, we should take notice that there is a chance that, if the consubstantiality between man and nature that has always been argued by science is true, the emancipation process might deliver us to nature at last without mediations. This would solve the problem by dissolving it: humans are nature. If the consubstantiality argument ends up being false, we are left with yet another unconceived. Whatever the solution is, it is exciting to work at it.

But the most important achievement of our entire argument is a simplification of thought. The heavy, artificial complication of the maieutics of capitalist intellectuality can be shed if we stick to what we have defined as silence. The different, and precise, usage of words and speech is not a novelty in general, and in particular to the readers of Giacomo Leopardi. What we do here is locate the causes of the misuses of words and speech in capitalism as we know it. By uncovering the intellectual cause of this problem, we have also, hopefully, supplied the springboard to a solution. By using words and speech carefully we simplify, not just discourse and social interaction, but also scientific analysis.

If nature as the material, the concrete, exists, what is being proposed here is a way to directly approach it without the mediation of a metaphysics. If nature is an illusion, then the approach proposed here is a way to get rid of a poorly metaphysics. A result such as the second might produce yet another metaphysics, of course, but it supplies a chance to be creative about it and to be open to any possibility. Such an opening is precisely what we lack in capitalism as we know it, which, as repeatedly seen, is perfectly sealed to anything that is not itself, i.e. its metaphysics. Thus, whether we at last gain the material, the concrete, or yet another metaphysics, what is being proposed in this volume is in both cases a chance to broaden human understanding, or even, in the most promising of cases, to revolutionize it.

In pursuing this approach, we are going straight ahead in opposing the vulgar Hegelianism of capitalism as we know it. It follows that a confrontation with the dominant, dialectical Marxism is also inevitable, for this last keeps winding up its Hegelian subtleties. To give a telling instance of the power of simple arguments as offered here versus the slow-moving apparatus of mainstream Marxism, the question of communism (which to the present author looks like a *conditio sine qua non* for anarchism), i.e. the elimination of private property, is perfect. Whereas, for the present approach, communism is a practical question with no time – in the sense of phases – involved (human understanding is time itself), for the Marxists' mainstream, communism becomes a burdensome sequence of subtle and controversial issues that comprise, as shown many times, perfectly metaphysical items (socialism, transition, the state, laws, planning, etc.) that can only be discussed in theory, that is in the metaphysics of capitalism, but the abolition of private property in fact takes an instant: you just abolish it.

There is no need to remind the reader that the Marxist approach has not only generated an enormous and sophisticated literature that has clogged up the issue, involving non-Marxist scholars as well. More importantly, it has produced the actual convolutions, inversions and hiccups of the history of socialist countries. Perfectly controversial metaphysical items have provoked the death and suffering of an uncountable number of persons, most of whom not only could do absolutely nothing to rescue themselves, but were also perfectly uninterested in such metaphysical questions. With the same type of logic, lives have been wrecked today in the EU and in the rest of the world. Governments, for instance, calculate that by killing n persons they avoid killing p persons, where $p > n$, and individuals approve, in the secret hope that they are not included in the set n. Some of these same people (the holders of alternative views) apply the very same reasoning the other way around, thinking that, by saving a few more people, they reduce casualties, i.e. in their flawed logic, avoid killing people. Meanwhile, it is real people who die or are maimed, to whom such idle metaphysics and its demented arithmetic are meaningless.

Yet, what we have just described is only a part of the immense tragedy of the metaphysics of capitalism as we know it. In fact, even the material victims are part of the same intellectual game. However ignorant, or isolated in both the cultural and geographical sense, or just unaware, the potential victims are playing the same intellectual game. Even when they are traditional, antiquated economic operators dressed in their folk garments, they can relate to capitalism only according to the rules of its metaphysics. Their death and their bewilderment are, and can only be, part of the metaphysical game, just like the tears and the horror of those who observe them. The same applies to the anarchists, or the hippies, and their semi-isolated economic efforts.

The only thing that could be done would be to use words and speech in a historical way to seek to signify the reach and power of the metaphysics of capitalism. The present chapter, in the first place, considered some important philosophical questions, in Section 5.2. Inevitably, the exploration of Marx the anarchist has been continued and furthered.

Section 5.3 introduced a definition of evil as the result of the enforced collectivization produced by the homogenizing effects of capitalist metaphysics. The help that words and language give to the task of evil has been also pointed out. A materialistic political economy as a destructive intellectual tool has then been outlined, going beyond the simple Humean framework by rehabilitating Epicurus through Marx the anarchist.

Section 5.5 developed the issue of emancipation, putting together all the arguments elaborated throughout the volume, in particular the difference between the imagined, the unimagined and the unconceived.

The implication of the whole argument has been sketched in 5.6 and will be further expanded in the next chapter, which concludes the book. The most important thing is that emancipation, i.e. the emancipation of human understanding towards 'liberty as chance', is a perfectly individual task. No organized violence can be involved in it, no groupings, other than natural, spontaneous groupings. This last thing happens all the time in reality, for less important issues, and therefore constitutes no difficulty for the point of view put forward here. No further discussion of the issue is needed.

Notes

1 '*Quam ob rem, at religio propaganda etiam est quae iuncta cum cognitione naturae, sic superstitionis stirpes omnes eligendae*' (2006, Book II, 149, p. 228).
2 Though he was only born in 1798.
3 Thucydides is mentioned to keep arguing that the phenomena described here as the metaphysics of capitalism are by no means unique to capitalism. Rather, in capitalism, they are distilled, purified and systematically employed as if there were nothing else. But there is much else, just like in Thucydides's times. I should thank Fiorinda Li Vigni for making me explore Thucydides, with the usual disclaimers.
4 I owe this idea to Flavia Di Mario, with the usual disclaimers. See Di Mario and Micocci (2015).
5 If all this is true, then the emphasis laid on the mass media by all sorts of thinkers is only yet another excuse not to face this general issue, and to justify their political defeats.

6 In order to take it, you may need some psychological conditioning or reconditioning by specialized personnel. This is allowed, and even praised (you are struggling to be part of society), and even increases GDP. But if, to cope, you need drugs or alcohol, this is allowed only as long as you do not get caught. If you are caught, claim some artistic pretension, or personal circumstances, and you are pardoned.

7 Here, the iterativeness of capitalism helps a lot, making all conjunctures similar and thus allowing for generalizations.

8 It is plausible to suppose that, rather than subscribing to the neo-liberal ideology, they longed to rid themselves of the task of devising their own economic policies, of which they had proved incapable. Italy is a perfect instance of such baseness.

9 This argument draws from and develops conversations I had a long time ago with Luciano Vasapollo, who is not responsible for anything I am saying here.

10 The subject matter of this book is the social sciences. An enlargement to the natural sciences is obviously well beyond what is possible here.

References

Ammiano Marcellino (2001) *Storie Res Gestae [Histories]*, 2 vols, Mondadori, Milan, Italy.

Badiou, A. (2009) *Logics of Worlds Being and Event II*, Continuum, London.

Benn Michaels, W. (2008) 'Against diversity', *New Left Review*, 52, 33–6.

Berkeley, G. (2004) *Principles of Human Knowledge and Three Dialogues*, Penguin, London.

Biscuso, M., and Gallo, F. (1999) *Leopardi Antitaliano [Anti-Italian Leopardi]*, Manifestolibri, Rome.

Cicerone, M. T. (2006) *Della Divinazione De Divinatione [On Divination]*, Garzanti, Milan, Italy.

Chomsky, N. (2008) '*Linguaggio e libertà* [Language and liberty]', in Chomsky, N., *Anarchismo [On Anarchism]*, pp. 136–58, Marco Tropea, Milan (originally published 1970).

Di Mario, F., and Micocci, A. (2015) 'Smith's invisible hand. Controversy is needed', *ESHET Conference*, Rome, 15–18 May.

Hegel, G. W. F. (2008) *La Fenomenologia dello Spirito [Phenomenology of Spirit]*, Einaudi, Turin, Italy.

Leopardi, G. (1998) *Canti [Cantos]*, Feltrinelli, Milan, Italy.

Lotz, C. (2014) *The Capitalist Schema Time, Money and the Culture of Abstraction*, Lexington, Lanham, MD.

Marx, K. (1990) *Differenza tra la Filosofia di Democrito e Quella di Epicuro [Differences Between the Philosophy of Democritus and that of Epicurus]*, Editori Riuniti, Rome.

Marx, K. (1992) *Early Writings*, Penguin Books, London.

Marx, K., and Engels, F. (1985) *The German Ideology*, Lawrence & Wishart, London.

Meillassoux, Q. (2010) *After Finitude: An essay on the necessity of contingency*, Continuum, London.

Merker, N. (2009) *Filosofie del Populismo [Philosophies of Populism]*, Laterza, Bari, Italy.

Micocci, A. (2000) 'Leopardi Antitaliano [Anti-Italian Leopardi]', *Il Cannocchiale Rivista di Studi Filosofici*, 3, 199–209.

Micocci, A. (2002) *Anti-Hegelian Reading of Economic Theory*, Mellen Press, Lampeter, UK.

Micocci, A. (2008/2010) *The Metaphysics of Capitalism*, Lexington, Lanham, MD.

Micocci, A. (2012) *Moderation and Revolution*, Lexington, Lanham, MD.

Micocci, A. (2014) 'Unusual Humean issues in materialistic political economy', *Journal of Philosophical Economics*, 7, 2, 22–6.

Moretti, F., and Pestre, D. (2015) 'Bankspeak: The language of World Bank reports', *New Left Review*, 92, 75–99.

Nussbaum, M. (2015) 'Transitional anger', *Journal of the American Philosophical Association*, 1, 1, 41–56.

Orlean, A. (2014) *The Empire of Value: A new foundation for economics*, MIT Press, London.

Pardjanadze, N., and Micocci, A. (2000) '*I Nichilisti Russi* [The Russian Nihilists]', *Il Cannocchiale Rivista di Studi Filosofici*, 2, 183–202.

Patou-Mathis, M. (2015) '*No, gli esseri umani non hanno sempre fatto la guerra* [No, human beings did not always make war]', *Le Monde Diplomatique Il Manifesto*, July–August, 18–19.

Rousseau, J.-J. (1975) *Emile*, Editori Riuniti, Rome.

Sallustio (1994) *La Congiura di Catilina De Coniuratione Catilinae [Catilina's Plot]*, BUR, Milan, Italy.

Schmitt, C. (2014) 'Hegel and Marx', *Historical Materialism*, 22, 3/4, 388–93.

Smith, A. (2009) *The Theory of Moral Sentiments*, Penguin Classics, London.

Sotiris, P. (2015) 'Struggle not destiny', *Historical Materialism*, 23, 2, 157–75.

Stiglitz, J. E. (2005) *I Ruggenti Anni Novanta [The Roaring Nineties]*, Einaudi, Turin, Italy.

Tacito (2000) *Storie [Histories]*, Garzanti, Milan, Italy.

Tacito (2007) *Annali [Annals]*, Rizzoli, Milan, Italy.

Thucydides (2005) *Le Storie [Histories]*, 2 vols, UTET, Turin, Italy.

6 Conclusions

6.1 Preliminary thoughts

In the experience of the present writer, the most common reaction to the argument that has been presented in this book is a refusal to follow the reasoning to its conclusions, and/or a set of irrational oppositions. As a matter of fact, there is little else one can do against an argument that explains human behaviour in general with the tools of political economy – for this is what has been done in this book. If you recognize what has been described as realistic, you thereby admit that all it takes to sketch human understanding in capitalism as we know it is political economy. The implication is that all other subjects (psychology, anthropology, linguistics, sociology, etc.) say the very same things as political economy, which they are supposed not to do. The possibility that this may be true terrifies the less-bold reader: who is right, the present author, with his radical method, past thinkers and unusual Marx, or present-day analyses that do not acknowledge such radical questions?

The paradox that contributes to the common reaction described above is that, whereas the human sciences, like common discourse, paint a picture of human understanding as a very complex set of processes, the present description instead sketches it as a simple, logically flawed thing. In so doing, it nonetheless implies the realistic possibility of a much richer individual endowed with immense – or better said, unutterable – potential. In other words, the complex and convoluted human being of capitalism as we know it is criticized and replaced with a simple and straightforward – but bare and hard to prove – infinite set of intellectual and emotional possibilities. Whereas the former is manageable with the words of a flawed metaphysics, the latter is not. This is the core of the problem that has been analysed, which further contributes, in the less-bold reader, to the emotional, irrational reactions that have been mentioned above.

The argument developed in this book, furthermore, comes down to the fundamental issue that few have acknowledged as such in the literature, that there is a reciprocal connection between the arid, unoriginal, uselessly complex and convoluted social man of capitalism and the presence of a manageable social, political and economic organization. In fact, such a connection is, it has been argued, an indissoluble tie. The imperfect, socialized human being of capitalism who rationalizes everything in words is thoroughly impotent outside society, for there he/she faces not only the unpredictability of real oppositions (the unimaginable), but also the possibility of perfectly undetermined events: the unconceived. This type of human individual is typical of capitalism but is also, *mutatis mutandis*, a constant in history and anthropology. If we want to find a non-social man by means of the human sciences, we must either set ourselves the task of retrieving the natural man, which Rousseau signalled as impossible, or look for pre-social, perhaps pre-agricultural, human organizations.

There is a third possibility, which is in fact what is being proposed here: individual emancipation. The difficulty is that attempting to achieve this is a highly risky endeavour. We can only start progressing along the path towards it, without knowing whether we will ever be successful. Such a path, moreover, requires the courage to accept the radical arguments put forward in the preceding chapters, or any alternative argument endowed with a similar degree of radicality. It is against this possibility that, as said above, most people react by displaying the pseudo-emotions and pseudo-reasoning of capitalism as we know it, which we can now summarize as follows: what does not follow the mediating, dialectical rules of the metaphysics of capitalism is impossible, and, even if one wanted to achieve it, it would take a transition period, and that would mean an enormous amount of time (and, implicitly, of pain).

We have shown in the preceding chapters the logical error inherent in stating that what does not follow the rules of capitalist metaphysics is impossible. Stating instead that the transition takes enormous amounts of time is a way to score a point easily, for it cannot be challenged: on the one hand, the very idea of transition implies a process that necessarily requires time. On the other, by bestowing a transition upon a radical break, one makes the whole enterprise look unfeasible, for, if it is radical in the sense proposed here, one cannot tell how it would come about. Hence, it would take a long time, if at all. Marx, with his Epicurus (see Section 5.5), however, has opened our eyes to the fact that man's sensitivity is time, and time is also change. The phenomenical features of events of the natural type are only reflected in man's sensitivity, whereas time and appearance consume each other. Univocal explanations are useless stratagems to pretend a mental sanity that is only capitalist (or any other) metaphysics. Transition is only a verbal construction.

If all the above is correct, there is a side issue that cannot be avoided: the role of the intellectuals, especially of the progressive kind. An intellectual, for our purposes here, is somebody who decides to play the part of a 'man of consequence' on issues where theory (any theory) and politics overlap. To be such a social figure, you need to plant one foot in academia and another in the mass media, including books of the popular kind. Your life depends, however, upon the survival of the political, economic, social and intellectual set-up that allows you to perform that role. To survive, in other words, you must work at a level of analytical depth that does not challenge the prevailing metaphysics. To be successful, you are better off proposing yourself as an opponent of 'the system' in the normal sense, i.e. by tackling one issue at a time, like the awareness-raisers mentioned in Chapter 1 do. The reader can pick his/her favourite example of an intellectual hero of the capitalist time.

Such intellectual leaders can only survive, as a consequence, by going along with the big deception of capitalist time politics: the confusion between subversion and revolution, typically developed and spread by left-wing parties. Admitting that revolution signifies the elimination of social ties and of institutional organization is impossible for such people. To preserve the prevailing metaphysics, they would rather undergo any repression, and even death. Such are the managers of the emotional opposition to radical thinking. They know repression both for having undergone it and for having inflicted it, but perfectly ignore the pain of isolation that they inflict on radical thinkers and radical books. They are the self-nominated managers of the words and language of the metaphysics of capitalism.

While producing, with the usual, consummated tone of scandalized necessity, protestations that humankind cannot be reduced to political economy or economics, they rename or slightly alter the very intellectual categories of these disciplines, as we have endeavoured to show in the preceding chapters, to describe human behaviour and propose their recipes for salvation. Socialism, welfare economics, corporatism and what have you are hailed, not only as the panacea for this or that critical conjuncture of capitalist history, but also as true 'revolutions', 'changes' and 'ruptures'. When such big goals are not 'practical' or 'feasible', the intellectuals are ready with lesser goals: for instance, in our dark, neo-liberal times, they are ready to salute any group that claims not to worship the so-called Troika as the 'radical left', or any actually fascist group as 'centre right', while, needless to say, having endless debates with each other.

It goes without saying that this makes the struggle for a more just world, where everybody can choose what to make of their life, even more imperative. If there were no division of labour of the capitalist kind, we would not relinquish intellectual leadership to such a minority, nor would we trust the results of their labour. A world without private property and the slavery of work is as urgent as the emancipation from the metaphysics of capitalism and cannot be trusted, as progressive intellectuals do, to class struggle, for this last, as Smith and Marx knew well, is one of the tools that are necessary to preserve capitalism. With this, we are back to the need for radical thinking.

The fear intellectuals have of radical thought is in fact, if everything argued so far in this book holds, perfectly logical and understandable if you look at it from the point of view of the 'practical' capitalist person we have introduced earlier. Nothing prevents us common people, however, from taking heed of the reasoning of La Mettrie and Hume and running the risk Marx ran of being misused and misinterpreted. Limpid, logical thought, however unsettling, does no harm, for it targets only those who are open to it already. Plus, if the metaphysics of capitalism is what we have described so far, those who are inside it are not even capable of recognizing radical thought. Intellectuals can only concentrate on minor issues, or go searching forever for what lies, they like to think, below the folds. The ideas that the future is undetermined and time is man's sensitivity are both missed.

The problem with the intellectuals is part of a more general problem, discussed throughout the preceding chapters, caused by the metaphysics of capitalism. The excess of determination of everything in capitalism, i.e. the constant attempt to always put things in their right place within the invented general order, causes the presence of a high degree of vagueness in just about everything. The apparent precision of the scientific laws of the natural and human sciences can only exist when coupled with the unredeemable vagueness of the laws themselves and of the words and concepts they refer to. As a consequence, at the political level, a behaviour can be a private vice as well as a public virtue, and vanity can inform of itself the actions of the social man, as Mandeville proposed (see Chapter 2). Nonetheless, we still can be respectable human beings at home and in public, as anyone can easily see.

Not only can nobody mark the border between vice and virtue in what we do as private individuals and even as states (or war would not exist, for we would be able to oppose reasonableness to it, for a major instance). Also, as proved by Adam Smith's desperate attempt to extricate himself from Mandeville's embrace, there is a grain of truth in everything. Every deed, every opinion, every theoretical reason can be argued, with the aim of reaching that grain of truth. Such a reaching is always achieved, for the system is geared to allow that very useless result. The vagueness and lack of logic in reasoning and words grant the possibility of always being precise in one's use of them, while contributing to the general vagueness.

As a consequence, intellectuals can deny that political economy can be as effective and complete as any other discipline in sketching the behaviour of the capitalist individual, an argument that contains a grain of potential, theoretical truth. Having done that, they can, as repeatedly said, describe the capitalist individual by using the tools of political economy. Throughout the preceding chapters, we have been discussing a few examples of this typically capitalist incoherence. Words such as choice, decision, efficiency and the like can, despite all the mathematics that is attached to them, convey as many meanings as the complicated, iterative mind of the capitalist individual can conjure up under the guidance of the latest intellectual fashion.

In other words, it is worth emphasizing, the generalized excess of determination makes every concept and every action amenable to modification and inversion, i.e. vague. Again, there is nothing new here, for the seeds of this condition have been clear since the eighteenth century. This time, instead of our usual philosophers, we will consider a satirist. The condition of the capitalist individual in fact is very similar to that of Gulliver in Lilliput (Swift, 2010): the country is plagued by political problems that are simultaneously idiotic (how to break eggs and the shoe-heel question) and serious in their implications (the state is divided by such issues), and that is worsened by the possibility of external invasion. Gulliver is a foreigner to Lilliput, and he therefore concludes:

> I desired the secretary to present my humble duty to the emperor, and to let him know that I thought it would not become me, who was a foreigner, to interfere with parties; but I was ready, with the hazard of my life, to defend his person and state against all invaders.
>
> (p. 37)

Gulliver's decision is illogical and unjust, and yet it looks perfectly reasonable to him and to any superficial observer. Let the reader apply it to the innumerable examples of present-day political life. In terms of individual freedom, we are a long way behind the pre-capitalist situation of Don Quixote (de Cervantes, 2013). In his imaginary world, which resembles Spain, individuals were free to go crazy in peace, because the others felt free to go along with the game played by the mad person or not. It is when some practically minded actors seek to bring Don Quixote back to sanity and to his home that the poor man dies. Meanwhile, he has done no harm: unlike Gulliver, he has fought imaginary enemies and even paid for the damage he has caused. The fiction is real to one mind only, while the others are free either to disregard it or to play along with it for a variety of describable and undescribable reasons. Socialized alienation is not innate. It is a characterizing feature of capitalism.

In capitalism as we know it, everything is compulsion and melancholy, and only half-intuited. The general compulsion enforced by the metaphysics is ignored, while all sorts of other compulsions that ensue from it (unjust laws, repression and unequal distribution of wealth, for a few typical instances) are elevated to the dignity of fundamental issues in which the loss of individual lives is irrelevant, for the goal is too high. The goal itself, however, is only formal, and the outcome of the actions undertaken to reach it is irrelevant. The toppling of a foreign dictator becomes the creation of a better world, and never mind if, in toppling him, you have caused more death and suffering than the dictator himself. Worse, the death and suffering become irrelevant twice over when the toppling of the dictator has caused international terrorism and mass migration, which (one at a time) come to represent the most threatening issue of the day.

There is almost no need to mention that, in the iterative functioning of capitalism as we know it, the victims of terrorism and the threat of immigration will soon be replaced by new, similar dangers. For these, new Gullivers will be ready to give their lives, despite caring nothing about the way of breaking eggs or the fashion in heels. A gloomy shaggy-dog story is constantly told, made up of an infinity of sinister stories that succeed each other. The more absurd and unrealistic the stories, the better they fulfil their role. The opposition groups contribute to this unfolding of absurd events by fighting them on the same grounds. A 2.5 or 2.8 per cent tax is opposed as an alternative to an unjust 3 per cent tax.

The sad, iterative capitalist game goes on, despite reality itself, with its endless possibilities, being present all around it, and above all with the incommensurable power of the unconceived. The enormous difficulty in rendering the above, which has been pointed out throughout the book, can be overcome by means of a historical political economy that looks backwards in order not to participate in a constructive way to the metaphysics of capitalism. A materialistic political economy describes; it cannot and must not prescribe. The task of emancipation as a whole must be entrusted, above all, to what has been called silence.

6.2 Right and wrong

In an intellectual world of iterations that cannot come to a firm conclusion, it is easy to claim that some form of pluralism is at work, and that everything can be adjusted after an appropriate debate. Instead, the very opposite is true. Everyone is compelled to take part in endless, seemingly eternal, activities. Whatever one does, although helping the present conjuncture (or you would not want to do it), cannot help the constant return of a new conjuncture that requires new, perfectly similar action.

The end of an economic crisis brings growth and another economic crisis, just as the end of a period of growth brings forth another period of growth after a crisis. Each of these is perfectly unexplained, for it is unanimous wisdom among the economists that crises come regularly but cannot be foreseen, let alone interpreted in their causes or even consequences. All we must do is keep working and bear with the boredom of the usual items of economic theory being endlessly iterated in favour of or against the present politics or the economic conjuncture. In these conditions – as the same applies to any field of capitalist life – there is no room for the individual to flourish.

There is, in fact, only room within the capitalist division of labour. You can – theoretically – choose to keep quiet or to become an opinion leader, because it takes the same lack of creativity to do both. There is no substantial difference between intellectual and menial labour, despite all the empty rhetoric about it. The very need for efficiency prevents the possibility of creativity. This is most openly displayed in the constant search to reward 'merit' and capacity, which are sought by iteratively presenting, over and over again but in a wider sense, intellectual objects similar to the 'collective intellect' discussed in Section 3.3. Competition and merit, as anybody with eyes and ears can find out by him/herself, are but names for a race to be as faithful to the system – i.e. mediocre – as possible. Students' intellects are thereby stunted in their prime.

Everybody runs, but there is no cynosure. The constant running must aim nowhere, or capitalism would progress towards its completion, opening the door to the stationary state, or to a socialist, similar, continuous aimless hastening. Yet, sometimes, what is clear-cut cannot help making itself visible, at the micro or macro level. Ecological disasters or nonsensical political acts afford a glimpse of non-dialectical possibilities. At that point, as many individuals as possible rush even more frantically, like bees in their hive, to patch up and seal the leakage that has let fresh air and sunlight in. Objects that are too big to handle for the metaphysics of capitalism are dissected into parts and classified into substreams of the given scientific disciplines, or covered in wax and left alone.

It is at this point that the simultaneous vagueness and precision of the capitalist words, language and concepts can display all their power in maintaining the status quo. Plus, what words and language cannot reach and settle, statistics and the social sciences do. When an incumbent disaster appears too close, calculations of probability and statistics relegate it to the realm of the metaphysics again. The long-term loss of soil fertility, to continue the attention we have paid to agriculture throughout the book, is transformed from a fact into an ongoing process. Such a transformation implies, with the typical conjunction of vagueness and precision we have insisted upon so many times, the possibility of being amenable to mending. Mending itself is, in turn, another process, as dialectical as the former in its functioning. It will, therefore, take time, the longer the better, and keep people busy and awareness high. Meanwhile, all sorts of romantic features can be dug up from a romanticized past to make this dialectical feast all the more complex by the addition of sentimental aspects (Micocci, 2015).

Next comes the sheer glory of consequences, to make the phenomenical object of study part of an inextricable network of complexity. Some people are economically ruined by the loss of fertility; food availability is threatened; scientists make proposals that are challenged and limited by the multinational agricultural corporations that are not ready to supply the market with what is required; protesters protest; awareness-raisers raise awareness; and so on and so forth. The simple object this huge game had started with becomes a complex, yet solvable (one issue at a time), cobweb of problems. There is a general failure to notice that no one ever asked the simple question: have we started from the beginning, identifying objects unequivocally?

The answer to the above question, of course, if everything so far argued is correct, is no. It follows that the useless complexity of the metaphysics of capitalism not only alienates individuals in the ways so far described, but also puts the very survival of humankind and, more importantly, of planet Earth itself at risk by not grasping concrete reality and by wasting time and resources on metaphysics instead of nature. Once again, the key to everything is time. If we do, see and feel something, we do not do, see and feel other things. It is, therefore, imperative and urgent that we direct our gaze towards the concrete.

In the metaphysics of capitalism, despite the incapacity to see the general dangers we have just described, there is nonetheless, as has been argued in the preceding chapters, a general feeling of continuous threat. Like all dialectical things, the threat, with the power of its determinations, appears capable of hiding the features of the world you cherish. It can be political, economic, bellicose, environmental or anything else you can conjure up by means of the maieutics of capitalist metaphysics. Survival itself thus becomes yet another dialectical task, lest you end up on the butcher's table of history. When it concerns the interaction of organized societies, this desperate attempt to reverse the course of history (the Hegelian trajectory of the Spirit) becomes the source of unspeakable cruelties.

The unimportance and expendability of the individual lead to the use of bellicose or terroristic methods, for these are the most effective in instilling speakable terror, hatred and pain by their allowing the misguided perception of snatches of natural feelings. The victims become, in their being but individuals, the source of commotion, while they are simultaneously – because of their unimportance to the workings of the dominant intellectuality – the best target for destruction. The same misguided snatch of naturalness makes you weep for the dead, while simultaneously killing the living. The metaphysics justifies it all in the ways already explained. Your awareness not only can be worn and cast off at need and at will, but can also be tuned to the useful target and to the useful intensity.

Thus, everything appears in a continuous flow, and the only hope for survival is to go along with the flow. It follows that a continuous state of intolerance ensues towards what obstructs, or may potentially obstruct, the flow. If no one cares for individuals, and there is a flow (never mind its direction), the only hope for individuals is to make themselves as inconspicuous (most often this means unoriginal) as they can. This rule equally applies to the common person, the progressive intellectual and any other person of consequence. For the others, those who do not comply, there is only oblivion and isolation, bestowed on them by the incapacity of the metaphysics of capitalism to notice, understand and counteract radical ideas.

One is left to wonder how many great pieces of work of the past 150 years have been lost because of the mechanism described above. Eighteenth-century thinkers, and Marx, could survive in the collective memory and in the records because they were old enough (the former) or hijacked by Hegelians (the latter), but, even if we could count and assess the ideas and suggestions that have been consigned to oblivion, and even retrieve and reconsider them, it would not matter, as already said many times over. The flow is inexorable in its necessity to make everything equally dull. Capitalist life is a race won by those who can bear boredom.

The most important absurdity that ensues from all this, however, is that the question of what is right or wrong is evaded. In the metaphysics of capitalism, in fact, right or wrong apply to two main sets of issues: moral and ethical questions, and what does not fit the flow of the metaphysics (important examples of the second are scientific mistakes or failures to abide by the rules of your discipline; this latter is well known in economics and political economy). Both sets of issues, however, are not amenable to any clear-cut solutions. Let us look in more detail, for there are a number of side issues that will help clarify what has been argued in the book.

In the first place, despite constantly appearing – for the reasons explained in the preceding chapters – simultaneously solved and unsolved even in their common, vague meaning, moral/ethical right and wrong acquire a paramount importance and are argued about all the time. In a world that is unable to attribute precise, exact meanings to words and concepts, the only way to assess whether a decision is sound is by resorting to ethics. Whether it is a religious ethics or a political ethics such as in fascism, there is nowhere else to turn for the capitalist human being. It follows that the possibility of liberalism is erased from the list of possible occurrences, just like the possibility of communist anarchism. Both, in fact, entail the need to look at the concrete, disregarding ethics and politics.

No wonder, therefore (see Micocci, 2012), that what we have called capitalism as we know it presents heavy, fascistic features in practice. Ethics informs of itself all political decisions, and even political opposition. There are even people who seek to consider, and even introduce, a business ethics, i.e. a fascistic regulation of what clearly needs no ethics, or would not work in the neutral, mechanical way prescribed by the theory. Funnily, most of those who support or oppose business ethics, with a flawed move typical of capitalist metaphysics, omit to mention that even the economic mainstream's assumption of a lack of ethics is based on an ethics (e.g. the sanctity of contracts, or the legitimate power of the nation-state to set legal limits). The outcome is that an endless field is open for infinite discussion of what kind of ethics, whose ethics, cultural differences, and so on.

The general result that interests us here is, however, that the possibility of utopias is denied. Liberalism and communist anarchism are not even considered. In their place, all sorts of 'practical' idea are instead discussed, the most ridiculous of them being socialism and neo-liberalism. The important condition for all this, it is easy to see, is that things are kept vague by using precise terms. The intellectuals can thus accuse the liberalism of neo-liberalism of terrible crimes, while others can point out that there is nothing, or little, or much, of liberal ideas in it. Socialists can defend what no person in his/her right mind would even dream of defending – for instance, Castro's Cuba or the People's Republic of China (I put forward these examples only because it is still too irresistibly fashionable to bash the USSR).

In sum, wrongness on methodological grounds having little momentum, right and wrong are established either by discussion – with the limits set by the metaphysics of capitalism – or by ethical decree. Both these aspects are hopelessly intermingled and overlap heavily. As long as this hopeless situation is kept, there is no way for the two main ideas of the nineteenth century, liberalism and communist anarchism, ever to be considered. What we have instead is a lack of new ideas of the same 'grand' type as those, and a creeping fascism that continually throws a communitarian ethical dust in the mechanisms of capitalism as we know it. Meanwhile, catastrophes appear on the horizon, helping the system abandon ideas in order to cope with them (in the iterative way described).

Right and wrong could instead indicate – simply – a way to be exact. If words and language had univocal meanings to convey, which means that we could direct our study straight to the concrete (within the limits pointed out throughout the book), we would be presented with a wide number of solutions to right and wrong questions, for they are eminently concrete questions. They would be visible at once, because they would lack that halo of ethical vagueness–precision they possess in capitalism as we know it. Life would be simpler, and we would be presented with problems that require the taking of individual responsibility for their answer.

6.3 A historical political economy

In the recent past, there have been long discussions about Veblen's idea that economics and political economy should not be taxonomic but evolutionary, to which the present author even contributed (Micocci, 2004). Looking at the subject from the perspective put forward here, it appears clear that such a question is not worth posing. Although, in fact, a taxonomy of any kind is absolutely needed, even when we want to emphasize the evolutionary character of economic facts, posing evolution – Darwinian or Lamarckian – as a characterizing feature of economic change is nonsensical.

We simply do not know enough about the way nature, including time, develops. We do not even know whether what we call nature exists. Finally, even if the first two points above are wrong, we have seen in the preceding chapters that we have good reasons to doubt the validity of the cause–effect connection. Most importantly, in any case, what we deal with in economic analyses is not nature. It is the metaphysics conjured up by the intellectuality of the current mode of production, in our case capitalism. Thus, evolution might apply only in that, like any other intellectual category of capitalism, we take it in the empty sense produced by the flawed logics of the metaphysics. It might be a method of study, if you do not reject the metaphysics, or just one of the many objects of the study of the metaphysics itself, if you do reject it.

The taxonomy part is, instead, more intriguing, for a taxonomy, including the way one orders the items when one builds it, is a necessary step for the study of any empirical subject, whatever one believes about their actual reality. In order to study a mode of production, we need to order and classify all its many objects, dividing them, for instance, in terms of their function. Luckily, this is fairly simple in the simplified intellectual and emotional life of capitalism. All we need to do is to steer away from the useless network of complications that is constantly re-proposed (as already discussed so many times) by both economics and political economy.

The categories to be organized and classified are, thanks to the simplified, iterative functioning of capitalism as we know it, the very same as those supplied by economics and political economy (see also Micocci, 2008/2010, 2002). Being entirely metaphysical, they constitute the very capitalist object we are looking for. All we need to do is free ourselves from the need to prescribe, and watch them from outside. That is what the historical approach within the materialistic attitude grants. It hardly need be said that, in this way, we can produce, not only the new observations we need to help the process of emancipation, but also the banal economic analyses that overlap with the economics and political economy produced by the metaphysics of capitalism.

Does this make political economy a non-economic subject? From the strictly technical point of view, the answer to this question is no, because, as said above, we necessarily produce economic considerations, and political economy is sufficient to paint the picture of capitalist society in all its aspects. From any other point of view, and in general, it is evident that such economic considerations are eminently historical and only serve purposes of historical analysis. The whole thing, in fact, revolves around the issue of emancipation, the first obstacle to which is precisely the existence of the state and the economy, in that these two supply the main and most common ammunition to the intellectual artillery of the metaphysics of capitalism. Going beyond politics using time, as suggested by Marx, is one of the first outcomes of the revolutionary process.

As we have taken as a working hypothesis of this book that a society of humans might continue to exist, the issue is whether political economy can contribute anything to such a society. It has been signalled in the preceding chapters that the answer to this question is in the negative. Planning, for an obvious instance, is an engineering and/or agronomic issue. No purpose can be served by a historical political economy other than that of contributing to the building of the present by means of an understanding of the past.

It is precisely this last function that is crucial to the functioning of human society, including social functions as technical as planning. By enhancing the intellectual and emotional independence of the human individual, a historical political economy contributes to that silence that we have seen to be the main tool for emancipation and for the quest for the material. A direct observation of reality, at least in the first phases of emancipation (for we do not know what might happen next), can replace the present artificial, intellectual reasoning that – in the extreme case of mainstream economics – can even do without reality itself to deliver its decisions. By baring reality of its metaphysical features, we reduce the risk of inflicting wounds on nature and on our fellow humans.

What we must do, in other words, is free ourselves from our capitalist subservience to economics and political economy and from the capacity these two have (for this much cannot be denied to them) to be of application to any field of human life. The cultural dominance of these subjects is the signal of the loss of individual humanity in the capitalist person. More precisely, and much worse, it is the signal that the capitalist human individual is homogeneous, and anything concerning it can be generalized. Even worse than that, some of these individuals might have retained their individual, non-generalizable characteristics. Yet, as explained in the course of the book, this simply does not matter. Their human features are there, visible to anybody, but they do not count. They do not fit the metaphysics.

One can only hint at the atrocious isolation these individuals feel, despite their inner sense of peace for doing those natural things that cause them so much social pain, but even this, as we have sought to prove in the course of this book, is impossible to transmit. If one conveys it in words, it becomes just another item to peddle in the iterations of capitalism as we know it. Its only purpose – if it causes any reaction at all – would be that of producing an occasional outburst of empty rhetoric.

To signify the generalized absurdity of the intellectual labours of capitalism as we know it and of its metaphysics, we can thus point to the fact, already hinted at in various parts of the book, that the common reader, i.e. the person well within the grip of the metaphysics of capitalism, would say that this is just extremism. Things, he/she would say, are not as extreme as the present author makes them out to be. Although this attitude is easy to identify as the typical application of vulgar Hegelian dialectics, one cannot help admitting that it is the correct interpretation of capitalist reality. Things are (pointlessly) complex and bland, and what is proposed here is indeed extreme.

In the oblique and crooked language of the metaphysics of capitalism, the above means that what is argued here is cynical, truly sceptical, and not amenable to compromise. It cannot participate in the general conversation managed with the flawed maieutics capitalist intercourse is all about. In even simpler words, either you take it or you leave it, and leaving it is the only socially reasonable option; taking it is socially unreasonable. This is how the matter stands. If what is being proposed here is correct, it points to a fatal flaw in the general intellectuality of capitalism, and to the revolutionary implications that mending this flaw brings about.

The best option for those who oppose what has been argued so far is, of course, that of dismissing it or, even better, disregarding it. If so, then one might be pushed to think that the present argument is correct, because the means of capitalist intellectuality cannot tear it apart. Naturally, the present argument can be torn apart, even if its author is obviously unable to see how. It is for the reader to do so, in all instances. Yet, even if the argument is wrong, is the general question of the limits to individuality in capitalism incorrect? Considering that eminent authors, some of whom have been considered in the preceding chapters, have posed the same problem, it is possible to hypothesize that it is a legitimate question.

Even if the logical argument proposed here is wrong, the present author therefore begs the reader to stay with the problem of the limits to individuality in capitalism as we know it. Reality is too sad, dull and boring to make one doubt the importance of this question.

6.4 Liberty as silence

The problem that remains to be solved and articulated in detail is that of silence itself. It is evident that its results cannot be outlined a priori with any hope of hitting the target, or it would not coincide with liberty. The question remains of how to go about it in practice, as the typical capitalist person would say. There is no answer to such a query either, and this is very lucky, besides being inevitable. There is even the chance that, if nature exists and humankind is consubstantial to it, future social arrangements might prove to be rather similar to the present ones.

The truly crucial issue, dealt with in Section 5.5, is that of abstract thinking. Such a term does not just mean the capacity to produce a type of thinking severed from the metaphysics of capitalism as we know it. That would be a perfectly feasible task, open to about anybody willing to engage in it. The consequences, in fact, given the incapacity of the dominant intellectuality to even take notice of it, may not be troublesome in most cases. If one has enough time on one's hands, and a degree of freedom from the cares of common life, non-metaphysical thinking is possible and something worthwhile engaging in for its own sake.

There is, however, more to be done if one wants to practice what we have called silence, and it has to do, obviously enough, with what Marx called sensuousness. One of the main limits of capitalist life, in fact, is that in it one can split functions from one another: cruel Nazi assassins can enjoy sex, music or art, because their absent or distorted sensibility can be replaced by a reasoning about the thing you are expected to enjoy. How are they to know, or even care for, what enjoyment is? What does it matter, if they do not even need to pretend enjoyment, in that, in the generalized metaphysics, what matters is the intellectual item conveyed in words? Who of us, for a less painful example, has not witnessed people signifying their enjoyment of a concert by dancing or rocking – out of time?

More relevantly, how do you recognize the alienated capitalist individual, or the few who may not be alienated? In Leopardi's poem quoted in Section 5.1, it is the sheep that are not alienated and are enjoying life, and yet they are the target of the invectives of the unhappy shepherd and are accused of lacking intelligence and sensitivity. The unhappy shepherd vents his bitterness and acquires, by doing so, a halo of both intelligence and sensitivity. There are grounds, however, to hypothesize that, by putting forward such intelligent and profound ideas, he is simply conveying his alienation from nature. There must be a way to reconcile language and nature.

The above is not the kind of issue this book can resolve. It suffices here to point at the limiting role organized societies play in enforcing the widespread individual incapacity to link abstract thinking with a sensuous belonging to nature. Although a complete separation is perhaps impossible, at least until someone invents a way not to feel sexual instincts or to do without eating – which is a most common attempt in capitalism as we know it, ranging from the vegetarians to extreme religious frenzies – there are no grounds to infer optimistic conclusions. The call for abstinence, purity and self-inflicted limitations is one of the commonest features of capitalism as we know it, and indeed of all organized societies.

As a consequence, liberty as silence is necessarily something that, to use Marx's words again, is beyond politics. It can be described, in capitalist parlance, as the acceptance of individual responsibilities. Each individual must face nature (the concrete) with the aim to see what it is, if it is anything at all. This is, inevitably, a task to be undertaken alone, entrusted to the bodily and intellectual capacities of each of us. All these characteristics, however, do not make it a lonely endeavour, for the simple reason that life is not arithmetical. Individual empowerment does not necessarily mean isolation from the others.

There is no denying the revolutionary momentum of this enterprise. Nor can we conceal the fact that it might appear terrifying to those used to the cosy comfort of the metaphysics of capitalism. We cannot deny the difficulty of the task either, but, now that we have listed the main difficulties, it is evident that we have simply described what life is out of the metaphysics of capitalism. Individual freedom is scary, and among the very things it brings in its wake in the mind of the capitalist individual is the end of communication. This is, naturally, a false problem.

Capitalist communication is, in fact, mainly perfunctory and highly technical in meaning. Most of the things we say are either necessary items for life's tasks or unnecessary attempts to signify our feelings (this task is unnecessary because feelings, to be communicated, must be in common, i.e. reduced to what we know and can iterate). A third category is constituted by the communication that replaces, and sublimates, emotions. We have been considering examples of this last in the course of the book. It is not surprising, therefore, that our society is defined by some as the society of information.

To these people, and indeed to everybody, social life is a continuous bombardment of information. Electronic devices are improved upon all the time to intercept and capture such information. People purchase them, and use them, to get hold of both social/institutional and personal information, but social life is not qualitatively different from what it was in the times of d'Holbach, La Mettrie, Berkeley and Rousseau, let alone Marx. The nature of information is the same. What has changed is the intellectual use we make of it.

Whether it is national or international news, or personal stuff, or just 'pass me the salt, please', information fits perfectly into the three categories of discourse we have seen above. It is necessary for the tasks of capitalist life. It helps us signify our feelings, i.e. their metaphysical nature and presence in the appropriate moments. Last, it replaces feelings by putting together the act of communicating and the emotion caused by the exaggerated impression that we are influencing ourselves or somebody else. However impotent to do anything, the capitalist human being can feel the thrill of uttering an opinion, banal, unoriginal and uninfluential as it may be.

Thus, life flows on. Despite the dullness of it all, there is room for each of us to distribute our intellectual time between supposed rational and emotional tasks. This, in turn, makes room for noticing that someone spends more time and effort on the latter rather than the former, or the other way around. In turn, this gives us the illusion that we are natural beings. The only alternative to all this is liberty as silence, with its undetermined nature and outcomes.

6.5 Final considerations

It is appropriate to conclude this book by finishing our tour of the anarchist Marx. We will consider here those parts of *The Holy Family* (Marx and Engels, 1956) that Marx himself wrote. In Chapter IV, Marx has a chance to discuss love; let us keep in mind that he is attacking the 'calm of knowledge', the misguided epigones of Hegel. What better subject than love to talk about natural objects?

> Object! Horrid! There is nothing more damnable, more profane, more massy than an object [. . .] How could [. . .] 'pure' criticism not see in love its *bête noire* [. . .] in love, which first really teaches man to believe in the objective world outside himself, which not only makes man an object, but the object of a man!
>
> (1956, p. 32; emphasis in the original)

Marx's polemic continues against Hegel's *Phenomenology* and the ensuing hatred against anything that moves from its abode in the brain to become 'sensually manifest' (ibid.).

What is supposed to be in the brain, while actually residing in the concrete, we have argued in the preceding chapters, can only be conveyed by means of words. Capitalist love can, like any other thing, be spoken, because it too is, in the language of the present book, metaphysics. It does not take an explanation to observe that the same applies to any other object of feeling, unless our whole argument is perfectly wrong.

In describing 'Critical criticism's third campaign' (Chapter VI, concerned with Bruno Bauer), Marx points out that:

> The French Enlightenment [. . .] in particular *French materialism*, was not only a struggle against the existing political institutions and the existing religion and theology; it was as much an *open* struggle against *metaphysics* of the *seventeenth century*, and against all metaphysics. [. . .] *Philosophy* was opposed to *metaphysics* as Feuerbach, in his first decisive attack on Hegel opposed *sober philosophy* to *drunken speculation*.
>
> (1956, p. 168; emphasis in the original)

In fact, such metaphysics had been 'restored' in the nineteenth century by 'speculative German philosophy' (ibid.). French and English socialism and communism, however, have shown that materialism 'now *coincides* with *humanism*' (p. 169; emphasis in the original).

Needless to say, 'French and English materialism was always closely related to Democritus and Epicurus' (p. 170). As a consequence, we can go back to Chapter IV and conclude that:

> The propertied class and the class of the proletariat present the same human self-alienation. But the former class finds in this self-alienation its confirmation and its good, *its own power*; it has a semblance of human existence. The class of the proletariat feels annihilated in its self-alienation.
>
> (p. 51, emphasis in the original)

We must notice that Marx grossly misinterprets the effects on the proletariat of his own correct observation on the common alienation of all classes. The preceding chapters have hopefully shown, in fact, how capitalist alienation brings no revolutionary impulse in any class.

Marx, however, was perfectly right in individuating in private property, which in capitalism is a Hegelian notion, one of the main causes of dehumanization (p. 52). Very importantly, and very much against the orthodox Marxist interpretation, Marx unequivocally expresses the non-Hegelian and anti-Hegelian nature of revolution. The proletariat can be victorious 'only by abolishing itself and its opposite' (p. 52). With the disappearance of both the proletariat and the propertied classes, private property also 'disappears'. One wonders how Marxists succeeded in constantly overlooking, especially in their praxis, and in driving everybody else to overlook, the clarity of this statement and of all the others we have been considering.

In sum, the revolutionary, which Marx here identifies with the proletariat, but which can be any individual or any group that has 'experienced all the conditions of life of society today in all their inhuman acuity' (ibid.), 'cannot free [itself] without abolishing the conditions of its own life' (ibid.). More precisely, and as a warning to orthodox Marxists past and present and to the progressive intellectual, 'It cannot abolish the conditions of its own life without abolishing *all* the inhuman conditions of life of society today which are summed up in its own situation' (ibid.; emphasis in the original).

It is hoped that this book has enlarged the intuition of Marx and of the Enlightenment philosophers by showing that, if we use the multidisciplinary tools of political economy to analyse capitalism as we know it, we can only describe a place of human limitation and of destruction of the prerogatives of the individual. Still, some might prefer to live under capitalism as we know it. If the argument of this book is correct, this group are perfectly coherent with the metaphysics of capitalism. Those who claim that they do not like capitalism and want to reform it, however, are even more so.

References

de Cervantes Saavedra, M. (2013) *El Ingenioso Hidalgo Don Quijote de la Mancha*, Catedra, Madrid.

Marx, K., and Engels, F. (1956) *The Holy Family or Critique of Critical Critique*, Foreign Languages Publishing House, Moscow (reprinted in Scholar's Choice).

Micocci, A. (2002) *Anti-Hegelian Reading of Economic Theory*, Mellen Press, Lampeter, UK.

Micocci, A. (2004) 'Economics, taxonomy and dynamism', *Rethinking Marxism*, 16, 1, 73–94.

Micocci, A. (2008/2010) *The Metaphysics of Capitalism*, Lexington, Lanham, MD.

Micocci, A. (2012) *Moderation and Revolution*, Lexington, Lanham, MD.

Micocci, A. (2015) 'Traditional issues need novel thinking', in Figus, A., *Land and Water Will Save Us from the Crisis: The role of universities*, pp. 131–54, Eurilink, Rome.

Swift, J. (2010) *Gulliver's Travels*, Harper Collins, London.

Index

For Product Safety Concerns and Information please contact our EU
representative GPSR@taylorandfrancis.com
Taylor & Francis Verlag GmbH, Kaufingerstraße 24, 80331 München, Germany